THE STRUCTURE OF
FREUDIAN THOUGHT

THE STRUCTURE OF FREUDIAN THOUGHT

The Problem of
Immutability and Discontinuity
in Developmental Theory

by

MELVIN FEFFER

INTERNATIONAL UNIVERSITIES PRESS, INC.

NEW YORK

Library of Congress Cataloging in Publication Data

Feffer, Melvin.
    The structure of Freudian thought.

    Bibliography: p.
    Includes index.
    1. Personality.   2. Freud, Sigmund, 1856–1939.
3. Developmental psychology.   I. Title. [DNLM:
1. Personality development.   2. Psychoanalytic
theory.   3. Freudian theory.   WM 460 F295s]
BF698.F354   150.19'52   81-23610
ISBN 0-8236-6185-7   AACR2

        Grateful acknowledgment is made to the publishers for permission to use material from:
        The Standard Edition of the Complete Works of Sigmund Freud, translated and edited by James Strachey, Sigmund Freud Copyrights Ltd., The Institute of Psycho-Analysis, and The Hogarth Press Ltd.
        Introductory Lectures on Psycho-Analysis (Part III), by Sigmund Freud, translated and edited by James Strachey, published in the United States by W. W. Norton, Inc., by arrangement with George Allen & Unwin Ltd. and The Hogarth Press Ltd.
        New Introductory Lectures on Psycho-Analysis, by Sigmund Freud, translated by James Strachey, published by W. W. Norton & Company, Inc. Copyright © 1965, 1964 by James Strachey. Copyright 1933 by Sigmund Freud. Copyright renewed 1961 by W. J. H. Sprott.

To my wife—to my mother—and to my sons.
Would that I had been able to dedicate books to each singly.

CONTENTS

ACKNOWLEDGMENTS

Of the many who have helped, I should especially like to thank Nick Cariello, my editor. His comments — always thoughtful, provocative, and rigorous — worked improvements in the text that went far beyond style. I profited from discussing various parts of the manuscript with John Ceraso, my colleague at the Institute for Cognitive Studies at Rutgers University, Newark. If I have distorted those aspects of learning theory with which my analysis is concerned, this would clearly be in spite of his efforts. It is difficult to single out those of my students whose active involvement forced me to rethink issues that I was convinced I had solved. As a group I thank them. My wife was always there — for listening, for comment, and for support.

INTRODUCTION

The Freudian theory of personality development has, of course, been variously and, indeed, repetitively criticized. In reviewing this theory in the light of such criticisms, I have become increasingly impressed by two problems that I believe are justifiably attributed to the Freudian position. One problem is the theory's preformist conception of development. In the Freudian interpretation, essential characteristics of maturity such as purpose and delay are present in primitive functioning from the very start. Indeed, in terms of the theory, these characteristics must first be evidenced in primitive functioning if development is to occur at all. That is to say, the primitive individual must first be capable of purpose and delay before he can acquire these very same attributes in the course of development. The other problem is that the theory is internally inconsistent. At the same time that primitive activity is represented as evidencing purpose and delay, it is also represented—and primarily so—as mechanically reactive and blind. Yet the theory offers no explanation that can account for the simultaneous presence of such mutually exclusive qualities of behavior. These problems have become impor-

1

tant to my thinking because I believe that they have an essential connection to one another—a connection that has not yet been clarified. In my view, the theory's preformism and logical inconsistency have a common basis in that they reflect a particular form of cognitive activity—if you will, a particular "structure of Freudian thought." Hence my justification for adding still another critique of Freudian theory to the literature. In this inquiry, I will make the case for a cognitive connection between the preformism and logical inconsistency of the Freudian conception and will attempt to show the significance which these problems have for developmental theory when they are so understood.

One might well ask: What do I mean by the "structure of Freudian thought?" It will be noted that I am using the term "structure" as synonomous with form or organization. This meaning of structure derives from the constructionist assumption that is basic to my inquiry. My critique presumes that we know our world by actively organizing our experience—by literally forming our object of knowledge. By the structure of Freudian thought, then, I mean the organization we impose on our experience in terms of concepts that are provided by Freudian theory. I am proposing, in this regard, that when we interpret the events of personality development in terms of Freudian concepts—when, in terms of these concepts, we try to understand how the child becomes the adult—we have no choice but to organize these events into a relationship of discontinuity and immutability. On the one hand, we find ourselves distinguishing between the primitive behavior of the child and the mature behavior of the adult in such a way that these behaviors are separated from one another by an unbridgeable gulf. That is to say, we are forced to characterize the behaviors of the child and adult as discontinuous temporal events. On the other hand, and paradoxically so, we interpret these very same events as being connected to one another such that the child is seen as "father to the man." And when we do, we find that the temporal events which we have connected have become identical to one another — are immutable over time. It is this particular form of cognitive activity — this structuring of temporal events into a form of discontinuity and, at one and the same time, immutability — that I am characterizing as the structure of Freudian thought and that I view as underlying the problems of inconsistency and preformism attributed to the Freudian position.

I am suggesting, moreover, that these problems, as so understood, have a significance that extends beyond the Freudian position per se to the broader domain of developmental theory. In this regard, I will be advancing what is essentially a two-fold thesis concerning the problem of immutability and discontinuity in Freudian theory. First, I will make the case that this form of immutability and discontinuity is not unique to Freudian thought but is rather a general characteristic of cognitive activity that is necessarily evidenced under particular circumstances: namely, whenever an individual, in structuring temporal events, is required to solve an unsolvable problem. The second part of my thesis concerns itself with the nature of the unsolvable problem which the individual is forced to solve by virtue of interpreting development in terms of Freudian theory. Here I will argue that this unsolvable problem and its solution stem from a Cartesian world view that is basic to the Freudian position. That is to say, it is because the constructs of Freudian theory are derived from a Cartesian philosophy that we find ourselves connecting the primitive behavior of the child to the mature behavior of the adult when, in fact, we have so distinguished between these temporal events that they cannot be so connected. My critique of Freudian theory, then, can be seen as an argument for the following view: When interpreting personality development in terms of a theory that presumes a Cartesian philosophy, we struc-

ture the temporal events of child and adult behavior into a
form of immutability and discontinuity because the underlying philosophical assumptions of the theory place us in the
paradoxical situation of connecting what are unconnectable
events. The problems of preformism and logical inconsistency that have been attributed to the Freudian position are
the manifestations of this form of cognitive activity—a
form that is necessarily evidenced when the individual is
forced to solve an unsolvable problem.

I will try to show that this conception of the preformism and logical inconsistency of Freudian theory has two
major implications for the broader domain of developmental theory. First, it would follow from my thesis that the
same form of immutability and discontinuity will be evidenced by any conception of development that takes, as its
starting point, the presumptions of a Cartesian philosophy.
This implication will enable us, I believe, to see underlying
connections between theories of development that otherwise seem quite different. Thus, I will be making the case
that the conceptions of development advanced by instinct
theory and behaviorism—positions that have generally
been viewed as essentially different and, indeed, antagonistic
to one another—encounter the same problems of immutability and discontinuity as Freudian theory. And this, by
virtue of their common Cartesian presumptions.

A second implication derives from my view that this
form of immutability and discontinuity is evidenced as a
general attribute of cognitive functioning in solving an unsolvable problem. I will argue that this view of cognitive
functioning can serve as the basis for an alternative conception of personality development—one that is more coherent
than that afforded by the Freudian position. And by this I
mean that it can serve as a basis for reformulating, in a more
coherent way, those issues which this Cartesian conception
of development has served to structure so problematically—

issues such as the classic nature-nurture problem and the relationship between purposive and mechanistic modes of functioning. Indeed, it will be seen that the form of immutability and discontinuity evidenced by Freudian theory, instead of being encountered as a problem, is viewed in this alternative conception as a regular and essential condition for growth or development. In effect, then, I will be attempting to clarify the significance of my critique of the Freudian position for a "constructionist" alternative to the nature of personality development. Having said this, however, I am obliged to add a qualification: In comparison to my critique of the Freudian position, the constructionist alternative receives only the sketchiest of treatments. It is my hope that this imbalance will be corrected by a future work which presents an elaboration of the constructionist position comparable to that of the critique presented here.

In making the case for my thesis, I have exploited the views of various theorists who should be acknowledged at the outset. Their contributions are noted in the order in which I develop my line of argument. First and most important are the conceptions advanced by Piaget and Werner. The cognitive developmental position of these theorists is basic to the assertion presented in the first chapter that, in solving an unsolvable problem, we have no choice but to organize our experience into a form of immutability and discontinuity. The second chapter presents the argument that we are forced into this paradoxical situation when, in terms of a theory of development that presumes the Cartesian world view, we try to understand how the child becomes the adult. This argument relies on Asch's critique of the instinct and behaviorist solutions to the nature-nurture problem or, as he represents it, their solutions to the problem of "psychological invariance and change." The third and fourth chapters are devoted to a description and analysis of Freud's "conflict" approach to development and to the essential difficulties that have been noted in the literature regarding his theory. My purpose is to show that these difficulties, usually considered in isolation, have a common basis in the immutability-discontinuity problem and are rooted, as such, in Freud's Cartesian epistemology. In documenting this, I profit considerably from the views advanced by Hartmann and White. The critique of the Freudian position is completed by an analysis, in the fifth chapter, of the Freudian "conflict-free" approach to development. Here my intent is two-fold. I want to show, first, that contemporary ego psychology encounters the same form of the immutability-discontinuity problem as Freud's classical version and for the same reason. Second, the analysis focuses on the Freudian dichotomy between energy and structure — a dichotomy that a number of theorists have suggested is basic to the difficulties encountered by the Freudian position. I want to show that this view is correct as far as it goes, but that the problems associated with the energy-structure dichotomy have a more fundamental basis in Freud's Cartesian assumptions. In this chapter, I again focus on conceptions advanced by Hartmann and White, but now from a more critical point of view. In the final chapter, I deal with the task which faces a constructionist alternative to the Freudian theory of personality development. In doing so, I am concerned with reformulating, from the perspective of a constructionist conception of development, such issues as the relationship between purposive and reactive modes of functioning. In particular, I consider the implications of transplanting, as it were, some of the Freudian insights to the context of a constructionist philosophical framework. In an important sense, then, I acknowledge Freud's contribution in this final chapter by assuming what probably is now part of conventional wisdom, namely, that any contemporary theory of personality development must take as its starting point the product of Freud's genius.

A final comment: The case that I will be presenting is a complicated one. Accordingly, I have attempted to highlight the essential line of my argument by relegating much of the elaborative material to footnotes. With few exceptions, then, the footnotes are not critical to my thesis and need only be considered — at least in an initial reading of the text — when the reader seeks further clarification of a particularly complex point. In some instances, however, the footnoted content *is* critical to my thesis; here I would suggest that this content be considered in conjunction with the initial reading, even though this may disrupt the line of my argument. I trust that my reasons for relegating this particular content to footnotes will be evident in the context of my analysis. In any event, these footnotes will be distinguished by an asterisk.

1

THE TWO FORMS OF
COGNITIVE ORGANIZATION

I have suggested that Freudian theory serves to structure the temporal events of personality development into a relationship that is discontinuous and, at the same time, immutable. Moreover, I have proposed that this form of discontinuity and immutability reflects an organization that cognitive activity necessarily assumes when the subject connects a sequence of unconnectable events. This chapter has the two-fold goal of clarifying the theoretical basis for these assertions and of elaborating upon their implications so that they can serve to guide my critique of the Freudian position.[1]

[1] A major qualification should be noted here. As has been indicated, my inquiry is essentially confined to a critique, and does not advance an alternative conception of personality development. Accordingly, I present in this chapter only a selective account of my theoretical position — one that serves to provide the basis for the critical evaluation of the Freudian approach. Where the presentation may be "thin" as a consequence, I will provide elaborative material via footnotes.

I should add that when I speak of personality development, I am using the term "personality" in only the loosest sense, as referring to interpersonal behavior — behavior that is, in general, more heterogeneous

My theoretical viewpoint assumes two fundamental propositions. The first is that it is in the inherent nature of cognitive functioning to impose an organization on experience.[2] The object of knowledge, in this sense, is actively constructed by the knower. This assumption of the "constructionist" position is best understood, perhaps, when considered in relation to the opposing Cartesian view. The Cartesian view, in its classic form, assumes an external reality which is made up of "primary qualities," such as extension and number, and which objectively exists *as such*. That is to say, the primary qualities are assumed to exist independently of the knower. This view further assumes that other properties which also appear to be those of an external reality, such as odor and color, are really contributed by the physiological sense activity of the knower. Accordingly, these subjective "secondary qualities" are to be distinguished from the "independently constituted" primary qualities which have an objective existence. The constructionist viewpoint, in contrast, assumes no such distinction between the objective and subjective properties of external being. Reality in *all* of its aspects — whether in the form of the so-called

---

in nature than such forms of traditionally defined psychological functioning as memory and perception. Although adequate for the purposes of my critique, this definition would obviously require systematic articulation in an alternative conception of personality development.

Having said this, I should reiterate that it is indeed my intention that this critique serve as a springboard for a future extension of the constructionist position to the problem of personality development. The implications of the present critique for this alternative are explored in the final chapter.

[2] By experience, I do not mean phenomenal experience, but experience in the empiricist sense, namely, the effects of commerce with the external world. I add this in order to avoid any possible implication of my position that there is a more fundamental "raw material" of the known world that is somehow given to us *ready-made* and that we then organize by virtue of constructive activity.

primary or secondary qualities, and however articulated or diffuse—is, in its very warp and woof, a constructed reality. This does not mean that the constructionist position denies the existence of a reality external to the knower. It asserts, however, that we can only know this reality in terms of the characteristics of the knower and, more precisely, in terms of the modes of organization which the knower imposes on his experience. Our reality, in short, is a reality "as known."[3]

The second assumption is a proposition which Werner (1957) has advanced as the guiding principle for his own inquiry:

Developmental psychology postulates one regulative principle of development; it is an orthogenetic principle which states that wherever development occurs, it proceeds from a state of relative globality and lack of differentiation to a state of increasing differentiation, articulation, and hierarchic integration [p. 126].

[3] My view of the constructionist position has been particularly influenced by Cassirer's (1923) account of Kant's "second Copernican revolution" and its implications for cognitive functioning. Note also a parallel distinction between the Cartesian and constructionist positions in Langer's (1969) characterization of "mechanical mirror" and "organic lamp" theories of development. As I represent these philosophical views, the mirror and lamp metaphors are not entirely adequate. The image of the mind as a mirror that objectively reflects an external reality portrays the Cartesian assumption of the independently constituted primary quality, but does not capture the notion of a knower who imparts subjective "secondary" qualities to the event. On the other hand, the metaphor of the organic lamp implies an independently constituted "something" in the darkness—a "something" that is revealed by the light of knowing. As such, the image does not adequately convey the constitutive activity of knowing—namely, the activity of forming the object of knowledge. Finally, it should be noted that I am using the term "constructionist" to designate my point of view rather than the more commonly used "constructivist" because I think the former conveys more directly the sense of active form-building than does the latter.

This proposition has the same status in my critique that it has in Werner's theory. It determines the inquiry's range of applicability. The operative phrase, in this regard, is "wherever development occurs...." Thus, if one were to note a behavior sequence that could not be described as becoming more differentiated and hierarchically organized, this would not constitute disproof of the principle, but would indicate that the sequence did not involve development as so defined. Hence such behavior would not be subject to a Wernerian analysis. By that token, my critique only applies to forms of cognitive activity that can be characterized in terms of this orthogenetic principle. Only to the extent that a form of cognitive activity can be described with respect to its degree of differentiation and hierarchic integration is that activity subject to the argument which I shall be presenting.[4]

These propositions can be elaborated by the following assertions:

(1) In structuring the object of knowledge, cognitive activity is limited to two forms of organization: a hierarchic form and a pars pro toto form.

(2) The expression of the hierarchic form is an indication that the subject is structuring the object of knowledge within his explanatory limits. The expression of the pars pro toto form is an indication that the subject is structuring the object of knowledge beyond his explanatory limits.

(3) Both the hierarchic form and the pars pro toto are simultaneously evidenced in the subject's activity of structuring the object of knowledge, although at different levels of organization.

---

[4] Werner (1957) has stated in this regard: "This principle has the status of a heuristic definition. Though itself not subject to empirical test, it is valuable to developmental psychology in leading to a determination of the actual range of applicability of developmental concepts to the behavior of organisms" (p. 126).

(4) Regardless of which form it takes in structuring the object of knowledge, cognitive activity can be characterized with respect to its degree of differentiation and hierarchic organization.

(5) If a temporal sequence of events is organized in a hierarchic form, by that token these events are being structured into a relationship of continuity and change. If, in contrast, a temporal sequence is organized as a pars pro toto, such events are being structured into a relationship that is immutable and, simultaneously, discontinuous.

(6) These assertions apply to cognitive activity at all levels of maturity.

With respect to the first assertion, a hierarchic form of organization can be described as one in which events are distinguished from one another and, at the same time, connected to one another as particulars of a more inclusive unity. This organization can first be exemplified in regard to a spatial array—namely, in the response of a ten-year-old to Piaget's (1950) class inclusion problem.[5] As part of the usual procedure, the child is shown a large number of wooden beads, most of which are red in color and two of which are blue. After the child has stated, in response to standard questions, that both the red and blue beads are made of wood, he is asked the critical question: "Are there more red beads or more wooden beads?" Our ten-year-old answered the question in the following way: "More wooden beads. [Why are there more wooden beads?] Because some of them are blue and some are red, but all of them are wood."

By his response, the subject is indicating that he has structured the class inclusion problem in a certain way. On the one hand, his distinction between the colors suggests that he has organized the beads into two groups. Even

---

[5] The responses to the class inclusion problem are taken from the protocols of subjects in Feffer and Gourevitch (1960). They can be considered as typical of their age groups.

though a given bead in such and such a place might be segregated from another bead in a different place, the child has brought these together in terms of a common property of "blueness" on the one hand, and "redness" on the other. At the same time, his response indicates that he has further unified the beads, as so distinguished, in terms of a more inclusive property of being wooden. The child, then, is evidencing a hierarchically organized "class inclusion" response. He is distinguishing between classes (each of which has, in itself, served to unify subordinate events) and is, simultaneously, connecting these classes as particulars of a still broader unity.

The pars pro toto has been defined as a form in which the part "stands for" the whole. It, too, can be exemplified by the child's behavior on the bead problem, but now in the response of a younger subject—a response that is developmentally prior to the hierarchically organized class inclusion response (Piaget, 1950). This younger subject, after affirming that the red and blue beads were made of wood, answered the question "Are there more red beads or more wooden beads?" in the following way:

> There's more red beads than wooden beads. [Why are there more red beads than wooden beads?] Because there's only two blue beads and there's a whole bunch of red beads. [Are the red beads made of wood?] Yes. [Are the blue beads made of wood?] Yes. [Then are there more wooden beads or more red beads?] More red beads. [Why are there more red beads than wooden beads?] Because there's a whole bunch of red beads and there's only two blue beads.

After indicating that all the beads are wooden, the child has gone ahead and contradicted himself. He has said, in effect, that "some" of the beads are more than "all" of the beads. Thus, his response that there are more red beads than wooden beads seems to suggest that the "part," somehow, has taken the place of the "whole." However, in designating this intriguing behavior as a pars pro toto, I have something more in mind than the intuition that there has been a reversal of the relationship between what is ordinarily understood as "part" and "whole." Rather, I am suggesting that such behavior can be designated as a "pars pro toto" with reference to the following three related ideas: that the younger child's red grouping represents an activity that is *isolated* relative to the older child's response; that this isolated activity is *functionally equivalent* to the activity represented by the older child's more inclusive wooden grouping; and that this isolated activity is a *part of the whole* as represented by the older child's more inclusive grouping activity.

Thus, I am suggesting, first, that our subject, like the ten-year-old, is structuring the event in terms of separate cognitive activities. He is able to understand, on the one hand, that all the beads are made of wood and, on the other, that they differ in terms of color. Yet, unlike the ten-year-old, he is unable to so distinguish between the beads and, *simultaneously*, unite them as being similar in terms of their property of woodenness. Although capable of both cognitive activities at different times, he cannot integrate these at one particular time into the hierarchic relationship we designate as "class inclusion." It is by realizing this essential isolation between the child's separate cognitive activities that we can begin to understand his contradictory behavior. When the child justifies his response that there are more red beads than wooden beads by saying that there are more red than blue beads, he is distinguishing between the beads in terms of color and, in the course of doing so, this activity is isolated from his earlier activity whereby he structured all the beads as being wooden.[6]

---

[6] The inability to distinguish between the beads in terms of color and, simultaneously, unite them in terms of woodenness, is not simply

But our understanding of the child's response as a pars pro toto is incomplete until we consider an additional feature of the situation. If, for the moment, we take the older child's hierarchically structured solution as a point of reference, we can say that the problem which has been posed for the younger child has this essential characteristic: Its solution requires the child to connect the beads, which he is able to distinguish via their color properties, in terms of a more inclusive property—*when he is unable to do so*. And we can say, further, that in spite of his inability to connect the red and blue beads in this way, *the child goes ahead and "solves" the problem nevertheless*. That is to say, the child's isolated focus on the difference in color is being offered as a solution to the problem. And, further, he is solving this problem in the only way that he can, namely, in terms of those as yet isolated color categories which he is able to impose on the material and which will become integrated into a hierarchic organization in the normal course of development. (Another, more precise way of saying this is that the child is responding to the question "Which are there more of?" in terms of the only organization he can impose on the event that *is* responsive to the question "Which are there more of?" In this sense, we can explain the child's behavior by saying that he attaches the property "more of" only to the redness of the beads and not to the woodenness of the beads because, while he is not yet capable of structuring the event in terms of the more inclusive grouping of woodenness, he is nevertheless capable of structuring the event in terms of an organization of color groupings in which the property "more

---

due to the fact that the property of color is perceptually dominant over that of wood. The identical form of difficulty is evidenced by the child when faced with the problem in which the inclusive class is "children" and the constituents are "boys" and "girls." ("There are ten children in a school; eight are boys and two are girls. Are there more children or more boys?")

of" can be attached to the color grouping of red.) It is under these circumstances that the child's activity takes that particular form which we are designating as the pars pro toto. For one can note what, in my view, is a highly significant feature of the younger child's solution. His solution is similar to that of the older child in that it is a function of the particular organization or unity that he is able to impose on the material. When the younger child solves the problem of "which has more," he is comparing the beads in terms of their color: There are more beads in the grouping of red than there are in the grouping of blue. When the older child solves the problem, he is comparing the more inclusive category of wood to a subcategory of color: There are, if you will, more beads in the grouping of wood than there are in the grouping of red.[7] It may be seen, then, that in solving the problem, the younger subject is using the category of "red" in the same way that he would have used the category of "wood" had he, like the older child, been able to integrate the color properties in terms of this more inclusive grouping. Accordingly, it may be said that even though the groupings imposed on the material by these subjects differ with respect to their inclusiveness, they are *functionally equivalent* in that they serve to solve the problem by connecting partic-

[7] A clear expression of this type of solution is evidenced by the subject who, after saying that there were more wooden beads than red beads, justified his response in the following way:

Because there's a lot—there's a lot of red beads and there are only two blue beads. I mean there's—all the red have only about—maybe 20 beads and they have—22 r—bl—wooden beads because they have two blue beads. [Why does that make it more wooden beads than red beads?] Because the red beads are wooden too. [Yes, but you said there were more wooden beads than red beads. Why are there more wooden beads than red beads?] [No response.] [I think you said it already, but can you tell me once more, so I'm sure I understand?] Because—the red beads are wooden and—and the blue beads are wooden—and there are only about 20 red beads, but there are 22 blue—re—wooden beads.

ulars within a given domain (in the case of the younger child, by connecting spatially segregated beads in terms of their color). It is, in part, because of this attribute of functional equivalence between the two solutions that we are able to characterize the activity of the younger child as evidencing a pars pro toto organization. For we must assume that the child is structuring the problem in terms of an organization that is available to him and, clearly, not in terms of the more inclusive organization that he is yet to evidence. At the same time, his grouping is functionally equivalent to a more inclusive grouping — one which, in the sense of solving the problem, serves in place of this more inclusive grouping. It is this functional equivalence between such different groupings which I have in mind when I use the term "standing for" in the expression "part standing for the whole."[8]

But the terms "part" and "whole" themselves remain unclear until we make explicit an aspect of our discussion which has been implicit thus far. In suggesting that we take the older child's hierarchically structured solution as a point of reference, I am implying that there are really two different perspectives or "knowing activities" involved in our analysis. We have, on the one hand, the perspective of "advanced cognition," which poses the problem and sets the standard for its solution in terms of an organization that is integrated or hierarchic relative to that of the younger child. And we have, on the other hand, the perspective of the younger child who, by definition, understands and solves the problem in terms of those activities which are available to him. In the final analysis, it is this distinction between

---

[8] It may be noted that the concept of functional equivalence reflects the constructionist assumption that cognitive activity, at all levels of maturity, actively imposes an organization on the object of knowledge. Piaget (1952) has treated this issue in terms of his concept of "functional invariance."

cognitive perspectives that permits us to say that when the younger child solves the problem under these circumstances, his solution takes the form of a pars pro toto. For it is only when we take the organization of advanced cognition as a reference point that we can see the younger subject's groupings to be subcategories or "parts" of a more inclusive whole. And, clearly, it is only with advanced cognition as a point of reference that we can say that one of these "parts" is serving as a functional equivalent to the more integrated grouping or "whole" which the subject *fails* to evidence. Thus, when I say that the younger child's solution to the problem evidences a pars pro toto form of organization, I mean that there is a functional equivalence between "part" and "whole" as seen from the perspective of advanced cognition. When the younger child states that there are more red beads than wooden beads, he is solving the problem by using a "part" (or what in the ontogenetically advanced hierarchic response would be the subcategory of red) in the same way that the older child uses the "whole" (or what in the hierarchic response would be the inclusive category of wood).

Our second assertion has already been implied in the above analysis, namely, that the expression of the hierarchic organization is an indication that the subject is structuring the problem within his explanatory limits, while the expression of the pars pro toto organization is an indication that the subject is structuring the problem beyond his explanatory limits. Thus, we see that the older subject has, indeed, evidenced a hierarchic form of organization in solving a problem that is within his explanatory limits or, if you will, a problem that he is capable of solving. And the younger subject has evidenced a pars pro toto when faced with a problem that is clearly beyond his ability, but that he solves nevertheless. But it is obvious that this assertion raises a troublesome and critical question: In what sense can it be said that one can structure a problem *beyond* one's explanatory limits? Have we not contradicted our fundamental constructionist assumption that the object of knowledge is known only in terms of the cognitive activity of the subject and hence must, *by definition,* be within the explanatory limits of such knowing activity? That is to say, are we not implying that the problem has such and such properties which exist outside the knowing activities of the subject and, hence, which are constituted independently of such knowing activity? No such contradiction need be present if one keeps in mind the two perspectives which we have distinguished in our analysis. The distinction between the perspectives of primitive and advanced cognition enables us, without contradiction, to represent the subject as structuring the problem beyond his explanatory limits—as solving an unsolvable problem. For while it is true that from the viewpoint of advanced cognition the younger child is structuring the class inclusion problem beyond his explanatory limits and hence as a pars pro toto, it is also true that when one takes the perspective of the younger child in viewing the event which is being so structured, this same solution to the class inclusion problem is hierarchic in nature. If, instead of the class inclusion question, we were to ask the younger subject, "Which are there more of, the red or blue beads?", the child's answer that there are more red beads than blue beads gives evidence that he is able, in terms of color, to unify beads that differ, for example, with respect to spatial location. He is, in other words, imposing a more inclusive grouping of color upon what one would presume to be diverse events. As so understood, the child's response is as much a form of hierarchic organization as is the older child's response to the class inclusion question. But if this is indeed our interpretation, then it would apply equally to the same response when it is offered as a solution to the class inclusion problem itself: When the younger child structures the class inclusion problem solely in terms of color groupings, i.e., in the same way that he has structured the question "Which are there more of, red or blue beads?", then we can say that he has structured the problem hierarchically. We can say further that he has structured the problem within his explanatory limits, namely, that he has solved the problem in terms of cognitive activities that are available to him. It is only from the viewpoint of *advanced* cognition that the subject is structuring the problem beyond his explanatory limits and, accordingly, as a pars pro toto. These implications of the distinction between the perspectives of primitive and advanced cognition are formally represented as *levels of organization* in the third assertion: Both the hierarchic form and the pars pro toto are simultaneously evidenced in the subject's activity of structuring the object of knowledge, although at different levels of organization. In this sense, the third assertion is a more precise way of expressing the content of the previous assertion. Namely, it can be said that the younger child's activity at one level of organization serves to unite subordinate particulars, while at another level of organization, this structuring is itself but a "part" — a subordinate particular — of the more inclusive construct implied in the older child's class inclusion response. Although the younger child is solving the problem in terms of the differences between isolated groupings — groupings that are subordinate to the more inclusive category used by the older child — each subordinate grouping, in itself, serves as the basis for unifying a domain of diverse and still more subordinate particulars. Accordingly, there is no contradiction in ascribing the pars pro toto and the hierarchic forms of organization to the younger child's activity. But this is the case only if we characterize such constructive activity in terms of *levels* of organization.

The fourth assertion follows from this argument: Regardless of whether it takes a hierarchic or pars pro toto form, cognitive activity in structuring the object of knowledge can be characterized with respect to its *degree* of differentiation and hierarchic organization. Even though the younger child's pars pro toto solution to the class inclusion problem can also be characterized as being hierarchically organized, this structuring must be *less* hierarchic than that evidenced by the older child's class inclusion response since it is, in itself, a constituent of that response.

Having so clarified these four assertions, we are now ready to consider the fifth: If a temporal sequence of events is organized in a hierarchic form, then, by that token, these events are being structured into a relationship of continuity and change. If, in contrast, a temporal sequence is organized as a pars pro toto, then such events are being structured into a relationship that is immutable and, simultaneously, discontinuous. This assertion follows from the two fundamental propositions of my theoretical position. Just as it can be said, in terms of our constructionist assumption, that the child connects beads that he is able to distinguish with respect to spatial location, so too can it be said that the subject connects events that he is able to distinguish as following one another in time.[9] If, moreover, we are able to characterize such cognitive constructions in terms of the orthogenetic principle of increasing differentiation and hierarchization, then the assertions which we have thus far elaborated would apply here as well. We can say, then, that a hierarchic structuring of a temporal sequence is one in which successive events are being distinguished from one an-

---

[9] This statement presumes that developmentally prior constructions of space and time have already taken place and that these less differentiated knowing activities are being further integrated as constituents of more hierarchically organized forms of knowing. Clarifying the process whereby such "categories" of experience are so progressively formed is the central issue for a constructionist conception of development.

other and, at the same time, are being connected to one another as particulars of a more inclusive unity. As in our earlier analysis, this organization can be illustrated by the child's response to a Piagetian task, but now one which highlights the structuring of a temporal sequence. In Piaget's (1950) conservation of quantity task, the child is first given a ball of clay and asked to make another like it. After the child indicates that he is satisfied that the two balls are identical, one ball is left in front of him as a standard of comparison, while the other, also kept in sight, is deformed into a sausage. The child is then asked if the ball and sausage possess the same or different amounts of clay. The child whose behavior on this task exemplifies the hierarchic form of organization will maintain, first of all, that the standard and the deformed event have the same amount of clay. Moreover, if the examiner tries to influence his judgment by suggesting that the sausage has more clay than the ball because of its increased length (e.g., "But isn't the sausage longer than the ball?"), the child will counter this suggestion by indicating that the increase in length is compensated or corrected by the decrease in circumference (e.g., "Yes, but it's also skinnier"). Finally, if the examiner deforms the sausage into successive instances of increasingly longer and narrower sausages, the child in response to the conservation question will, each time, stoutly maintain his initial judgment that the amount of clay remains the same and, each time, will defend his judgment by noting the compensatory relationship between the perceptual or "figural" properties of the event.

It may thus be seen that the subject has imposed an organization on the temporal events — ball into sausage 1, sausage 2, etc. — one that is formally identical to the hierarchic structuring imposed by our class inclusion subject on the spatial array. Just as the blue and red beads were distinguished from one another in terms of their perceptual qualities, so too is our "conserving" subject distinguishing between the temporal sequence of events in perceptual terms, namely, the deformed event is becoming longer and narrower. And just as our class includer is able to unite the discriminated blue and red beads as different particulars of a more inclusive category of wood, so too is our conserver simultaneously connecting the perceptually discriminated temporal events in accordance with a more inclusive unity. The subject has grasped the principle that the difference in a given figural dimension is exactly compensated by the difference in its polar dimension, and that this compensatory relationship applies to all the events which have been discriminated in this temporal sequence. As such, each successive event particularizes this "compensation" rule and, as so understood, possesses an invariant or "conserved" quantity of clay. To emphasize the hierarchic nature of this form of structuring: The rule whereby the successive events are being connected has a relationship of *inclusion* with respect to the states which have been perceptually discriminated. Each state, as perceptually discriminated, is understood as an exemplification of that rule.[10]

On what basis, then, do I say that a hierarchic organization of temporal events structures such events into a relationship of change and continuity? I would suggest, in this regard, that when we use the term "change," we implicitly mean by this, first, that *something* has changed; second, that this "something" is, in itself, invariant or immutable at one level of organization; and, third, that this invariance is evidenced, in different forms, at another level of organization. In regard to the conserving response, this "something"

---

[10] The subject may offer other responses to justify his conserving judgment, such as "You can roll the sausage back into the ball." I am focusing on the compensation rule because it serves, more clearly than these other responses, to illustrate the hierarchic nature of the conserver's structuring of temporal events.

can be said to be a given amount of clay—an amount which exists as an invariant over the time represented by the successive events which have been discriminated. We see, moreover, that by virtue of the rule of compensation, this invariant amount of clay is represented as taking successive and different particular forms: ball to sausage 1, sausage 2, etc. These forms are seen as particulars of the rule and, as so understood, are connected to one another as different perceptual manifestations of the invariant amount of clay. It follows, then, that for the conserver, the perceptual differences between ball and sausage are indicative of a change in perceptual form with respect to this invariant, more inclusive realm of being. The relationship between the hierarchic organization and the notion of change can be stated more formally: If two successive states of being are different from one another, then such differences are indicative of a change from one state to another only in reference to an invariant, more inclusive realm of being—one that is manifested in each of these different states. Indeed, if successive states were understood as different from one another, but not as different forms of the same underlying realm of being, then such states would not be taken as indicative of change, but as isolated, discontinuous happenings.

It can be suggested, further, that when we use the term "continuity," we mean something very much related to what we mean by the term "change." By "continuity," we mean that *something* is continuous; that this "something" is, in itself, invariant at one level of organization; and that this invariance is evidenced in different forms which are discriminated at another level of organization. One might well ask, then, is there any difference in meaning between our notions of continuity and change? I would suggest that there is. When we use the term "continuity" rather than "change," we are focusing on one level of organization rather than another with respect to the hierarchic structuring we are imposing on temporal events. In the notion of change, we are focusing on the *differences* between states, but in relation to an implicit underlying invariance. In the notion of continuity, we are focusing on the underlying invariance or *sameness* of these states, but in relation to their differences. That is to say, the different states have a relationship of continuity by virtue of the fact that, at each point in time, they represent the presence of an invariant state of being. In regard to the conserving response, then, the different shapes of ball, sausage 1, sausage 2, etc., are continuous with one another by virtue of their each having the same amount of clay or, put more concretely, there is, "in" each of the different forms, the "same clay" in the "same amount." One might say, therefore, that in spite of their differences, these states are continuous with respect to one another by virtue of an underlying sameness which each event exemplifies in its different perceptual form.

On further reflection, however, it may be seen that there is a more precise way of formulating this state of affairs. One should say, rather, that it is precisely *because* of their differences that temporal events in a hierarchic organization are continuous with each other. For if each event were considered to reflect an underlying invariance and yet were judged as showing *no* differences with respect to one another, then these events would have to be viewed as *not* having changed. That is, if an underlying state were viewed as being manifested in a given form, and this form were identical to one which followed, then such successive events would have a relationship of immutability — one which, in a sense, would directly reflect the invariance of the underlying state. Thus it can be said that the experience of continuity is, by all means, an experience of sameness, but of a sameness via, or through, differences. An experience of this sameness without such differences could only take the form of immutability.

To sum up, then, the continuity-change relationship is a correlative one. The different events in a temporal sequence are structured into a continuity-change relationship when these events are connected to one another in terms of being different manifestations of a more inclusive invariant state. Under these circumstances, such differences, on the one hand, are indicative of a change in relation to an implicit underlying invariant; on the other hand, there is a continuity between these events to the extent that one focuses on the invariant state which is revealed via these different forms.[11]

We can illustrate the pars pro toto structuring of temporal events by again referring to behavior on Piaget's conservation task, but now as it takes the form of a "non-conserving" solution given by one our younger subjects. This non-conserver, in typical fashion, stated that the ball-deformed-into-sausage had more clay than the ball that had served as the standard, and gave as his reason the fact that the sausage was longer than the ball. And he said this even though the deformation had taken place in full view. This same child, however, on being asked, "What happened to the ball?", indicated that it had become the sausage, and further answered the question "Where is the clay that was in the ball?" by saying that the clay was "in" the sausage—that it had become part of the sausage. Upon being pressed to show the examiner where in the sausage one could "find" the clay that came from the ball, the subject vaguely indicated by word and gesture that it was "spread out" in the sausage.

I consider this behavior illustrative of a pars pro toto for two reasons. First, the non-conserver is solving the prob-

---

[11] My analysis of the continuity-change issue has been significantly influenced by Kaplan (1960). It may be apparent to some readers that the continuity-change relationship, as so represented, has more than an accidental connection to such philosophical issues as "the one and the many," "being and becoming," and "permanence and change."

lem in terms of an activity which is a constituent of the more integrated response given by the conserver. Like the conserver, the non-conserver is able to distinguish between ball and sausage in perceptual or figural terms. But unlike the conserver, for whom the perceptual discrimination is merely a necessary but not sufficient condition for his solution, the non-conserver is solving the problem precisely in terms of this perceptual discrimination. Earlier, we saw that the conserver's judgment of quantity was a function of his ability to integrate, via his rule of compensation, the differences along one perceptual dimension with the differences along the other. The non-conserver, in contrast, bases his judgment of quantity on his discrimination of the ball and sausage in terms of a single, isolated perceptual dimension. In this sense, we can say that the non-conserver is solving the task in terms of an activity which is "part" of the hierarchically organized activity basic to the conserving solution. We can, moreover, interpret the non-conserver's solution in the same way that we did the younger subject's response to the class inclusion problem: The subject is being given a task which requires for its solution a cognitive organization that he has not yet attained. Nevertheless, he solves the task, and on his own terms. Not yet having progressed developmentally to the point where he is able to solve the problem in terms of the more inclusive compensation rule, the non-conserver solves the problem precisely in terms of the "part" activity of which he *is* capable, namely, that of distinguishing between the ball and sausage in perceptual terms. Thus we can say that the non-conserver's perceptual activity, in solving an unsolvable problem, is serving a function equivalent to the more inclusive rule represented by the older subject's conserving response.

Second, his non-conserving judgment notwithstanding, the "ball-into-sausage" are not discrete, isolated events for our subject. As far as he is concerned, the sausage perpetuates the earlier existence of the ball. And, in particular, the clay in the ball continues its existence in the sausage in that it continues to be concretely and perceptually "spread out" in space. It may be said, then, that the subject's perceptual activity serves to do more than merely distinguish between ball and sausage. His perceptual activity also serves to connect, albeit at a different time, the very temporal events which he has distinguished. Here, too, the non-conserver's behavior is formally identical to that of our younger subject on the class inclusion task. This subject, it will be recalled, was able at one time to connect all the beads as being wooden and, at another time, to distinguish between the beads in terms of their color. He was unable, however, to bring these two activities together in that he could not solve the class inclusion problem by connecting the color classes in terms of a more inclusive property of woodenness. Similarly, our non-conserver is unable to integrate the perceptual differences between ball and sausage in terms of a more inclusive rule and is reduced to connecting these events by means of the same perceptual activity that served to distinguish between these events in the first place. As such, this "part" perceptual activity is serving a unifying function equivalent to that served by the more inclusive rule. Accordingly, from this viewpoint as well, it can be said that this part activity is functionally equivalent to the whole — a whole which the non-conserver is yet to construct in terms of the compensation rule, but which he will construct in the normal course of development.[12*]

[12*] My interpretation of the non-conserver's connection of ball and sausage has been influenced by the classical Gestalt conception that such events are integrated in accordance with principles that govern perceptual functioning. As Asch (1952) has stated:

> In an important contribution Duncker... has discussed in detail the correspondence between the phenomenal properties of cause and effect.... In addition to spatio-temporal proximity between cause and effect, there are other important relations of similarity and identity between them. In particular, the form of the effect fre-

We can, accordingly, characterize the hierarchic and pars pro toto structuring of temporal events in the following way: When the conserving subject structures the temporal events of ball and sausage into a hierarchic organization, the constructive activity which serves to connect these events in terms of their similarity has a relationship of *inclusion* to the constructive activity which serves to distinguish between these events in terms of their differences. The perceptual differences between these events serve as the particulars of a more inclusive compensation rule whereby these events are the same. Such perceptual differences, then, can be said to represent functioning at one level of organization, while the rule of compensation can be said to represent functioning at a more inclusive level of organization — functioning which, in unifying these perceptual differences, can coexist simultaneously with such differentiating activity without contradiction. In contrast, when the non-conserving subject structures these temporal events into a pars pro toto, there is a relationship of *identity* between his connecting and differentiating activities. And I mean by this that the non-conserver, although connecting the temporal events of ball-into-sausage, is doing so on a very different structural basis from that of the conserver. In contrast to the rule of com-

---

quently corresponds to the form of the cause. A hot object transmits heat to its neighborhood; a wet object moistens things in contact with it; a moving object sets others objects in motion... [pp. 101–102].

From this viewpoint, the events "ball-into-sausage" have been connected to one another in terms of their spatial and temporal proximity, and in terms of their similarity of color and texture — connections governed by Gestalt principles of perceptual organization. These same principles of organization are also considered to govern the formation of perceptual properties such as length and circumference. And it is in terms of these "Ehrenfels" properties (Köhler, 1947) that the events of "ball-into-sausage" are being distinguished from one another.

pensation which is a different and more inclusive form of cognitive activity than the perceptual events which it unifies, the activity which serves the non-conserver in connecting these events is but another instance of the very same form of functioning which has served to distinguish between these events in the first place. We have seen, moreover, that these differentiating and connecting activities of the non-conserver are isolated from one another. They are elicited at different times by the examiner's questions, and their contradictory implications are not yet realized by the subject. Accordingly, it can be said that the similarities and the differences which the subject is thereby imposing on temporal events are sequential and isolated instances of constructive activity at the same level of organization.[13]

It is from this relationship of identity between differentiating and connecting activities at the same level of organization that we can formally derive the discontinuity-immutability problem. On the one hand, we can say that the successive events of ball and sausage are being distinguished from one another. The subject perceives that the sausage is longer and thinner than the ball. However, he is not yet able to integrate these perceptual differences in accordance with the more abstract and inclusive rule of compensation. In being given a task which requires this rule, he is reduced to solving the problem in terms of what he *can* do, namely, dis-

---

[13] Indeed, as I will suggest in Chapter 6, when the subject brings these isolated perceptual activities in relation to one another, an essential condition of conflict is created whereby the pars pro toto becomes reorganized into a more hierarchic form. Thus the subject is seen as being faced with the contradiction: How can the sausage, which perpetuates the earlier existence of the ball, also have more (or less) clay than the ball? The conservation response, governed as it is by the compensation rule, serves to resolve this contradiction. Needless to say, the problems of clarifying how these separate and isolated events are "brought together," and what is the nature of the process involved in the subsequent reorganization are central for Piagetian theory.

criminate between these events with respect to one or the
other perceptual dimension. Clearly, then, the subject cannot view the perceptual differences between ball and sausage
as different particulars of a rule which he has not yet acquired. Nor can he view these differences as the particulars
of the connecting activity which he *does* evidence, since such
connecting and differentiating activities are but sequential
and isolated instances of functioning at the same level of
organization. Hence, in basing his judgments of quantity on
the perceptual differences between ball and sausage, he can
only understand such differences in quantity as isolated happenings rather than as particulars of a more inclusive, invariant realm of being. The judgments of "more" and "less"
clay occur, then, as discontinuous events.

On the other hand, we have seen that the subject is
perfectly capable of connecting ball-into-sausage in terms of
a perceptual process which I have suggested is governed by
Gestalt principles of organization (see footnote 12). Thus,
the sausage *perpetuates* the existence of the ball; the clay
now present in the sausage is the *same* clay that was earlier
in the ball. It may be seen, then, that the subject's perceptual activity, like the rule, is serving to define an invariant
realm of being — one which exists over the time represented
by the successive events which the non-conserver has
distinguished. As I have emphasized, however, the non-
conserver's activity, in so connecting ball and sausage, is
isolated from the activity which has served to distinguish
between these events. Accordingly, the invariant realm of
being which is thus defined by the subject's connecting activity is isolated from the differences between these temporal
events. The amount of clay, defined as an invariant by the
subject's perceptual activity, cannot be particularized in
terms of the perceptual differences between ball and
sausage. As such an invariant, it cannot simultaneously be
represented, at another level of organization, as taking suc-

cessive and different perceptual forms. It follows, then, that in contrast to connecting ball-into-sausage as a continuous event — in a relationship of sameness that is expressed via different forms — the non-conserver is connecting ball-into-sausage in a relationship of sameness with *no* differences. That is to say, in a relationship of immutability.

In sum, just as the continuity-change relationship is a correlative one, so too is the relationship between immutability and discontinuity. Immutability and discontinuity are the fundamental properties of a pars pro toto organization whereby the cognitive activity that serves to distinguish between temporal events is a separate and isolated instance of the same form of cognitive activity that serves to connect these same events. Essentially, the child when focusing on the similarity between ball and sausage, cannot at the same time consider these events in terms of their differences. Accordingly, either the quality of discontinuity or that of immutability will be evidenced as a function of whether the subject focuses on the differences between the successive events or their connection. To the extent that he focuses on the differences, then the quality of discontinuity comes to the fore. To the extent that he focuses on their similarity, then the quality of immutability takes precedence.[14] We thus have the anomalous situation in which the child sees the clay as existing in immutable form, all the while that he also sees it as discontinuously increasing or decreasing. In this re-

[14] At this point, my interpretation converges with Goldstein's (1940) and Hanfmann's (1939) view that the "pathological concreteness" and "over-abstractness" which coexist in the thought disorder of the brain injured and schizophrenic are derivable from the same form of thought, namely, one in which the similarity of events cannot be considered simultaneously with respect to their differences (see also Feffer, 1967). At the same time, this convergence should serve to underscore my departure from a more common usage of "pars pro toto" — one that tends to restrict the term to instances of "paralogical thinking" or formal thought disorder. (See Arieti [1959] and Kasanin [1944] for a discussion of paralogical thinking in schizophrenia.)

spect, our non-conserver is functioning like Orwell's barn-
yard commissar, who justifies a contradictory practice by
saying that all the animals are equal but some are more
equal than others. For our non-conserver, the clay in
the sausage, by virtue of its concrete perceptual extension, is
the same clay that was earlier in the ball. And yet, by virtue
of its *greater* perceptual extension, namely, its increased
length, the sausage has more clay than was earlier in the
ball.

How then, it may be asked, are these considerations
relevant to our thesis regarding the Freudian theory of
development? I have suggested in this regard that a theory
of development is a set of concepts that serve to organize
our experience of temporal events such that these events are,
on the one hand, distinguished from one another in terms of
their relative maturity and, on the other hand, connected to
one another in terms of their underlying similarity. As so
understood, these concepts (or theoretical "constructs") not
only guide our highly refined and consciously manipulated
scientific efforts, but govern our everyday common sense activities as well. It is clear, for example, that we are guided in
our everyday raising of children by common sense distinctions we make between the primitive behavior of the child
and the mature behavior of the adult-to-be: distinctions between impulsiveness and foresight, between helplessness and
independence, between an eye-for-an-eye vindictiveness and
a flexible forbearance. And it is equally clear that our
childrearing practices also involve the common sense con-
viction that there is an underlying connection between the
temporal events which we have so distinguished. We have
proverbs which not only connote this connection in a
general way ("The child is father to the man"), but which
also represent opposing intuitions regarding the nature of
this connection ("One cannot make a silk purse out of a
sow's ear" versus "As the twig is bent, so will the tree be

formed"). At this common sense level, then, a temporal sequence of events is being organized by a theory of development. The behaviors of the child and adult are being distinguished in terms of their relative maturity, and are also being connected to one another in terms of an underlying unity. It follows, then, that the assertions we have considered in relation to the child's structuring of the conservation problem would apply, as well, to common sense theories as they serve to structure the temporal events of child and adult behavior. Moreover, if we presume my final assertion, namely, that our previous considerations apply to cognitive activity at *all* levels of maturity, then it follows that just as a common sense structuring of temporal events is limited to the hierarchic and pars pro toto forms of organization, so too are these forms of organization the only ones which are available to "refined" theories of development.[15] If, then, I am able to establish that a refined theory of development encounters problems of immutability and discontinuity, I should be able to derive these problems from a relationship of identity between differentiating and connecting constructs. And, in this context, I mean by a relationship of identity that the construct which serves as the basis for distinguishing between primitive and mature behavior also serves (although at a different time) to define

[15] The characterization of scientific theory as "refined common sense" is borrowed from Pepper (1942). This characterization can be misleading, however, if by this one assumes that there is, on the one hand, only common sense cognition and, on the other, only refined theoretical cognition. In my view there are a multitude of forms whereby temporal events can be structured. Where these forms have a developmental relationship, it can be further said that the less hierarchically organized form serves as a constituent of the more hierarchically organized form. Though too sharp a dichotomy may thus be implied by "refined" versus "common sense" cognition, the distinction does serve to emphasize my view that cognitive activity at all levels of maturity is always a structuring of experience and, hence, evidences the two forms of organization that I am proposing.

the underlying unity whereby such differentiated events are being connected. Moreover, I would offer the following interpretation of such an identity relationship between differentiating and connecting constructs: Although the theorist has been able to posit a construct that serves to distinguish between the temporal events of child and adult behavior, he has not been able to offer a more inclusive construct that can serve to connect these temporal events as so distinguished. Yet he has gone ahead and posited a connecting construct nevertheless. He has solved this unsolvable problem by means of a construct that he *has* been able to posit, namely, by means of a construct that has served to distinguish between these events in the first place. Finally, I would argue that when someone else, in turn, interprets the temporal events of personality development in terms of such constructs, he too is forced to structure such events in the form of an identity relationship. The cognitive activity whereby he distinguishes between the primitive behavior of the child and the mature behavior of the adult becomes a separate and isolated instance of the same form of cognitive activity whereby he imposes a connection upon these temporal events.[16]

My critique, then, will attempt to show that this relationship of identity between the differentiating and connecting activity of the subject underlies the problems of preformism and logical inconsistency that have been attributed to the Freudian position. I will argue, in this regard, that Freudian theory views the functioning of the child as being reac-

---

[16] Note that two separate ideas are involved here. One is that when the theory posits identical connecting and differentiating constructs, these represent separate and isolated instances of the same form of cognitive activity on the part of the individual who has proposed the theory. The other is that such an identity relationship between differentiating and connecting constructive activity is again involved when another individual uses these concepts in interpreting the temporal events of personality development.

tive or mechanical in nature, and that it distinguishes such functioning from the behavior of the adult which it views as having a purposive directionality. Freudian theory posits, moreover, that the behaviors of the child and the adult have an underlying connection. Common to their behaviors, as so distinguished, is a core of functioning which the theory under certain circumstances represents as being identical to the mechanical reactivity of the child and, under other circumstances, as being identical to the purposive directionality of the adult. I will argue, then, that Freudian theory structures the problem of development in terms of an identity relationship. It advances a construct that serves as a basis for distinguishing between primitive and advanced behavior, while that same construct also serves to define the underlying unity whereby such differentiated states are being connected. Accordingly, I will make the case that when the subject interprets personality development in terms of this identity relationship between differentiating and connecting constructs, he is forced to structure the temporal events of child and adult behavior into a form of immutability and discontinuity. When he focuses on the similarity between primitive and mature functioning, this similarity takes the form of an immutable event. He ascribes properties to mature functioning that are present from the very beginning in primitive behavior. That is, he interprets development in a way that has traditionally been termed "preformist." On the other hand, when he focuses on the differences between primitive and mature functioning, he is forced to represent the characteristics of mature behavior as discontinuously coming into being. And as so represented, these characteristics contradict the fact that they have also been represented as being present in primitive functioning from the very outset. Hence the problem of logical inconsistency.

Finally, the reader should distinguish between two central ideas in my argument and should note their connection with the two basic presumptions of my theoretical approach. One critical notion is that the problem of immutability and discontinuity in a refined theory of development derives from a relationship of identity between constructive activities — from the fact that a constructive activity is serving to connect a sequence of temporal events when this same form of constructive activity is also serving to distinguish between these events. This notion is based on my assumption that cognitive activity structures the object of knowledge. Were my critique to be based, instead, on an assumption of the independently constituted event, I could hardly make the same assertion. The second critical idea is that this identity relationship is indicative of a pars pro toto and, accordingly, of the fact that the subject, using the concepts of this refined theory, is structuring a problem beyond his explanatory limits. Clearly, then, I am extrapolating from my analysis of the child's cognitive activity to an analysis of scientific cognition. This extrapolation presumes that constructions of reality by refined theories are as subject to development as constructions of reality by common sense cognition; and it presumes, further, that where such development does occur, it takes the form of increasing hierarchization. Thus, we are able to characterize refined Freudian theory as structuring the problem beyond its explanatory limits only if we assume, first, that relative to the Freudian conception, a more advanced theoretical construction of development is possible *in principle* and, second, that if such a construction *were* to be evidenced, it would be more hierarchically organized than the Freudian conception. This permits us to take the hypothetical theoretical construction as a point of reference in our analysis of Freudian theory, just as we took ontogenetically advanced cognition as such a point of reference in our analysis of the younger child's behavior on the bead problem. In so doing, we can interpret the "connecting" construct in the Freudian interpretation as a "part" that is functionally equivalent to the integrated unity or "whole" represented by this more advanced hypothetical conception of development. That is to say, we can interpret this concept in Freudian theory as serving to connect unities which have been differentiated when, in fact, no more inclusive concept (as represented by our hypothetical theory) is available to Freudian theory. By so interpreting the Freudian conception (namely, as one that connects realms of being when it lacks the more inclusive concept for doing so), we are able to account for the identity relationship between constructs and, by logical derivation, the forms of immutability and discontinuity that Freudian theory encounters.

In short, it is in terms of using a more hierarchically organized, albeit hypothetical, conception as a reference point that we can make the case that an identity relationship, from which we logically derive the immutability-discontinuity problem, is indicative of a pars pro toto structuring of the problem beyond the explanatory limits of the theory. And we are able to posit such a hypothetical reference point only on the basis of the orthogenetic principle that constructive activity manifests an increasing hierarchization with development—a principle that, accordingly, serves to elaborate the constructionist assumption.

2

THE CARTESIAN ASSUMPTIONS OF
INSTINCT THEORY AND BEHAVIORISM

In the last chapter, I suggested that if a theoretical conception of development advances a construct that serves as a basis for distinguishing between primitive and advanced behavior, and that construct also serves to define the underlying unity whereby such differentiated states are connected, then from a logical viewpoint that conception must structure the problem of development as one of immutability and discontinuity. I have proposed, moreover, that this identity relationship between differentiating and connecting constructs occurs when the theory lacks a construct that is inclusive of the states it has differentiated, but posits a connection between these states nevertheless. Thus, I have suggested that the identity relationship can be interpreted as a pars pro toto form of organization which is evidenced when the theory structures the problem of development beyond its explanatory limits.

It can now be proposed that the explanatory limits of a theory of psychological development are given by its underlying epistemology. By this, I mean that the differenti-

ating and connecting constructs which are being advanced
in a conception of development derive from the theory's assumptions regarding the relationship between the subject
and object of knowledge. The present chapter advances my
argument for this assertion. It does so by focusing on the
classic positions of instinct theory and behaviorism in regard
to the problem of development. First, I will describe these
positions as they are represented by Allport and Bertocci in
their controversy concerning the functional autonomy of
motives. This controversy will serve to draw our attention to
what appears to be a fundamental antagonism between the
conceptions of development advanced by instinct theory
and behaviorism, namely, that one view encounters a problem of immutability and the other a problem of discontinuity. I will then turn to the positions of instinct theory
and behaviorism as these are represented by Asch. My intent here is to make the case, using Asch's analysis, that in
spite of this mutual antagonism, each conception of
development does, in fact, encounter an identical form of
the immutability-discontinuity problem. Finally, I will argue
that instinct theory and behaviorism encounter the same
form of the immutability-discontinuity problem because
they assume the same Cartesian epistemology. It is here that
my thesis will serve to clarify the connection between this
epistemology and the forms of immutability and discontinuity which these positions encounter in their conceptions
of development. I will argue that the basic constructs of
both positions embody a Cartesian view of the relationship
between the subject and object of knowledge and, because
of the explanatory limits which are thus given, serve to
structure the temporal sequence of child and adult behavior
in terms of an identity relationship and, hence, into a form
of immutability and discontinuity.

THE ALLPORT-BERTOCCI CONTROVERSY

The exchange between Allport and Bertocci centered

on a conception that Allport (1937) had proposed as an alternative to the prevailing views of instinct theory and behaviorism regarding the nature of development. In Allport's opinion, neither of these positions did justice to the fact that the behavior of the child developed into adult motivation which was both diversified and purposive. On the one hand, Allport suggested, the behaviorist conception that habits were acquired via conditioning could account for the diversity of adult motivation. However, this approach left the development of such behavior almost entirely to chance factors of external stimulation, and treated interests and dispositions as purely reactive or mechanical in nature. As such, the directed, long-term purposiveness which he saw in adult interests was being inadequately represented in the behaviorist conception. On the other hand, Allport recognized that instinct theory did, indeed, represent the purposive directionality of adult motivation. Yet because of its conception that such purposive striving was innate, it did not at the same time deal with the uniqueness or the qualitative diversity of adult behavior. As Allport (1937) noted:

> The enthusiastic collector of bric-a-brac derives his enthusiasm from the parental instinct; so too does the kindly old philanthropist, as well as the mother of a brood. It does not matter how different these three interests seem to be, they derive their energy from the same source. The principle is that a very few basic motives suffice for explaining the endless varieties of human interests [p. 143].

It followed for Allport that since each adult had his own unique pattern of purposive interests and strivings while the child did not, there was a developmental process of individuation that was not being represented by either of these approaches.[1] The concept of *functional autonomy*

---

[1] Allport also criticizes Freudian theory in similar terms. Since, however, the Freudian approach receives extended treatment in later

was Allport's attempt to represent this process. In his view, this concept combined the best of both approaches in that it embodied behaviorism's view of qualitative diversity and instinct theory's emphasis on the purposive directionality of adult motivation. As such, the principle of functional autonomy stood "midway" between the behaviorist view and the instinct approach by characterizing "adult motives as infinitely varied, and as self-sustaining *contemporary* systems, growing out of antecedent systems, but functionally independent of them" (p. 143). In terms of this conception, adult motives had a point of origin in the organic tensions of infancy in that they were initially acquired as conditioned instrumental activities, as behaviors which, in relation to environmental events, served to reduce physiological drive. However, this bond between adult motives and the organic tensions of infancy was historical and not functional in that it was broken as the individual matured. As Allport notes in one of his illustrations, the ex-sailor may have initially acquired his love for the sea as an incident of his effort to make a living. In Allport's words, "the sea was merely a conditioned stimulus associated with satisfaction of his 'nutritional craving' " (p. 145). But as a wealthy man, even though he was no longer required to have commerce with the sea in order to satisfy a physiological need, his "hunger for the sea persists unabated" (p. 145). What was initially a conditioned instrumental activity became independent of the drive that it was originally designed to satisfy:

> The pursuit of literature, the development of good taste in clothes, the use of cosmetics, the acquiring of

---

chapters, this content is omitted here. It should also be noted that I do not attempt to deal with the issue of individual differences versus nomothetic laws (an important concern of Allport's), even though the issue is closely related to the problem of continuity and change as I am posing it.

an automobile ... all may first serve, let us say, the interests of sex. But every one of these instrumental activities may become an interest in itself, held for a life time, long after the erotic motive has been laid away in lavender [p. 146].

In noting, moreover, that adult motives were not reducible to either instinctual givens or to physiological satisfaction, Allport was emphasizing that such activity could not be viewed as being powered by energy from organic sources. Rather, adult motives were "contemporary systems" that were self-sustained by virtue of their "lack of completion":

The child who is *just learning* to speak, to walk, or to dress is, in fact, likely to engage in these activities for their own sake, precisely as does the adult who has an *unfinished* task in hand. He remembers it, returns to it, and suffers a feeling of frustration if he is prevented from engaging in it. Motives are always a kind of striving for some form of completion; they are unresolved tension, and demand a "closure" to activity under way [p. 154].

It may thus be seen that in emphasizing an infinite variety of purposive behaviors that became independent of their instinctual source, the principle of functional autonomy was directed toward representing the qualitative diversity and uniqueness of adult motivation. In this sense, the concept of functional autonomy represented Allport's attempt to account for a process of change in terms of which the undifferentiated child became the differentiated adult — a process that he felt was neglected, in particular, by instinct theory. But if Allport was so directed toward representing the quality of change in development, Bertocci (1940), as a proponent of instinct theory, addressed himself to what he saw as the opposite weakness in Allport's conception. And that was

his failure adequately to represent the continuity of
development:

> ... because Allport is concerned to emphasize the
> uniqueness of personality against an instinct-theory, his
> own theory must adequately deal with the basic prob-
> lem of the psychology of personality, namely, the unity
> and continuity as well as uniqueness and differentiation
> of personality.... But will the principle of functional
> autonomy do justice to the datum, namely, the observ-
> able continuity of personal development? [p. 517].

In developing his argument, Bertocci capitalized on
Allport's own criticism of the behaviorist conception of
learning (namely, that it emphasizes chance reactivity) and
asked in regard to the concept of self-sustained instrumentalities: What is to prevent *all* acquired behavior from becoming self-perpetuating? And if such were the case, would
one not then have the individual jumping on his horse and
galloping simultaneously in all directions? Clearly, for Bertocci, the concept of intrinsically energized contemporary
systems raised havoc with the continuity of personality:

> ... if mechanisms do cut loose not only from the
> original but also from all innate purposive drives, the
> unity and longitudinal consistency of any acquired per-
> sonality is no longer guaranteed [p. 521].

But, he noted, there was a more fundamental difficulty
in Allport's account. This had to do with the fact that
Allport accepted the behaviorist interpretation as to how the
instrumentalities were acquired in the first place, namely,
through an association between behavioral and environmental events by virtue of the reduction of physiological
need. It was not, Bertocci commented, that he had difficulty
in accepting the behaviorist's starting point that the infant
felt bodily comfort owing to the presence of mother. The

mother, he agreed, became functionally related to the infant's need for bodily comfort. What concerned him was what followed in the behaviorist's conception:

> ... the magic begins when we are told that her absence provokes a longing for the "comfort of her companionship," especially if "companionship" means more than simple bodily comfort. For whence this desire for social, aesthetic, or mental companionship in an organism which by definition wants only physical comfort.... A white rabbit and a black cat have suddenly appeared in the tall white hat which a moment ago contained only one innocent white rabbit! [p. 519].

It followed for Bertocci that if such discontinuity was encountered in traditional behaviorist theory, then it was doubly a problem in Allport's approach since he accepted the mechanistic drive-reduction model as a starting point and ended up with purposive, intrinsically energized adult motives:

> ... if the non-purposive "push" of infancy gives way to the purposive "pull" of increasing maturity, we are left with another mystery. Whence the purposes which later appear in human behavior? By what magic are these new purposes born? Are they sprung full-born from the head of Zeus? [p. 518].

The systematic implications of this criticism were, perhaps, most clearly indicated in Bertocci's formal analysis of the conception of novel motives:

> Let us first be clear as to the meaning of *created*.... The creation of an entity involves the creation *outright* of an entirely new or novel quality or thing, the abrogation of its continuity with what preceded it so far as human knowledge is concerned. To maintain that new interests or purposes are created involves, therefore,

the premise that new interests or needs occur in the organism ... without any continuity in essential *quality* and *direction* with the givens [p. 511].

Having thus scored the discontinuity encountered in the principle of functional autonomy, Bertocci in turn offered his own alternative to account for the qualitative diversity of adult motivation. Congruent with McDougall's instinct theory, Bertocci started with the assumption that the organism, without benefit of learning or training, had "instinctive propensities" for acting in particular ways toward environmental objects. The maternal instinct, for example, was aroused by the stimulation of the infant's presence and found expression in a specific mode of behavior (the instrumentality) in relation to the object. Instincts could thus be differentially "realized" through instrumentalities, as goal-directed behavior, depending on the nature of the external circumstances. As an artist might seize upon whatever materials were at hand—bits of cloth, oil paint, or raw granite—in order to express his creative impulse, and in doing so manifest different forms of creative activity, so too did an instinctive propensity realize its essential nature by exploiting particular environmental circumstances by means of this or that instrumentality. In one culture, the maternal instinct could realize itself in relation to the infant in terms of swaddling; in another, in terms of rocking. Moreover, as a specific alternative to Allport's notion that adult motives functioned as autonomous contemporary systems, Bertocci proposed that the instrumentality also could function independently of the original instinct. However, he posited an energy source for this "autonomous" instrumentality that was very different from the intrinsic motivation suggested by Allport:

To use a crude figure, mechanisms are like the horse-riders ... [they] can switch from the saddle of one

horse (propensity) to the back of another.... But they
do not drive themselves! [pp. 521–522].

Thus, in his account of change, Bertocci guarded
against the discontinuity of functional autonomy by substituting *another* instinct as the energy source of an instrumentality that had apparently become autonomous. As Bertocci
saw it, if the ex-sailor's love for the sea was no longer serving
to realize a nutritional instinct, it was nevertheless realizing,
and thus being powered by, another equally fundamental
instinct. It was this continuing presence of the innate propensities as the basic motive source that provided the con-
sistency and continuity of personality:

> ... we can appeal to the mysterious concept of on-
> togenetic emergent evolution to account for the
> appearance of new needs.... Or we can appeal to an
> instinct-theory which attempts to delineate what these
> basic drives ... are in the first place [p. 520].

This way of avoiding the problem of discontinuity in
accounting for the development of motivation is clearly seen
in Bertocci's view of purposive behavior. Bertocci had no
doubt that such behavior typified adult motivation. Indeed,
to his way of thinking, purpose was a primary datum to
which any theory was required to address itself. But it was
not an emergent which thereby distinguished adult motivation from that of the child. Rather, purposive striving was
given in the propensities to start with and, as such, characterized the behavior of the child as well as that of the adult:

> In the last analysis, the inadequacy of explanations in
> organic terms lies in their inability to account for the
> *functional* or *purposive* data of human experience. For
> this very reason, the hormist starts with the psychic
> level of purposive striving and maintains it throughout
> [p. 518].

THE IDENTICAL CONSTRUCTS OF INSTINCT THEORY AND BEHAVIORISM

It can be said, then, that when the positions of Allport and Bertocci are seen from the other's perspective, each is subject to an essential problem. Allport attempts to do justice to the differentiation and uniqueness of adult motivation and hence to the dimension of change in development. His efforts are criticized by Bertocci, who points out that the concept of functional autonomy is especially vulnerable to the weakness of behaviorist doctrine. Namely, that in terms of this formulation, change becomes discontinuity. Yet Bertocci's alternative to the discontinuity of functional autonomy only manifests the weakness that Allport's principle had attempted to correct in the first place. In accounting for the continuity between the adult's purposive behavior and that of the child, Bertocci relies on the continuing presence of the innate propensities which evidence purposiveness at the "psychic level" in earliest infancy. In so investing the organism at the outset with that which is evidenced in maturity, Bertocci would appear to exemplify the essential implications of Allport's criticism that continuity in the hands of instinct theory becomes preformism, or an immutable sameness. In their mutual criticism, then, the interchange between Allport and Bertocci (and, by proxy, between behaviorism and instinct theory) has assumed a particular form.[2] Each theorist, in his attempt to correct for what he views as a distortion of the continuity-change relationship engendered by the other's position, is open to the criticism by the other that he, too, has distorted the relationship, albeit in the opposite direction.

It might thus appear that the Allport-Bertocci contro-

[2] It should be clear that I am confining myself to Allport's concept of functional autonomy and am not characterizing his general theoretical position.

versy represents a conflict between essentially different and mutually antagonistic conceptions of development. And, indeed, this is how the controversy between instinct theory and behaviorism has generally been portrayed in the literature. A notable exception to this portrayal, however, has been the Gestalt position regarding these theories, a position that has been particularly well represented by Asch (1952) in his approach to the continuity-change problem (or, as he terms it, the issue of "psychological invariance and change"). Although Asch acknowledges the obvious differences between instinct theory and behaviorism, he suggests that these differences are more apparent than real in that they stem from the same theoretical perspective regarding the problem of continuity and change in development. Thus, on one level, Asch characterizes instinct theory and behaviorism in very much the same way that Allport and Bertocci characterize each other's position on the issue of the functional autonomy of motives. As does Allport, Asch criticizes instinct theory for the immutability that is given in its view of "original man." He notes that in its account of the continuity in development, instinct theory posits, as its basic unit of analysis, the "instinctive propensity," which is "prewired" to the object by means of a specific mode of behavior — the instrumentality. Only the instrumentality, he notes, can be altered as a function of experience and even this modification is assigned minimal weight by instinct theory. What is emphasized, instead, is that the instinctive tendency and its allied emotions are beyond the reach of experience and thereby constitute the same underlying core of both the child's and the adult's behavior (for example, the maternal instinct as this is evidenced in the behavior of the child cuddling her doll and the mother nursing her child).

And, as does Bertocci, Asch criticizes behaviorist doctrine for the discontinuity that is given in its view of "modified man," that is to say, for the discontinuity that is evidenced in the process whereby the behavior of the child becomes that of the adult as a consequence of external stimulation and experience. As Asch describes it, classical behaviorism starts with the organism in a state of primary need, such as hunger or sexual excitation, a state that elicits restless activity made up of random, or trial-and-error, behavior. This activity can be exemplified by the paradigm of the hungry cat in a cage in which the escape route is closed by a latch; some food is then placed outside the bars, just beyond the cat's reach. Under these conditions, a typical sequence of trial-and-error behavior would consist of the cat's extending its paw between the bars of the cage, followed by biting at the bars, and then shaking anything that is loose in the cage. As Asch has noted, these responses are understood as being random in that, unlike the instrumentality of instinct theory, they are not inherently directed toward external events which would serve, objectively, to reduce the primary need. Even though such movements (as biting the bars of the cage) may be elicited by "native action tendencies," they are "blind" in relation to the goal (namely, they do not reflect the fact that pressing the latch is a necessary instrumental activity for the reduction of hunger). Instead, the particular sequence of movements is understood by this conception as a mechanical repetition of those behaviors which have served in the past to bring about the reduction of primary need. The response that is evidenced first in the sequence is the one that has been "reinforced" the most frequently and consistently, the response evidenced second in the sequence is the one that has been reinforced the next most frequently, etc. It follows from this conception of change, then, that if a given movement in this random sequence *does* serve to reduce the primary need under these circumstances, then this particular behavior becomes differentially strengthened in relation to the other responses of the sequence. It has a higher probability of occurrence than it did prior to such reinforcement. Thus, in the behaviorist paradigm, the cat in its blind, mechanical repetition of past reinforced behaviors might sooner or later accidently push the latch which opens the door of the cage at which point he is able to escape and eat the food. If, now, the cat is repeatedly put back in the cage under the same conditions of hunger, the act of pushing the latch may be observed to occur earlier and earlier in its sequence of activities, until at some point the cat promptly pushes the latch and eats the food. It may thus be said that a mediating activity has been acquired, or that a habit has been formed. And this is further understood to mean that an activity that had a relatively low probability of occurring under these conditions now has a high probability of occurring by virtue of the reinforcement history derived from the experience in the cage. As Asch characterizes the behaviorist viewpoint, acquired behavior, whether that of lower animals or man, and whether nonsocial or social in nature, is an initially produced sequence of random activities which become differentially highlighted to the extent that they happen to mediate, or are instrumental to, primary need gratification.[3]

As has been suggested, moreover, the similarity between Asch's critique and that of Bertocci goes further than one of noting the behaviorist emphasis on change. Like Bertocci, Asch considers change, as so conceptualized in behav-

---

[3] Note that, in an important sense, the habit which is so acquired is "already there" in the existing response repertory of the organism, but at a lower probability of occurrence. Dollard and Miller (1950), for example, have asked in this regard: "But if the correct response must always occur before it can be rewarded, what novelty is added by learning?" And they answer: "The new feature is that the particular response rewarded now occurs regularly to a specific cue, whereas previously its occurrence at just that time and place may have been exceedingly infrequent" (p. 37). It will be seen, in the analysis of Freudian theory, that this view can be understood as being a characteristic example of the form which the immutability-discontinuity problem takes in Cartesian conceptions of development.

iorist theory, to be discontinuous in the sense that such acquired mediating behavior is subject to "chance factors" of
external stimulation. In the behaviorist account, he points
out, what is acquired is fortuitous. Such mediating behavior
has no intrinsic relation to the essential properties of man,
as defined by what is given in man's original nature. Regardless of its characteristics, an act is retained if it satisfies.
Asch underscores this fortuitousness of acquired characteristics in "modified man" by noting that, from the behaviorist
viewpoint, anything — even properties which are antithetical
to one another — can be so acquired.

> Tendencies to kill and to love, to pursue truth and to
> cheat, to compete and to cooperate — each of these stands
> in exactly the same external relation to the nature of
> men; they are so many habits and tendencies that men
> may or may not acquire [p. 74].

Clearly, then, Asch's criticisms are similar to those
made by Allport and Bertocci in their respective evaluations
of each other's position. However, Asch's analysis goes beyond the Allport-Bertocci controversy in suggesting that
there is a more fundamental commonality which underlies
the apparent differences between instinct theory and behaviorism. Their differences notwithstanding, he asserts, the approaches of instinct theory and behaviorism represent the
same traditional answer to the problem of invariance and
change in psychological development.

> Both doctrines agree in formulating the proposition
> that what is invariant in human beings is given before
> experience and that the effects of experience, since
> they depend on external conditions, on circumstances
> not directly related to the properties of men, furnish
> the contingent aspect of men [p. 75].

Asch is suggesting here that both theories understand
the developmental relationship between the child and adult

in identical ways. Both positions view the *continuity* of development in terms of the notion of an inherited inner "nature"—an inner nature of specific trends and capacities that are given "before experience" and that reveal themselves most clearly in behavior at the earliest stages of life. Regardless of whether man's inherited nature is seen in terms of the primary needs of behaviorism (such as the sexual and hunger drives), or as the extensively organized propensities of instinct theory (such as the sexual and life-preservative instincts), the construct of an inherited inner nature provides the basis for understanding the similarity between the child and adult. Namely, this construct serves to define a common invariant core that underlies the diverse behaviors of child and adult and that is, itself, beyond the reach of experience. At the same time, Asch suggests, both positions understand developmental *change* as a modification of behavior that was originally governed by this native core—a modification that is seen as being fortuitous, as stemming from "nurture," or, as they see it, from experience with external events that are not "directly related" to man's inner nature. This is the case whether such differences are understood as minor modifications of the instrumentality by instinct theory, or as major modifications of random behavior into habits by behaviorism. In sum, then, Asch is asserting that the so-called "nature-nurture controversy" between instinct theory and behaviorism is only a controversy with respect to *what* and *how much* is acquired and not with respect to a conception of the process that underlies development. That is to say, both approaches understand the continuity and change of development in terms of identical conceptions of nature and nurture. Their difference lies in merely giving differential weight to the nature and nurture constructs in their relative emphasis on original or modified man.[4]

[4] For a parallel critique of the nature-nurture controversy in the area of comparative animal behavior, see Lehrman (1970).

THE CARTESIAN WORLD VIEW OF INSTINCT
THEORY AND BEHAVIORISM

My thesis exploits Asch's contention that both positions understand the problem of development in terms of
identical constructs. Although he does not explicitly state it,
Asch's analysis suggests that the distinction which both approaches make between the native inner core of the propen-
sities/primary needs and the externally influenced mediating
activity of the instrumentalities/habits reflects the epistemology of a more fundamental Cartesian world view — one
which bifurcates nature into separate and mutually alien
states of subjective and objective being. In so characterizing
the Cartesian world view, I am following Burtt (1924) in
applying the term "Cartesian" to those philosophical positions in which an independently constituted reality is distinguished from a subject of knowledge who, by virtue of
the material nature of his senses, contributes subjective and
illusory qualities to the known event. In this sense, one can
so designate the views of Galileo and Newton as well as Descartes, although I do not intend by this to otherwise equate
their philosophies. The seeds of this world view, Burtt suggests, are given in a conception set forth by Galileo whereby
he distinguished between "primary" and "secondary" qualities of being. Although lengthy, Galileo's treatment is worth
quoting because of its importance to my argument:

> ... I feel myself impelled by the necessity, as soon as I
> conceive a piece of matter or corporeal substance, of
> conceiving that in its own nature it is bounded and
> figured in such and such a figure, that in relation to
> others it is large or small, that it is in this or that place,
> in this or that time, that it is in motion or remains at
> rest, that it touches or does not touch another body,
> that it is single, few, or many; in short by no imagina-

tion can a body be separated from such conditions: but that it must be white or red, bitter or sweet, sounding or mute, of a pleasant or unpleasant odour, I do not perceive my mind forced to acknowledge it necessarily accompanied by such conditions; so if the senses were not the escorts, perhaps the reason or the imagination by itself would never have arrived at them. Hence I think that these tastes, odours, colours, etc., on the side of the object in which they seem to exist, are nothing else than mere names, but hold their residence solely in the sensitive body; so that if the animal were removed, every such quality would be abolished and annihilated [quoted in Burtt, 1924, p. 85].

In its classic form, then, the basis for the Cartesian world view starts with the assumption that there are, on the one hand, the "primary" qualities of the object, such as size, extension, and number. These properties are objective in the sense that they are intrinsically connected to the object, namely, the object cannot be conceived of apart from such attributes. Being intrinsic to the object, they are *independently constituted* in that they do not require the perceiving individual for their existence. On the other hand, there are the "secondary" qualities of the object, such as fragrance and color. These properties have a different ontological status. Since one can conceive of the object without its necessarily having such attributes, then it follows that these attributes are not intrinsically connected to it. It further follows, however, that since they *are* experienced as properties of the object, then this must be a function of what the perceiving individual brings to the object by experiencing it through his material physiological senses. Rather than being independently constituted, then, these secondary qualities are subjective in that they exist only as a function of the knower; they are, in Galileo's words, "mere names" which reside solely in the subject.[5]

In elaborating on this Cartesian view, Burtt suggests that the distinction between primary and secondary qualities was instrumental to impressive advances made in our knowledge of the physical world. Indeed, he suggests, this view of reality has come to serve as the metaphysical foundation of modern science and as the dominant world view of our age. However, he proposes, these advances were gained at a price — a price that is implied in the very distinction between the primary and secondary qualities of being. And that price was a fundamental isolation between the subject and object:

> The gloriously romantic universe of Dante and Milton, that set no bounds to the imagination of man as it played over space and time, had now been swept away. Space was identified with the realm of geometry, time with the continuity of number. The world that people had thought themselves living in — a world rich in colour and sound, redolent with fragrance, filled with gladness, love and beauty, speaking everywhere of purposive harmony and creative ideals — was crowded now into minute corners in the brains of scattered organic beings. The really important world outside was a world hard, cold, colourless, silent, and dead; a world of quantity, a world of mathematically computable motions in mechanical regularity [pp. 238–239].

Burtt points out, moreover, that the isolation between subject and object is to be seen on a formal level as well, where it is expressed as a "problem of knowledge." Classically, the problem has been stated in the following

[5] The terms "primary quality" and "secondary quality" were coined by Locke, although it is clear that Galileo's argument here provides the basis for this terminology (see Windelband, 1901).

way: If objective nature is made up of the pure primary attributes of size, number, extension, etc., while subjective nature (in Galileo's terms, our "sensitive body") is the basis for the "illusory" secondary qualities, then how is valid knowledge possible? If he can only add distortion to the object in the process of experiencing it, how can the subject ever come to know the primary qualities in their true form, namely, *as* primary qualities? One implication of the Cartesian view, then, is that it characterizes the subject in *material terms* whereby he can never know the "real" or primary qualities of the independently constituted object since he contaminates the object in the course of knowing it. The subject, in this material sense, is never coordinated in a relationship of knowing with the real object. He is doomed to perpetual isolation from it.

It is critical to my thesis, however, to note that the opposite implication is also given in the Cartesian view. Galileo's proof that such properties of size and number exist as primary qualities is based on the proposition that these are the properties which are necessarily conceived by mind, when mind conceives of the material body. Since, however, these qualities are qualities *as known,* it follows that this proof, from the very outset, must assume a subject who in *mental terms* knows and, in this sense, *is* coordinated with the real object. Indeed, it can be generally asserted, in this regard, that an epistemology which assumes that *such and such* properties are independently constituted must, by that token, implicitly assume that these properties are properties as known and hence must implicitly assume, as well, a subject of knowledge who knows the properties which are being defined as independently constituted. It can be said, then, that the distinction between the primary and secondary qualities of the real object not only serves to dichotomize the subject and object into isolated realms of inner and outer being, but also implies the classic Cartesian dichotomy between different aspects of the subject — on the one hand, a material body of the senses which inherently distorts and hence which is isolated from an independently constituted reality, and on the other, a realm of pure mind which knows and hence is coordinated to this objective reality.[6]

In the light of this world view, we can now refocus on Asch's contention that instinct theory and behaviorism have an identical conception of the developmental relationship between the child and adult. As Asch has suggested, both positions derive developmental *change* from experience with a fortuitous reality that serves to modify the natively given behavioral properties of the primitive organism. The behavior of the child is seen as evidencing inherited action tendencies in their purest form and, accordingly, as differing from the behavior of the adult to the extent that the adult's behavior evidences mediating responses that have been acquired as a function of experience. And, Asch asserts, both positions derive developmental *continuity* from a core of human nature that governs such originally given behavioral properties and that underlies the activity of both the child and adult. I will argue that the view of development which is thus being advanced by instinct theory and behaviorism embodies the divergent implications of a Cartesian epistemology whereby one aspect of the subject is isolated from an independently constituted reality, and the other aspect of the subject is directly coordinated to this reality. Specifically, I will argue that developmental change as understood by instinct theory and behaviorism presumes a Cartesian isolation between the material subject and the independently constituted object, while the view of developmental continuity advanced by these positions presumes a subject of pure reason who is directly coordinated to this reality. And

[6] For those further interested in how the distinction between the primary and secondary qualities is expressed in Descartes' dualism of mind and body, see Windelband (1901).

I will suggest, further, that if this is the case, then my assertions regarding the two forms of cognitive organization can serve to articulate formally the implications of Asch's analysis that there is a deeper structure which both theories have in common and in terms of which they organize the problem of development as a form of immutability and discontinuity.[7]

To this end, I will first make the case that a Cartesian isolation between the subject and object underlies and, indeed, is necessary to the conception which both theories advance regarding the problem of developmental change — or, as they view it, the problem of acquired differences between the child and adult. In particular, I will argue that this implication of the Cartesian epistemology is revealed by the typical experimental situation — in this case, the paradigm of the cat in the cage — which has served to clarify the processes involved in the acquired response.[8]

In terms of the conception of acquired differences, if a subject's action in a particular situation is immediately followed by reinforcement, and if this action already has the highest probability of occurrence in that situation, then this experience can only serve to perpetuate such behavior under

[7] Asch's analysis of instinct theory and behaviorism has been significantly influenced by Köhler (1947), who views introspectionism and behaviorism as assuming an elementaristic "machine theory" of functioning. Thus, Asch (1952) notes that this machine theory "... is the most significant point of agreement between the two doctrines and the technical ground for the preceding ideas they share" (p. 76). Clearly, then, my analysis and Asch's differ with respect to what we consider the more basic commonality underlying the immutability-discontinuity problem that instinct theory and behaviorism encounter. This is not the place, however, to explore the nature of the relationship between a machine theory of functioning and the Cartesian viewpoint. The problem will be considered in connection with White's (1963) conception of development in Chapter 5.

[8] Even though both positions are understood here as proposing the same conception regarding the differences between the child and adult, behaviorism traditionally has been far more concerned with this issue than instinct theory. Hence the paradigm is a behaviorist one.

similar circumstances. The experience of reinforcement merely strengthens the probability of an already most probable response. In order, therefore, to bring about *acquired* behavior — that is, in order to shift the subject's hierarchy of response probabilities such that a less probable response becomes more probable and vice versa — the experimental situation must be so constructed that the subject's most probable response is *not* directly followed by reinforcement. To this end, the experimenter constructs the cage with bars through which food can be seen and smelled. And he places this food outside the cage, just beyond the hungry animal's reach, but on the side *opposite* to where the escape latch is located. In doing so, the experimenter is defining the cat's world as having an essential property, namely, that of a latch which, if pressed, results in tension reduction. And he is further constructing this world so that the activity of pressing the latch has a low probability of occurrence in the cat's repertory of available responses. He deliberately evokes other more probable responses such as reaching through, biting, and scratching the bars that are adjacent to the food. By that token, then, we can say that the experimenter is also constructing a world of properties (e.g., the food's proximity to the cat, the intervening bars) that are readily responded to by the subject. But now he is defining such properties as unessential in that, when so responded to, tension reduction does not directly follow.

Clearly, then, the experimenter is literally constituting the properties of the subject's world. In his omnipotence, he is creating a world for the subject by defining for him what is essential and unessential, hidden and obvious. And he is doing so on his own terms, not the subject's. The experimenter is constructing this world in accordance with his assumption that, as a necessary condition for the acquired response, the subject's most probable response must be coordinated to the unessential properties of the world and must, by that token, be isolated or "blind" with respect to its essential properties. In order for the hungry cat to learn from his experience in the cage, he must first, if you will, distort the real world that has the essential property of a "latch to be pressed" into a world that has the unessential property of "bars to be clawed and bitten." The experimenter, in other words, is designing an experimental situation that will elicit a *random* sequence of behavior as the necessary basis for the acquired mediating response. In this sequence, since the more probable responses, by design, are not followed by reinforcement, the less probable one of pressing the latch will eventually occur and, as a consequence of reinforcement, will become increasingly strengthened until it attains the highest probability of occurrence in the subject's repertory of available responses. It can thus be said that acquired mediating responses and, hence, the acquired differences between the child and adult, are a reshaping of random activity into a pattern of responses that are coordinated to a set of independently ordered events; independently ordered in the first place so as to elicit a random sequence of behavior. Clearly, however, the reinforcement that governs this reshaping can only be fortuitous as far as the subject is concerned. As a necessary condition for the shift in the hierarchy of probabilities, the events that determine this reinforcement have been isolated from him by design (that is, in order to elicit a random sequence of behavior).[9]

Note, moreover, that the isolation which is so engendered by this experimental paradigm is not merely between the external event and the subject's overt behavior. It is also between the external event and the natively given core of the subject. If we take a given sequence of random activity and

[9] I have been influenced here by Goldstein's (1939) analysis of the isolation engendered in the organism's functioning by the experimenter's method of investigation.

push its reinforcement history back far enough, then we can only arrive at a sequence of random behavior given *before* any experience of reinforcement — before, in effect, any experience with the essential properties of an independently constituted world. Thus, if we were to ask, each time, what were the determinants of a particular set of response probabilities, we would be directed to successively earlier reinforcement experiences, until we would arrive at what, in Dollard and Miller's (1950) approach, are behaviors natively instigated by the arousal of physiologic drives. We would arrive at an "innate hierarchy of responses" whereby the differential probability of occurrence in a given sequence is evidenced without previous external reinforcement — where "the order of the response is primarily determined not by learning" (p. 36). By this infinite regress, in other words, we would be driven back to native action tendencies that direct such random behavior and that are revealed in their clearest form at the earliest stage of life. In the final analysis, then, when representing natively determined behavior as being modified by experience, this conception must characterize such behavior as being pre-wired to unessential aspects of the world and as being isolated from its essential aspects. For if it were not so pre-wired to unessential aspects of the world, then this behavior could not be randomly organized. If this is so, then it follows that the native core which directs such blind random behavior must also be interpreted as being isolated from the essential (that is, reinforcing) aspects of the world.

In sum, a particular relationship between the subject and object is being presumed in this view of the acquired differences between the child and adult. If we take the experimental paradigm for eliciting random behavior as a metaphor for this relationship, we can say that this conception must assume that the subject faces a world of independently constituted, essential properties from which he is inherently isolated and in relation to which he engages in blind, distorting activity. This, truly, is a subject who is in a world, but not of it. As such, this conception of acquired differences can be said to presume one of the basic implications of the Cartesian world view, namely, that of a subject who contributes subjective distorting qualities to an objective reality of primary qualities and who, by virtue of this, is isolated from this independently constituted event.

It should be noted, however, that this same experimental paradigm can be interpreted as indicating that instinct theory and behaviorism hold the divergent implication of the Cartesian view as well — and this in their conception of developmental continuity. Indeed, the conception of continuity advanced by these theories can be said to be the obverse of their conception of developmental change. We have seen, in this regard, that the experimental paradigm is so designed that, given the arousal of primary need, the subject's most probable response is not followed by reinforcement. And for good reason. For if it were so followed, the probability of this most probable response would be further increased, and no change in the subject's overt behavior would occur. Note the implications of this experimental paradigm for the conception of behavioral continuity: Continuity — the absence of change — can be accounted for precisely by the fact that, given the arousal of primary need, the probability of the subject's most probable response *will* be increased by reinforcement. This implication of the experimental paradigm, then, serves not only as the basis for a conception of acquired differences, but also as the basis for behavioral continuity and, when extrapolated to the relationship between the child and adult, as the basis for a conception of developmental continuity. As so understood, the continuity between the child and adult takes the form of overtly expressed and commonly held mediating responses. The common expression of such mediating responses in the behavior of the child and adult is further understood as a function of a particular history of reinforcement: These responses have served, in childhood, to reduce primary need in a direct and consistent way; consequently, they continue in adulthood to have a high probability of occurrence with respect to essential events. By the logic of the previous analysis, moreover, if we push this reinforcement history back far enough, we arrive at an assumption which, in certain respects, is similar to that underlying the conception of acquired differences. We end up with the assumption that there are tendencies in man's nature which serve to direct behavior toward external events without the benefit of experience. Now, however, such natively directed activities are seen, not as being coordinated to unessential properties of the world (for if they were, change would follow), but on the contrary, as inherently coordinated to events that serve directly to bring about tension reduction and, in so doing, promote individual and species survival (as, for example, sexual activity and mothering). In the final analysis, then, the continuity between the child and adult derives from the assumption of a natively given, pre-wired *adaptive* coordination between the subject and object. Even though the behavior of the adult might differ from that of the child by virtue of evidencing acquired mediations, his behavior is also similar to that of the child in the degree that it continues to evidence such natively given adaptive mediations.

In sum, if one accepts my argument that the conception of change advanced by behaviorism and instinct theory presumes a Cartesian isolation between the subject and the independently constituted essential event, it follows that the conception of continuity held by these theories presumes the divergent view that the subject is inherently coordinated to the essential event. That part of the adult's overt behavior which is like the child's is derived from one side of the Cartesian dichotomy, namely, from an underlying native core of primary needs that govern preformed connections to essential reinforcing aspects of an independently constituted world. And that part of the adult's overt behavior which is different from the child's is derived from the other side of the Cartesian dichotomy, namely, such behavior is shaped by an independently constituted world of essential reinforcing events to which the native core is blind. To paraphrase Asch, then, the essential difference between a behaviorist focus on acquired mediations and instinct theory's concern with man's inherent nature stems not from a disagreement as to fundamental constructs. It stems, rather, from a disagreement concerning how much of the native inner core is connected to a world of essential events and how much of the inner core is isolated from this independently constituted world. From instinct theory's emphasis on the coordination of the natively given core to the world of essential events we can derive its theory of the instinctual drives. From behaviorism's emphasis on the blindness of the natively given core to the world of essential events we can derive its theory of acquired habits. The antagonism between these theories thus stems from a difference in the relative weight which each position assigns to these divergent implications of the Cartesian world view.

THE IMMUTABILITY-DISCONTINUITY PROBLEM ENCOUNTERED BY INSTINCT THEORY AND BEHAVIORISM

How, then, are these divergent assumptions of the Cartesian epistemology relevant to the forms of immutability and discontinuity that instinct theory and behaviorism encounter in their conceptions of development? I have suggested that events in a temporal sequence have a continuity-change relationship when that sequence is so structured that prior and subsequent events are being distinguished with respect to particular properties and that, as so distinguished, these events are being connected as different sequential particulars of an underlying more inclusive unity. The continuity-change relationship, then, is a relationship between temporal events as hierarchically structured. The similarity in these events, as represented by the underlying invariant, has a relationship of inclusion with respect to the events that have been distinguished. The continuity-change relationship, moreover, is a correlative one. In the notion of change, we are focusing on the differences between these events in relation to the more inclusive unity, namely, these differences indicate that a change has occurred with respect to this underlying realm of being. Correlatively, in the notion of continuity, we are focusing on the more inclusive unity but in relation to such differences. Sequential events are seen as having a relationship of continuity in that they reflect, via their different properties, this underlying invariance.

We can, accordingly, ask this question in regard to the conceptions of development advanced by instinct theory and behaviorism: Can the child and adult, as distinguished from one another in terms of the conception of acquired differences, be understood as different particulars of a more inclusive unity? In the light of our analysis, I believe that the answer is clear. We have seen that in their conceptions of acquired mediations, both positions view the difference between primitive and mature behavior as a function of two quite separate and, indeed, antagonistic influences. At one pole are external independently constituted circumstances, defined as having such and such essential properties. At the other pole is the organism's inherent nature which directs random activity—that is, activity which is isolated with respect to these essential properties. The adult differs from the child to the extent that these essential properties have served to organize random behavior into acquired mediating responses. By the same token, the child differs from the adult to the degree that he has not yet had this formative experience, thereby evidencing more than the adult, the random behavior which is organized by his blind original nature. The child and adult, if you will, are marching to the very different drummers of a distorting inner nature on the one hand, and an external reality of essential events on the other. It follows, then, that this conception of acquired differences must carry with it the same implication that has been classically represented by the problem of knowledge in Cartesian epistemology. If the problem of knowledge has pointed to an unbridgeable isolation between a distorting subject and the independently constituted object, this same isolation must exist between the child whose behavior is a function of a distorting inner nature and the adult whose behavior is a function of an external reality of essential events. Just as there is no more inclusive unity in the Cartesian world view that can serve to connect the distorting subject with the independently constituted object,[10] so too there is no more inclusive unity available to this conception of acquired differences that can serve to connect the behavior of the child, as so distinguished, with the behavior of the adult.

And yet we have also seen that the conception of development advanced by instinct theory and behaviorism *does* posit a connection between the primitive activity of the child and the mature activity of the adult. As Asch has asserted, both positions suggest that the child and the adult, however they may differ with respect to acquired mediations, are similar by virtue of sharing an identical nature that is given before experience and that serves as a core of functioning, common to the behavior of both the child and adult. It follows from my thesis, therefore, that in so uniting the behavior of the child and adult, this concept of a common core of functioning has a relationship of identity with one or

[10] For an analysis of this point, see Windelband (1901).

the other of the constructs that have served to distinguish between the temporal events of child and adult behavior. That is, my thesis would suggest that instinct theory and behaviorism, unable to unite the acquired differences between the child and adult as particulars of a more inclusive construct, must be uniting these temporal events in terms of constructs that *are* available and, in particular, in terms of constructs that have served as the basis for distinguishing between the child and adult in the first place. In this regard, we have seen that the conception of acquired differences assumes an original blind nature as the basis for the child's prior random behavior. And, as so defined, this behavior is distinguished from the adult's subsequent mediating activity, which, in turn, is organized or defined by the essential properties of an independently constituted reality. My thesis would suggest, therefore, that the presumption of a blind inherent nature and the presumption of an independently constituted reality — presumptions that are the basis for distinguishing the behavior of the child from that of the adult — are the very constructs that serve to connect these same sequential events. That is to say, these constructs serve to define the core of functioning that is *common* to the behavior of both the child and adult. It is largely with respect to which construct serves to define this common core of functioning that instinct theory and behaviorism differ. As we shall see, instinct theory defines this common core of functioning primarily in terms of an independently constituted reality, while behaviorism defines it primarily in terms of a blind inherent nature.

It is in terms of these two identity relationships that one can formally explicate what is only implied in Asch's critique of behaviorism and instinct theory, namely, that by virtue of a common epistemology, these theories are advancing the same conception of development — one that encounters identical problems of immutability and discontinuity.

To that end, let us consider, first, the implications which follow from the identity relationship in which the child and adult, as distinguished in terms of acquired mediations, are being connected in terms of the construct that has served to define the *prior* event of primitive activity, this construct being the presumption of a blind inherent nature that directs the child's random behavior. As advanced in Chapter 1, my thesis suggests that in so connecting the sequential states of primitive and mature behavior, this construct serves a function equivalent to that served by an inclusive construct in a hierarchic organization: The construct serves to define a realm of being which is common to both primitive and mature functioning and which thus exists as an invariant over the span of time represented by these sequential states. We have seen, however, that in contrast to an inclusive construct, the presumption of a blind nature also serves to define the primitive random functioning of the child, thus distinguishing such functioning from the mature mediating activity of the adult.[11] As an underlying invariant, therefore, such natively directed random activity, in being so identical to primitive functioning, must be as isolated from the mediating behavior of the adult as the random activity of the child and the mediating behavior of the adult are isolated from one another. It follows, then, that the sequential events of primitive random activity and mature mediating behavior cannot be understood as different particulars of this underlying invariant; they cannot be understood as having a relationship of change. Since, however, the conception of acquired differences *does* posit that these events follow one another over time, such events can only be viewed as being discontinuous with respect to one another.

[11] My analysis here is in agreement with Asch's contention that both positions hold the view that man's original nature is revealed most clearly at the earliest stages of life. Note, however, that this applies only to man's blind nature and not to his inherent adaptive nature which is

It may be seen, then, that if one focuses on the acquired differences between the child and adult within the
context of this identity relationship, one can derive the
problem of discontinuity which instinct theory has attributed to the behaviorist view of developmental change.
To paraphrase Bertocci, the subsequent mediations of the
adult have magically come into being with no continuity in
essential quality with the assumed givens of primitive blindness. But it may also be seen that if we shift our focus to the
underlying invariant and to the connection which this invariant affords, then one can derive a problem of immutability from this identity relationship as well. Since the
prior event has been defined as having the same properties
as the invariant state which underlies the prior *and* subsequent events, the prior event itself can only be perpetuated
in immutable form over the span of time represented by this
sequence of events. Via the invariant state, the prior event
of natively directed random activity stretches ahead of itself,
so to speak, to coexist with the subsequent event of acquired
mediations — even while such acquired mediations have discontinuously come into being. As so understood, the functioning of the child becomes an isolated and hidden core of
adult behavior — or, in the behaviorist lexicon, drive-in-
stigated activity which has a low probability of occurrence.
Such activity only becomes evidenced when, for whatever
reason, the acquired responses no longer continue to
mediate reinforcement, thereby resulting in a shift in the
hierarchy of response probabilities which characterizes the
adult's typical functioning. Such, then, are the implications
of this identity relationship. In this conception of develop-

---

the basis for the pre-wired coordination to essential events. As I will
argue, these pre-wired coordinations can only be understood as being
evidenced in immutable form and hence cannot serve to distinguish between primitive and mature functioning.

ment, adult functioning is represented as an acquired overlay of magically appearing mediating responses juxtaposed on an immutable core of natively directed random behavior—the child in the man, as it were, waiting to surface.

Let us now consider the implications of the second identity relationship available to these theories by virtue of their underlying epistemology. This is the identity relationship in which child and adult, as distinguished in terms of acquired mediations, are being connected in terms of the construct that has served to define the *subsequent* event of mature functioning, this construct being the presumption of an independently constituted reality that shapes the adult's mediating behavior. Based on the same line of reasoning as in the preceding analysis, we can say, first, that this construct is serving to define a realm of being which is common to both primitive and mature functioning and, accordingly, which exists as an invariant over the time span represented by the sequential states of random behavior and acquired mediations. Second, in contrast to an inclusive construct, the construct of an independently constituted reality also serves to define the mediating activity of the adult, thus distinguishing such functioning from the random behavior of the child. Accordingly, just as the random behavior of the child and the mediating activity of the adult are isolated from one another, so too is the underlying invariant of externally shaped mediating activity isolated from the random activity of the child. That is to say, the sequential events of random activity and acquired mediations can be as little understood as different particulars of an invariant realm of adaptive mediations as they can be understood as different particulars of an invariant realm of blind random functioning. It may be seen, then, that a focus on the acquired differences between the adult and child within the context of this second identity relationship also leads to a problem of discontinuity. And if we shift our focus to the underlying invariant of mediating activity and to the connection between the sequential events of child and adult behavior which this construct affords, then it will be seen that this conception of development encounters a problem of immutability as well. Since the subsequent activity of the adult is identical to the underlying invariant of externally shaped mediating behavior, this has the paradoxical effect of stretching the subsequent event back in time, via this invariant state, such that it coexists with the prior event of primitive random activity. In effect, we have mediating behavior which is present at the very outset of functioning and which is identical to that evidenced in the adaptive functioning of the adult. Thus, focusing on the similarity between the child and adult within the context of this second identity relationship enables us to derive the problem of immutability that behaviorist doctrine has attributed to instinct theory's approach to developmental continuity. That is, in addressing itself to this issue, instinct theory posits that the child and adult are similar by virtue of sharing innate adaptive propensities that govern pre-wired instrumental responses to essential events. And, to paraphrase Allport, continuity as so understood becomes preformism or an immutable sameness.

The foregoing analysis, accordingly, enables me to represent the implications of Asch's critique in the following way: Instinct theory and behaviorism have advanced solutions to the issue of "psychological invariance and change" which are based on a common Cartesian epistemology and which, by virtue of this, encounter identical problems of immutability and discontinuity. And this, in spite of what has commonly been accepted as the mutual antagonism and essential difference between these positions with respect to the issue of nature versus nurture. Indeed, it may be seen that the antagonism between these positions is but a reflection of the divergent implications of an epistemology that both theories accept. That is to say, both theories distinguish between the child and adult in terms of the respective influence of a blind original nature and an independently constituted reality of essential events. As so viewed, these theories do not differ in terms of their basic constructs. Rather, they differ, first, with respect to which of these constructs serves to connect the sequential events of child and adult functioning: in the case of behaviorism, a blind original nature; in the case of instinct theory, an independently constituted reality of essential events. Second, having so structured an identity relationship between the child and adult, these theories differ with respect to whether they focus on the differences or on the connection between these successive events. Thus, in regard to the mutual antagonism between behaviorism and instinct theory, it may be seen that each theory is criticizing the other not only from the viewpoint of the very assumption that it has exploited in connecting the child and adult, but also in terms of its respective focus on the difference and on the connection between these successive events. In criticizing the preformism of instinct theory, behaviorism is reacting to instinct theory's focus on the invariant of mediating behavior which serves to connect the primitive functioning of the child to the mature behavior of the adult. It is doing so, however, from the perspective of having implicitly connected the child and adult in terms of an original blind nature. Accordingly, in opposing this preformism, behaviorist theory with its characteristic focus on the acquired differences between the child and adult, can only encounter a discontinuity between the adult's mediating activity and the prior given of primitive blindness. By the same token, instinct theory, in criticizing this conception of change, is doing so from the perspective of having implicitly connected the child and adult in terms of an underlying adaptive nature. Accordingly, in opposing this discontinuity, instinct theory with its characteristic focus on the connection between the child and adult, can only encounter, in turn, the immutability or preformism of ascribing the adult's mediating behavior to the child.

The antagonism between instinct theory and behaviorism, then, can be understood, not as a difference in kind, but as one of focus within the constraints of the same epistemology. As so understood, the sins of one position are those of the other, but they are sins of omission, not commission. Thus, were these positions to shift their traditional emphasis in order to deal with the issue they so typically neglect, each would encounter the formal problem they have so easily seen in the other position. Were instinct theory to shift from its isolated concern with the similarity between the child and the adult, and deal instead with their differences, then this position would encounter the discontinuity inherent in its conception. Even though instinct theory may posit far fewer acquired mediations than behaviorism, the acquired mediations that *are* posited would still be discontinuous with respect to the prior state of random activity that the theory is now implicitly assuming. And were behaviorism to venture from its traditional domain and concern itself with the issue of how to understand the similarity between the child and adult, then it would have to confront its view that this similarity derives from an underlying immutable core of blind human nature. Moreover, given their Cartesian epistemology, the only recourse these theories have in dealing with such problems of discontinuity and immutability would be to restructure the similarities and differences between the child and adult in terms of the only other identity relationship that is open to them. But then, of course, the theory would merely encounter the immutability-discontinuity problem in the precise form that each has criticized in the other. Behaviorism would be forced to acknowledge the immutability of those few pre-wired adaptive connections, such as the reflexes, which it is willing to accord to original nature;[12] while instinct doctrine would continue to confront the discontinuity between the random activity of the child and the few acquired mediations which it is willing to accord to the adult, but now as these differences are being connected by an immutable, albeit relatively circumscribed, core of natively directed random activity.

In sum, I have argued that both instinct theory and behaviorism advance a conception of development in which the primitive functioning of the child and the mature functioning of the adult are distinguished from one another by virtue of their having been defined respectively by the Cartesian presumptions of a distorting inner nature and an independently constituted world of essential properties. As so distinguished, however, these sequential events cannot be connected in a relationship of continuity and change. And this, because there is no construct available to the Cartesian world view that is inclusive of the presumptions of a distorting inner nature and an independently constituted reality. Hence, there is no construct available to instinct theory and behaviorism that is inclusive of the random functioning of the child as distinguished from the mediating behavior of the adult. We have seen, however, that these positions nevertheless do advance a conception of development in which the behaviors of the child and adult are connected in terms of their similarity. Accordingly, it follows that these

[12] It may be further noted that behaviorism would also have to come to terms with the implicit form of immutability given in the view that the organism's repertory of available responses contains the response which will become the habit, but which in primitive random activity has a low probability of occurrence with respect to the essential event. In this sense we have the nascent adult in the child waiting to become accentuated by the reinforcement of an independently constituted reality. The relationship between this form of the immutability-discontinuity problem and the Cartesian epistemology will be elaborated in the analysis of Freudian theory.

positions are connecting these unconnectable events in terms of constructs that have served to distinguish between the child and adult in the first place. In the same way, formally considered, that the non-conserving subject connects the successive events of ball and sausage when he lacks the more inclusive compensation rule, so too do the conceptions advanced by instinct theory and behaviorism connect the sequential events of random behavior and acquired mediations. A construct that has served to distinguish between the sequential events is used in place of the more inclusive unifying construct that the theory lacks. It is from this relationship of identity between connecting and differentiating constructs that I have derived the various forms of immutability and discontinuity that instinct theory and behaviorism encounter in their conceptions of development. And it is from this relationship of identity that I am able to infer that these forms of immutability and discontinuity are the characteristics of a pars pro toto organization which refined cognition must take when structuring a problem beyond its explanatory limits — limits which, as I have argued, are contained from the very beginning in the epistemological presumptions of the theory.

3

FREUD'S CLASSICAL THEORY
OF PERSONALITY

In Chapter 4, I will be advancing the case that Freud's classical theory assumes the Cartesian epistemology in common with the instinct and behaviorist positions and, by virtue of this, encounters the same form of the immutability-discontinuity problem in its conception of personality development. More particularly, I will be arguing that this problem derives from the fact that Freud posits theoretical connections between causally determined and purposive modes of functioning when his philosophical presumptions serve to characterize these modes of activity as irrevocably isolated from one another. Thus, I will be making the case that Freud's theory, like that of instinct theory and behaviorism, encounters particular forms of immutability and discontinuity by virtue of attempting to solve a problem that its Cartesian viewpoint has rendered unsolvable. The present chapter provides the source material for this thesis, and accordingly, is devoted to a detailed description of Freud's theory.

As is well known, Freud's theoretical constructions evolved in several stages and over a long, productive career.

The reader may find it helpful in following my account to note that Freud maintained a fundamental idea throughout the changes represented by these successive versions of his theory. In all versions, Freud held that the behavior of the organism was governed by a principle of *minimal tension*. By that he meant that behavior, at all times, was directed toward a world of impersonal objects and interpersonal others in a way that served either to reduce a high state of tension or to maintain a low state of tension. Such behavior could be further distinguished, Freud suggested, as being causally determined or purposive. In common with other theorists, Freud understood causally determined behavior as an event that came about as a result of preceding conditions and that, in principle, was predictable from such antecedent conditions. This type of functioning was formally represented in Freud's theory by his "metapsychological" constructs of energy and structure. Behavior was understood, in terms of these constructs, as the activation of inert structures by psychic energy — structures that, in turn, served to organize, direct, and mechanically discharge this energy in accordance with the minimal tension principle.[1] Because Freud typically employed hydraulic metaphors for these energy and structure concepts (such as water flowing through a network of channels), I shall be referring to causally determined behavior as so represented in Freud's theory as a "hydraulic mode" of functioning.

In addition to hydraulic functioning, Freud also understood behavior as being purposively motivated in the sense that behavioral events were connected to one another as means toward a particular goal; that is, he understood such behavior not as determined by a prior condition, but as

[1] Freud's metapsychology has been similarly characterized by a number of psychoanalytic ego psychologists, notably Rapaport (1951b), White (1963), and Holt (1967).

chosen by the individual in order to achieve a future result. Just as Freud understood hydraulic events as being governed in accordance with the principle of minimal tension, so too did he conceptualize purposive activity. When the individual acted in deliberate, rule-following ways toward specific goals (that is, when he displayed means-end behavior which embodied the reality of social conventions), Freud interpreted the attainment of such goals as serving to realize a more fundamental end-state of maintaining or restoring a minimal level of tension. The constant feature of Freud's thinking, then, was his notion that human behavior was characterized by a particular relationship between hydraulic (causally determined) and purposive modes of functioning. Both purposive and hydraulically directed behaviors were governed by a more fundamental minimal tension principle or, if you will, were directed toward bringing about an end-state of minimal tension.[2]

It should also be noted that the relationship Freud posited between hydraulic and purposive modes of functioning applied, as well, to symptomatic behavior. That is, the symptom was also characterized in terms of hydraulic and purposive modes of activity directed toward bringing about an end-state of minimal tension. Freud, however, distinguished symptomatic behavior from normal functioning by conceptualizing the symptom as an alternative, pathological expression of the minimal tension principle — one that occurred when there was an interference with the normal expression of this principle. Even though Freud was to articulate increasingly refined conceptions of the symptom in his successive versions, this view remained the same: Symptomatic behavior could be understood as a pathological form of hydraulic and/or purposive activity that was

[2] My characterization of Freud's causally determined, purposive, and end-state modes of functioning has been influenced by Peters (1958).

evidenced in accordance with the minimal tension principle when the more adaptive forms of purposive and hydraulic behavior were blocked from expression.

Given this constant in Freud's thinking, the various versions of his theory can be distinguished along two dimensions. First, they can be distinguished with respect to the relative emphasis which Freud placed on the hydraulic as compared to the purposive mode of functioning, particularly as these were relevant to symptomatic behavior. Second, the various versions can be distinguished in terms of the particular ways in which Freud represented the interaction between the hydraulic and purposive modes of functioning, again as these particularly applied to the symptom. Three major versions of his theory, advanced roughly within the periods of 1893–1900, 1900–1917, and 1917–1940, can be so delineated. In the initial version, Freud (Breuer and Freud, 1893–1895) viewed behavior as being governed mainly by hydraulic processes. In this context, the symptom represented an alternative, mechanical form of discharge for energy which, in part, was being purposively blocked from direct expression. This view of the symptom as a hydraulic expression of blocked energy was retained in his second version (Freud, 1917b) of the sexual-ego instinct polarity. In this second version, however, Freud viewed symptomatic behavior as having purposive qualities as well. He saw the symptom as a "means" activity that was instituted by the ego instincts in order to avoid an anticipated increase of tension attendant upon the performance of a given sexual act. In Freud's (1933) final anxiety-defense paradigm, this characterization of the symptom as a purposively directed activity was both emphasized and refined. Now the symptom became part of a complicated defensive strategy whereby the ego, directed toward the more fundamental end-state of minimal tension, purposively mediated between the blind demands of a hydraulically organized id and an external antagonistic reality.

My thesis, for the most part, will apply to Freud's third version. In particular, it will apply to the connections that Freud posits, in this final version, between the hydraulic and purposive modes of functioning. It will be seen, however, that Freud's final view is a systematic outgrowth of his earlier positions and, moreover, that the changes in Freud's thinking are, themselves, relevant to my argument. Accordingly, the more detailed description of his theory starts with his earlier positions.

THE EARLY VERSIONS

In Freud's (Breuer and Freud, 1893–1895) initial conception of personality functioning, the symptom represented a mechanical discharge of energy that followed antecedent events in accordance with deterministic physical laws.[3] The antecedent events in this case were real-life traumatic happenings which subjected the individual to states of intense affective arousal. In accordance with the principle of minimal tension (called the "principle of constancy" in this initial version), such affect was seen as normally being discharged through channels of action and thought: action whereby the individual reacted appropriately in dealing with the traumatic situation, and thought in terms of which the individual brought the content of the traumatic experience into association with other "corrective" experiences. Such normal discharge served to reduce the high tension levels and was evidenced by the individual's conscious but attenuated (schematic) memory of the event. Under certain circumstances, however, these normal discharge processes were interfered with, and the affect remained in a bottled-up

[3] My description of Freud's first version is based, in particular, on the following in Breuer and Freud (1893–1895): the preliminary communication, the cases of Emmy von N., Lucy R., Katharina, and Freud's final chapter on the psychotherapy of the hysterias.

state. Since, however, the organism continued to function in accordance with the minimal tension principle, such affect, like water under pressure, tended to be discharged by other avenues. The hysterical symptom was one such avenue of discharge. In taking the place of conscious thought and action, the symptom served as an abnormal vehicle which discharged and thus gave a hydraulic form of expression to such "strangulated affect."

Even during this initial approach to symptom formation, Freud modified his views concerning the nature of the traumatic event as well as the conditions that prevented normal discharge. Although he started with the idea that various kinds of traumatic events could be antecedent to the hysterical symptom, and that these could occur at any time in the patient's life (in the case of Emmy von N., for example, the sudden death of her husband and being choked by her child), he gradually came to the position that the essential trauma was one of a sexual nature in that it largely involved sexual seduction or assault. He also pushed the sexual trauma back to successively earlier periods in the patient's experience (in the case of Katharina, for example, to early adolescence). Concerning the blocking of trauma-induced affect, Freud had initially posited four conditions, of which three were consistent with the hydraulic conception. First, the trauma itself was of such an extreme nature that it "overloaded" the normal modes of discharge. Second, the trauma could have been experienced in a particular context which prevented direct action, as, for example, the strictures of a social situation that prevented the individual from reacting immediately and emotionally to a particular event. Third, Freud suggested that the individual could have been in an atypical state of distress or fatigue (the "hypnoid state") when the trauma occurred and that the event, being isolated from the subject's typical experience, could not be corrected. A fourth condition which he proposed, however, involved a mode of organization very different from a hydraulic one. This was Freud's conception of repression as a defense against the occurrence of high tension levels. In this initial version, repression was characterized as a deliberate exclusion, or "suppression," of the traumatic event from conscious awareness (in the sense of "putting it out of mind") in order to prevent the re-experiencing of the tension associated with the event. The effect of conscious repression, like that of the hypnoid state, was to isolate the memory of the trauma from contact with other experiences and thereby prevent associative correction.[4] Although initially considering the defense of repression as one of several isolating conditions, Freud in this first version came to single out this purposive, directed process as the essential factor in the blocking of normal discharge. The first phase of Freud's theory thus culminated in a particular view regarding the relationship between purposive and hydraulic modes of functioning: In the background of every hysterical symptom, Freud proposed, there was a real-life sexual trauma. The affect brought about by this trauma had been, in accordance with the principle of minimal tension, intentionally and consciously "repressed" from direct discharge into thought or action. However, this purposive blocking of normal discharge set into motion, again in accordance with the minimal tension principle, a hydraulic displacement of this energy such that the energy was now converted into the hysterical symptom.

[4] Closely related to the isolation of the hypnoid state is another conception which Freud advanced during this period. Events could be similarly isolated because of the subject's lack of understanding. In comparing the case of Katharina with that of Lucy R., Freud notes that, where Lucy R. deliberately repressed the memory of a distressing event, Katharina's lack of memory for a reported seduction attempt was due to her ignorance of sexual matters at the time of the attempt. Freud maintained this view of isolation due to ignorance in his second version as well, as can be seen in the case of Little Hans (Freud, 1909).

Freud's second major conceptualization of personality organization and symptomatic behavior followed from an "unwelcome discovery" (Freud, 1914a, p. 17). In extrapolating from the earlier view he had proposed in *Studies on Hysteria* (Breuer and Freud, 1893–1895), Freud had come to believe that sexual traumas in early childhood were the causative agent in producing the symptom. And yet, to his dismay, he discovered that these sexual traumas of childhood had not actually occurred as reported by his patients, but were fantasies.[5] His revision was based on an accommodation to this finding. Freud proposed that these reported experiences (which at this point also included the observation of parental intercourse and threats of castration) were indicative of a "psychical reality" every bit as significant as the event which he had originally taken to be a physical reality. If his patients invariably produced such childhood fantasies, then it followed for Freud that, as children, the patients had brought something of an invariant nature to certain external situations—an invariant that transformed these situations in a characteristic way. This invariant, in his view, could only be an instinctual organization. In line with the sexual as well as the castration content of such fantasies, Freud (1917b) proposed two congenitally given organizations as the prime movers of normal and pathological behavior. These were the *sexual instincts* which functioned to preserve the species, and the *ego instincts*

[5] A summary, such as this, cannot do justice to Freud's reaction. As he notes in "On the History of the Psycho-Analytic Movement" (1914a):

> The firm ground of reality was gone. At that time I would gladly have given up the whole work.... At last came the reflection that, after all, one had no right to despair because one has been deceived in one's expectations; one must revise those expectations. If hysterical subjects trace back their symptoms to traumas that are fictitious, then the new fact which emerges is precisely that they create such scenes in *phantasy,* and this psychical reality requires to be taken into account alongside practical reality [pp. 17–18].

which served to preserve the individual (Freud, 1917b, p. 350).[6] Though this revision was a radical one in that it represented a shift from an emphasis on external environmental events to internal constitutional ones, Freud nevertheless maintained his fundamental notion regarding the relationship between the purposive and hydraulic modes of functioning. Influenced by the views of contemporary physics concerning the functioning of mechanical systems, Freud assumed that energy provided the force behind all psychological activity and, accordingly, interpreted the sexual and ego instincts in terms of this hydraulic view. Thus, he assumed that the functioning of both instincts was causally determined in that each required as the *source* of its energy a prior condition of excitation in a somatic substratum. These instincts, moreover, functioned in accordance with the principle of minimal tension in that an increase in such physiologically derived energy served as the antecedent condition for behavior which inherently served to lower energy levels. In this regard, the instincts functioned in accordance with the "aim" of maintaining minimal levels of energy and were inherently directed toward reality *objects* in terms of which this lowering of energy was effected. Hunger, for example, represented one such force behind the activity of the ego instinct in that it stemmed from a condition of nutritional deficit in bodily tissues and provided the energy for inherently directed activity with respect to food. By the same token, Freud designated the force behind the functioning of the sexual instinct as "libido" and derived this energy, as well, from the endogenous excitation of physiological structures, in this case, the mucous membranes of the mouth, anus, and genitals. Freud, however, was more detailed and systematic in regard

[6] In the interest of clarity, I will in general be referring to these groups of instincts in the singular, namely, as the "sexual instinct" and the "ego instinct."

to the libidinal energy of these "component sexual instincts" than he was ever to become in regard to the energy of the ego instinct. Although he interpreted the energy of the ego instinct in hydraulic terms, it is in his articulation of the properties of libidinal energy that his model of hydraulic transformations was evidenced in its clearest form. Freud saw libidinal energy, whether derived from oral, anal, or genital zones, as having a common property. These physiological sources contributed to a quantitative sum of libido in terms of which an increase was experienced as pain, and a decrease was experienced as pleasure. Freud likened this property of libidinal energy to an amoeba's activity in extending a part of its fluid-like protoplasm to engulf an external particle of food. In forming psychological attachments to objects, the organism similarly invested (cathected) objects with libidinal energy. Such objects almost literally received the fund of energy which the organism in like amount had discharged. As in the initial principle of constancy, then, the organism functioned hydraulically in accordance with the minimal tension principle, namely, in terms of maintaining the lowest level of sexual energy possible by virtue of being inherently directed toward discharge onto appropriate objects.

In this second version, the most immediate cause of symptomatic behavior continued to be a blocking of energy discharge such that an alternative pathological path was taken in accordance with the principle of minimal tension. As Freud (1914b) noted in regard to the blocking of libidinal discharge, ". . . in the last resort we must begin to love in order not to fall ill, and we are bound to fall ill if, in consequence of frustration, we are unable to love" (p. 85).[7] However, by virtue of his shift of emphasis to the "psychical reality" of the sexual and ego instincts, Freud now proposed

[7] An extended quotation from this passage serves to illustrate even more clearly Freud's (1914b) continued interpretation of behavior in terms

a very different basis for such blocking as well as a very different conception of the alternative paths the blocked energy could follow. The blocking of libidinal discharge was now seen as the expression of a basic antagonism between the sexual and ego instincts — an antagonism derived from the differential nature of the reality objects toward which the instincts were inherently directed. Freud (1913) speculated that the instinctual predisposition to act in particular ways toward such objects stemmed from adaptive responses which the individual's prehistoric ancestors had made to similar reality events and which had been passed on as part

of hydraulic functioning that is governed, more fundamentally, by the principle of minimal tension:

> At this point, our curiosity will of course raise the question why this damming-up of libido in the ego should have to be experienced as unpleasurable. I shall content myself with the answer that unpleasure is always the expression of a higher degree of tension, and that therefore what is happening is that a quantity in the field of material events is being transformed here as elsewhere into the psychical quality of unpleasure.... Here we may even venture to touch on the question of what makes it necessary at all for our mental life to pass beyond the limits of narcissism and to attach the libido to objects. The answer which would follow from our line of thought would once more be that this necessity arises when the cathexis of the ego with libido exceeds a certain amount. A certain egoism is a protection against falling ill, but in the last resort we must begin to love in order not to fall ill, and we are bound to fall ill if, in consequence of frustration, we are unable to love [p. 85].

It may thus be seen that behavior such as interest in one's surroundings, as well as symptomatic activity, is being interpreted as causally determined, namely, as being determined by the antecedent event of an increase in the amount of libidinal energy. And, further, in accordance with the minimal tension principle, such behavior serves to decrease the quantity of sexual energy.

Note, moreover, that "frustration" as an antecedent of the symptom does not apply to the energy of the ego instinct, but to that of the sexual instinct. In contrast to the ego instinct, the frustration of which could only lead to the death of the individual, the sexual instinct could be frustrated indefinitely, albeit with the possible result of symptomatic behavior.

of the individual's evolutionary inheritance. Thus, in functioning to perpetuate the species, the sexual instinct predisposed the organism to discharge libido by acting in directed ways toward sexual objects, including, significantly, the parent of the opposite sex. This conception of the sexual instinct is nicely exemplified in one of his case histories (Freud, 1909), in which he described a phobic fear of horses in a five-year-old boy. In his analysis of the events leading to this five-year-old's symptoms, Freud pointed to behaviors indicative of the child's "intensified sexual excitement" (p. 118), such as his masturbatory activity, his wanting mother to touch his penis, and his erotic interest in defecation. Freud then beautifully portrayed the content and direction of this sexual excitement in the following passage:

> But his father not only knew where children come from, he actually performed it—the thing that little Hans could only obscurely divine. The widdler must have something to do with it, for his own grew excited whenever he thought of these things—and it must be a big widdler too, bigger than Hans's own. If he listened to these premonitory sensations he could only suppose that it was a question of some act of violence performed upon his mother, of smashing something, of making an opening into something, or forcing a way into an enclosed space—such were the impulses that he felt stirring within him. But although the sensations of his penis had put him on the road to postulating a vagina, yet he could not solve the problem, for within his experience no such thing existed as his widdler required [pp. 134–135].

The ego instinct, on the other hand, in serving to preserve the individual rather than the species, provided the organism not only with built-in orienting responses to life-supporting events such as food, but also with defensive or fight-flight reactions to life-threatening events. Continuing his speculations on evolutionary inheritance, Freud (1917b) suggested that one such life-threatening event in the organism's prehistory was the castration of the son by the father for the incestuous act. Accordingly, the ego instinct, with its predisposition for responding adaptively to this still prevailing external danger, protected the individual from the tension-raising consequences of such direct libidinal expression.[8] However, an essential ingredient of the danger facing the organism was its own internal impulse, directed as it was toward the forbidden incestuous object. Accordingly, one could not flee from this danger in the same way that one might from a suddenly appearing dangerous animal. One could only protect oneself by an "inner flight" from this "inner danger." This protective reaction of the ego instinct took the form of instinctual repression— of blocking the incestuous impulse from direct expression, whether in the form of conscious thought or overt action. Note, however, that this repressive "putting out of mind" was no longer conscious, purposive suppression as Freud had initially conceived it. What had to be put out of mind was no longer the awareness of an external traumatic event (the memory of which would cause a re-experiencing in the future of the tension associated with the event), but an awareness of the internal, insistent, and *present* demands of the sexual impulse itself. Moreover, the act of repression,

[8] Freud (1933) maintained this view in his final version as well, but now within the context of a greater emphasis on experience. Thus he notes in regard to the male child's castration anxiety that "he has some grounds for this, for people threaten him often enough with cutting off his penis during the phallic phase, at the time of his early masturbation, and hints at that punishment must regularly find a phylogenetic reinforcement in him. It is our suspicion that during the human family's primaeval period castration used actually to be carried out by a jealous and cruel father upon growing boys..." (p. 86). This paradigm obviously had to be elaborated in order to handle the "castration complex" in women (see, for example, Freud, 1933, p. 87).

being an instinctive response, was itself unconscious and not subject to volitional control; and was thus unlike deliberate suppression. It was, in short, a "reflexive" (Alexander, 1932) or hydraulic process. In elaborating upon this conception, Freud (1915a) distinguished between two forms of repressive activity, "primal repression" and "repression proper." Primal repression referred to a process whereby the primitive sexual impulse, which by its nature existed in an unconscious state, was denied entry into consciousness. Freud (1917b) likened the process to a situation in which the passage between two rooms was guarded by a zealous doorkeeper who in his role as *censor* examined visitors in the outer reception room and denied them admittance to the main room if they represented danger. Just as a particular guest was in no way different, before and after admittance, so too was the instinctual impulse in no way changed in the process of becoming conscious, other than in terms of the dimension of consciousness. The second form of repression, that of repression proper (or "after expulsion"), involved already conscious experiences which, by virtue of their associative connection with the originally repressed dangerous impulse, were apparently automatically reacted to by the ego instinct as having the quality of a present and immediate danger. Under these circumstances, such conscious and otherwise innocuous experiences suffered the same fate in being expelled from awareness as the originally repressed impulse.

Given this concept of repression whereby libidinal energy was blocked from its inherent tendency toward discharge onto the sexual object (both in reality and as represented in thought), Freud saw the symptom process as consisting of two phases. The *initial phase* represented a direct continuation of Freud's earlier view that symptom expression was merely a hydraulic conversion of "strangulated affect" which could not be discharged in the normal way.

That is to say, the repressed libidinal energy took an alternative, pathological form of discharge. Freud suggested that two major pathological outlets were so open to blocked libidinal energy. One was that of diffuse anxiety. Thus, in his analysis of Little Hans's phobia, Freud (1909) pointed to a phase of apprehensiveness which preceded the child's specific fear of horses. In his interpretation, Freud focused on the fact that, prior to the symptom of diffuse anxiety, the child's sexual excitement had undergone a general inhibition. Among other things, Little Hans had made efforts to stop masturbating, and now showed disgust regarding elimination. Freud interpreted this inhibition as evidence of a blocking of libidinal discharge and a consequent heightening of libidinal excitement to the point where there was a "reversal of pleasure into unpleasure" (p. 34). The initial symptomatic expression of anxiety was thus seen as an alternative form of hydraulic discharge for libidinal excitement that had previously been expressed as positively experienced erotic behavior. As Freud put it, Little Hans's anxiety was a "transformation of his libidinal longing" (p. 136).

A second pathological outlet for hydraulic discharge was provided by the structures of the sexual instinct. In his conceptualization of the sexual instinct as a source of libidinal energy, Freud (1905) had presented a specific and systematic account of how the organization of the sexual instinct changed over time. In this characterization of sexual development, the oral, anal, and phallic components of the sexual instinct became differentially highlighted, with each component successively dominating the quality of sexual life. This developmental progression culminated in a hierarchically organized form of sexual activity in which the component instincts became subordinated to the primacy of genital activity. Thus, sexual behavior which involved oral and anal activity was characterized by Freud as developmentally advanced only if the activity of these component instincts led to genital intercourse. Freud's characterization of sexual development, then, was essentially a description of the progressive structuring of libidinal energy with respect to discharge.[9]

In spite of this hierarchic organization, however, Freud (1917b) suggested that these component instincts could take the place of one another in serving as vehicles for discharging libido. They represented, in other words, equivalent modes of libidinal discharge:

> ... the sexual instinctual impulses in particular are extraordinarily *plastic,* if I may so express it. One of them can take the place of another, one of them can take over another's intensity; if the satisfaction of one of them is frustrated by reality, the satisfaction of another can afford complete compensation. They are related to one another like a network of intercommunicating channels filled with a liquid; and this is so in spite of their being subject to the primacy of the genitals—a state of affairs that is not at all easily combined in a single picture [p. 345].

[9] The developmental trend of the sexual instinct toward increasing hierarchization is nicely expressed by Freud (1917b) in the following passage:

> For the present you should keep firmly in mind that sexual life (or, as we put it, the libidinal function) does not emerge as something ready-made and does not even develop further in its own likeness, but passes through a series of successive phases which do not resemble one another; its development is thus several times repeated—like that of a caterpillar into a butterfly. The turning-point of this development is the subordination of all the component sexual instincts under the primacy of the genitals.... This is preceded by a sexual life that might be described as distracted—the independent activity of the different component instincts striving for organ-pleasure. This anarchy is mitigated by abortive beginnings of 'pregenital' organizations—a sadistic-anal phase preceded by an oral one, which is perhaps the most primitive... [p. 328].

This dual property of sexual organization, whereby the component instincts were subordinated to genital primacy, and yet also represented substitutive forms of discharge for genital activity, was of fundamental significance to Freud's conception of symptomatic behavior. If repression by the ego instinct resulted in a blocking of libidinal energy from discharge onto the incestuous object via the genital mode, then the libido in true hydraulic fashion could be diverted to the equivalent modes of discharge afforded by the component sexual organizations. Since, however, these alternative paths were earlier, more primitive forms of organization, the alternative discharge was seen as a retrogression in the normal developmental process or, if you will, as a *regression*. Repression, then, could lead to regression as its consequence.

There was, moreover, a still earlier consequence of repression that was critical to the regressive movement from more advanced to more primitive discharge modes. Although some retention of earlier phases of sexual activity always appeared in the foreplay of mature sexual functioning, the behavior of some individuals suggested to Freud that they were investing an inordinate amount of libidinal energy in these primitive forms of sexuality. Freud further noted that this primitive activity was not a new emphasis as might be expected in regression, but was a long-standing characteristic of the individual's sexual behavior. Freud viewed this functioning as indicative of a *fixation,* or an arrest in the progressive structuring of libido such that a relatively greater amount than was usual continued to be directly discharged by the component sexual instincts. He likened libidinal fixation to a situation in which small groups of a migrating people, instead of continuing with the main body and struggling toward a common destination, separated themselves off by remaining at some of the way stations encountered on the route to the goal. This fixation

Freud (1917b) attributed to several factors. One factor, he suggested, had to do with constitutional differences between individuals with respect to the "tenacity with which the libido adheres to particular trends and objects" (p. 348). Libidinal fixation could also result from particular gratifying sexual experiences in childhood. However, whichever of these "complemental" predisposing factors predominated, a further necessary condition was required for the neurosis subsequently to develop.[10] This early fixation had to give rise to an equally primitive counter-activity of the ego instinct which blocked such libidinal gratification. The ego instinct, reflexively responding to the sexual impulses involved, instituted an act of repression. As Freud (1917b) expressed it, "the ego experiences a *repression* where the libido has experienced a *fixation*" (p. 352). The consequence of such repression was to consolidate the fixation of the libido in that the sexual impulses and their means of gratification were isolated from further experience such that they persisted in "unaltered" form (Freud, 1915a, p. 148).[11]

[10] For the purposes of my thesis, it is not necessary to distinguish between Freud's conception of the neuroses and the perversions.

[11] Primal repression, Freud (1915a) states:

... consists in the psychical (ideational) representative of the instinct being denied entrance into the conscious. With this a *fixation* is established; the representative in question persists unaltered from then onwards and the instinct remains attached to it [p. 148].

It would seem that Freud ambiguously views fixation to be both a cause as well as a consequence of repression. This ambiguity may well reflect the ignorance to which Freud readily admits concerning the constitutional basis of fixation. At any rate, the ambiguity continues to be reflected in Fenichel's (1945) summary of Freud's views. Of the various causes of fixation, Fenichel cites the probability of essentially unknown hereditary factors, as well as early experiences of excessive satisfaction and/or excessive frustration which lead to repression whereby the instinctual drives are isolated and, accordingly, do not participate in further development.

Freud's view of regression was intrinsically connected to this concept of fixation. If an inordinate amount of libido was fixated in earlier functions, then the chances were greater that difficulty would be encountered in discharging the remaining libido at the more advanced stages. In elaborating on his metaphor of migrating bands, he noted that the larger the number of individuals who remained behind, the fewer there were to deal with any enemies they might encounter on their route to the goal, and the more readily they would retreat to the way stations which had provided a haven for the laggards. Thus, if the objects of satisfaction in external reality were repressively denied to the individual because of the danger involved, the libido was passively "drawn" toward previous fixations, like energy flowing into sink-holes, via the "intercommunicating channels" of the component instincts. The libido was, in Freud's (1917b) words, "compelled to take the path of regression and strive to find satisfaction either in one of the organizations which it has already outgrown or from one of the objects which it has earlier abandoned" (p. 359). Freud also understood the drawing power of the previous fixations to result from the fact that, because of earlier primal repression, these *unconscious* primitive vehicles of libidinal expression remained free of the restraining influence of the ego instinct and accordingly represented an opportunity for direct and unfettered libidinal expression. Freud (1917b) noted that "by cathecting these repressed positions as it flows backward, the libido has withdrawn from the ego and its laws, and has at the same time renounced all the education it has acquired under the ego's influence" (p. 359). In thus serving to attract libidinal energy, the already repressed unconscious material acted in concert with the ongoing repressive activity of the ego instinct to produce the effect of regression.[12]

[12] The cooperation between the fixated unconscious content and the

Regression, then, was clearly distinguished from the repressive activity of the ego instinct by virtue of being seen as the consequence of such activity. That it was important to Freud that repression be so distinguished from its consequences can be seen in the effort he took to ensure that repression not be confounded with regression. Thus, Freud (1917b) noted that, from one point of view, repression proper (after expulsion) could be taken as a form of regression since it led to an expulsion of the impulse from the higher stage of consciousness to the primitive stage of the unconscious. However, Freud stressed, this aspect of the concept did not capture the essence of repression; for *primal* repression (as distinguished from repression proper) led to a very different consequence. In this form of repression, the primitive impulse was prevented from ever *reaching* the higher stage of consciousness. Hence, the essential aspect of repression lay not in the fate of the impulse, but in the defensive, directive activity of the ego instinct which led to both results. This distinction between the two aspects of repression, namely, the defensive *activity* of the ego instinct and the *effect* of such defensive activity on the libidinal impulse served, in turn, to highlight his formal distinction between repression and regression. In warning the reader not to confuse the two, Freud (1917b) emphasized:

Thus the concept of repression involves no relation to

---

repressing force of the ego instinct is described by Freud (1915a) in connection with his characterization of repression proper:

Moreover, it is a mistake to emphasize only the repulsion which operates from the direction of the conscious upon what is to be repressed; quite as important is the attraction exercised by what was primally repressed upon everything with which it can establish a connection. Probably the trend toward repression would fail in its purpose if these two forces did not cooperate, if there were not something previously repressed ready to receive what is repelled by the conscious [p. 148].

sexuality: I must ask you to take special note of that. It indicates a purely psychological process, which we can characterize still better if we call it a 'topographical' one. By this we intend to say that it is concerned with the psychical regions which we have assumed to exist, or, if we drop this clumsy hypothesis, with the construction of the mental apparatus out of distinct psychical systems.

... What we have hitherto spoken of as regression, however, and have related to fixation, has meant exclusively a return of the libido to earlier stopping-places in its development — something, that is, entirely different in its nature from repression and entirely independent of it. Nor can we call regression of the libido a purely psychical process and we cannot tell where we should localize it in the mental apparatus. And though it is true that it exercises the most powerful influence on mental life, yet the most prominent factor in it is the organic one [pp. 342–343].

It may thus be seen that Freud took pains to distinguish between repressive activity and its consequences because this distinction highlighted the systematically important antagonism that he had posited between the sexual instinct as a peremptory libidinal force which hydraulically flowed along whatever discharge paths were available to it and the ego instinct as a defensive, albeit hydraulic, organization which could oppose such blind libidinal discharge. This antagonism was crucial to the first phase of symptom formation in that Freud derived the form of the symptom from the hydraulic displacement that followed the ego instinct's repressive blocking. As evidenced in diffuse anxiety and regression, the displaceable libido took the form given to it by whatever pathological structures served as an alternative vehicle for discharge.

But in contrast to the initial phase, which clearly represented a continuation of Freud's earlier view of the symptom as a hydraulic conversion, the *second phase* of symptom formation involved a qualitatively different mode of functioning. This phase was constituted by a further *purposive* reaction of the ego instinct to the hydraulic consequences of its own earlier repressive activity. Of the two hydraulic consequences — that of diffuse anxiety and regression — let us consider, first, the ego instinct's further reaction to libidinal *regression*. In describing the initial phase of the symptom, Freud had suggested that the fixated unconscious material acted in concert with the repressive activity of the ego instinct in that it served to "attract" the repressed libido by affording an opportunity for direct, albeit more primitive, expression. Freud pointed out, however, that this opportunity was an illusory one. If the opportunity for direct expression was afforded, it followed that the danger associated with such direct expression also arose and, accordingly, re-evoked the prohibitive activity of the ego instinct. Each fixation, in thus serving as the focal point for regression, provided a focal point, as well, for the re-emergence of conflict. The old struggle between the sexual and ego instincts, but on this new battleground, constituted the basis for the second phase of symptom formation. But now the struggle led to a resolution different from that of the first phase. Instead of directly blocking the sexual impulse, the ego instinct attempted to avoid the consequences of direct libidinal discharge by means of a *strategy,* namely, that of permitting the regressed sexual striving to be expressed in a hidden or circuitous way. Symptomatic behavior came into being as "an ingeniously chosen piece of ambiguity with two meanings in complete mutual contradiction" (Freud, 1917b, p. 360). The symptom, by simultaneously expressing, and yet concealing libidinal discharge, represented a compromise reconciling the antagonistic demands of the sexual and ego instincts. As Freud (1917b) noted in regard to this second phase:

> We already know that neurotic symptoms are the outcome of a conflict which arises over a new method of satisfying the libido [p. 349].

> The two forces which have fallen out meet once again in the symptom and are reconciled, as it were, by the compromise of the symptom that has been constructed. It is for that reason, too, that the symptom is so resistant: it is supported from both sides [pp. 358–359].

In sum, the antagonism between the sexual and ego instincts was basic to both phases of the symptom's formation. In the initial phase, this antagonism as well as its resolution were essentially hydraulic or causally determined. There was libidinal energy, instigated by somatic excitation and blindly directed toward discharge in accordance with a constitutionally given genital mode of expression. And there was a reflexive repression of this libidinal energy, again in accordance with constitutionally given structures (although Freud did not clearly delineate the energy source and nature of these structures). The consequence of this antagonism was hydraulic regression—a diversion of the libidinal flow to other more primitive modes of discharge. In the second phase of symptom formation, the antagonism between the sexual and ego instincts involved a different force and was resolved in a different way. On the one side, there was the continuing push of libidinal energy for direct discharge along the primitive channels to which it had been diverted. That is, such activity continued to be interpreted by Freud in terms of the hydraulic metaphor whereby energy was organized, directed, and discharged via structure. Thus, Freud continued to understand such functioning as causally determined—as coming about by virtue of a prior event. On the other side, however, the activity of the ego instinct was now purposively directed toward coping with this hydraulic displacement of libidinal energy and its continuing push toward discharge. Namely, the symptom was a stratagem — a means chosen by the ego instinct for fulfilling in a disguised and circuitous form this continuing demand of the regressed libido for direct discharge along the primitive pregenital paths. Essentially, then, the ego instinct's activity was governed by the recognition that discharge in this concealed form would be less dangerous to the organism than direct hydraulic discharge. Thus, the ego instinct's activity, rather than being determined by an antecedent condition, was directed toward a future result and hence was purposive in nature. As a compromise formation, the symptom in the second phase reflected this particular interaction between purposive and hydraulic forms of activity.[13*]

[13*] It will be noted that Freud is quite inconsistent in his metaphorical descriptions of the instincts, at times, for example, seeming to characterize the functioning of the sexual instinct as being purposive as well as hydraulic in nature. Hence, relying solely on such descriptive material may not provide the most solid ground for my assertion that Freud viewed the activity of the ego instinct in the second phase of symptom formation as purposively governed while continuing to view the activity of the sexual instinct as causally determined. Freud's conception of the symptom as a "compromise" formation does, I think, provide the more formal and, accordingly, the more solid basis for this assertion. (My thanks to Nick Cariello for suggesting this point.) It can be argued that the compromise represented by the symptom in the second phase is, in fact, a compromise made only by the ego instinct, not the sexual instinct, and that this difference between the instincts reflects the basic distinction made by Freud between causally determined and purposive behavior. Thus, in both phases of symptom formation, Freud characterizes the functioning of the sexual instinct as being directed toward the most immediate discharge of libidinal energy in accordance with the principle of minimal tension. As so understood, the sexual instinct cannot, as it were, accept partial satisfaction, but is directed toward discharge as long as libidinal energy is not at its lowest possible level. And this via whatever structures are available, including those indirect and disguised routes provided by the symptom. Accordingly, it can be said that the activity of the sexual instinct is causally determined in that whenever libidinal energy is not at its

Freud also proposed that the ego instinct reacted in a similar fashion to the other major hydraulic displacement of the initial phase, namely, that of *anxiety*. In his analysis of a phobia in a five-year-old, Freud had suggested that Little Hans's initial apprehensiveness was a hydraulic resultant of libidinal blockage. He further noted that it was only subsequent to this diffuse anxiety that the youngster had evidenced the dramatic behavior that constituted the phobic symptom: Little Hans refused to go out of the house be-

---

lowest possible level—whenever there is *any* sum of physiologically derived libido that has not yet been discharged—the prior and sufficient condition for the occurrence of such sexual activity exists. The presence of any amount of libidinal energy is a sufficient cause for the energy to flow along whatever channels are available for discharge. (Hence the diversion of libidinal flow to the pregenital structures as a consequence of repressive blocking in the first phase and the uncompromising push or demand for discharge via these structures; and in the second phase, the further re-routing of libidinal energy along the indirect pathways provided by the symptom.)

In contrast, the ego instinct functions differently in the second as compared to the first phase of symptom formation. In the first phase, we see that the activity of the ego instinct, like that of the sexual instinct, is causally determined. The push of libidinal energy toward direct discharge in thought or action immediately and reflexively elicits a repressive blocking by the ego instinct. As long as the libidinal demand exists, a prior and sufficient condition is thereby created for the defensive reaction on the part of the ego instinct. In the second phase, however, a very different state of affairs exists. Rather than reflexively blocking the libidinal energy whenever it pushes toward discharge, the ego instinct now permits *some* discharge of libidinal energy in a disguised and circuitous form. It can be said, then, that in contrast to its functioning in the first phase and in contrast to the functioning of the sexual instinct in both phases, the ego instinct is accepting partial satisfaction with respect to the discharge of its *own* energy (granting, of course, that Freud never clarifies the nature of this energy). If this is indeed the case, then we can say further that the activity of the ego instinct is not being causally determined. For it can be argued that were the activity of the ego instinct to be so determined, then such activity would result in *no* expression of libidinal energy, no matter how circuitous—that is, in no compromise. And this because of the danger involved. The activity of the ego instinct would, in other words, be directed toward complete tension reduc-

cause he feared that he would be bitten by a horse — one that fell down and kicked its legs. In his interpretation of Little Hans's symptoms, Freud (1909) proposed the following relationship between the initial anxiety and the subsequent phobia:

> An anxiety-hysteria tends to develop more and more into a 'phobia'. In the end the patient may have got rid of all of his anxiety, but only at the price of subjecting

---

tion — toward the complete satisfaction of protecting the individual from *any* danger of castration, no matter how slight. (Indeed, this is precisely how one would characterize the ego instinct's activity in the first phase of symptom expression, namely, its indiscriminate and uncompromising repression of any libidinal demand.) Thus, the compromise represented by the symptom is one whereby the ego instinct permits a partial satisfaction of the sexual instinct (and, by doing so, provides the prior and sufficient condition for the continuing demand of the sexual instinct for complete and immediate discharge), but at the cost of giving up complete satisfaction with respect to its own instinctual energy.

Now, if this analysis is valid, it follows that the activity of the ego instinct in the second phase is *not* being completely determined by the prior event of physiologically derived energy and, as such, constitutes an exception to the principle of minimal tension, *at least insofar as the principle pertains to causally determined functioning.* How, then, can we account for what seems to be a fundamental departure on Freud's part from his most cherished principle? The answer is that there is no inconsistency, at least on this level of analysis, if we realize that Freud is viewing the activity of the ego instinct as being purposively governed. As I will elaborate in a subsequent section, Freud (1911b), in his "Formulations on the Two Principles of Mental Functioning," views the compromise activity of the ego instinct as being governed by the "reality principle," namely, activity which is directed toward minimal tension in the *long run.* As such, this activity is distinguished from the functioning of the sexual instinct which is governed by the "pleasure principle," namely, activity which is directed toward minimal tension in the short run — toward the immediate reduction of tension. As so understood, then, the compromise activity of the ego instinct does not constitute an exception to the principle of minimal tension. On the contrary, such compromise activity is being governed precisely by this principle, but in regard to the anticipation of future events — that is to say, such activity is being governed by purpose.

himself to all kinds of inhibitions and restrictions . . . it is these defensive structures that appear to us in the form of phobias and that constitute to our eyes the essence of the disease [pp. 116–117].

The phobic symptom, then, was created in order to avoid the outbreak of the anxiety state. And by this Freud meant that the ego instinct actively attempted to reduce the nameless fear of anxiety by attaching it to an external danger. The reason for this defensive action, in Freud's view, was that it was easier to avoid a known external danger than it was to avoid the internal danger of the instinctual impulse. As so interpreted, the phobia reflected the ego instinct's purposive coping with the diffuse anxiety that had come about as the hydraulic consequence of its own previous activity.[14] Freud noted, moreover, that the form and content of the phobia

[14] In order to more clearly represent the line of development in Freud's thinking, I am taking certain liberties with his analysis of Little Hans. As this analysis is being presented, Freud appears to be distinguishing clearly between the two phases of the symptom picture in terms of the differential influence of the sexual and ego instincts as hydraulic and purposive modes of functioning. Actually, this is not quite the case. At the time of his analysis of Little Hans (1909), Freud had not yet advanced his concept of the ego instinct. It was only subsequently that Freud (1911a, 1911b) explicitly formulated the ego instinct as a purposive defensive organization. Accordingly, in the case of Little Hans, he is more ambiguous than our presentation would imply regarding the differential nature of the forces underlying the initial phase of repression and the subsequent phase of the phobia. Thus Freud (1909) notes with respect to repression:

It is hard to say what the influence was which, in the situation we have just sketched, led to the sudden change in Hans and to the transformation of his libidinal longing into anxiety. . . . Whether the scales were turned by the child's *intellectual* inability . . . or whether the effect was produced by a *somatic* incapacity . . . this question must be left open until fresh experience can come to our assistance [p. 136].

Early in the case, moreover, Freud answers his question "Where did the material for this phobia come from?" (p. 26) in the following way:

Probably from the complexes, as yet unknown to us, which had contributed to the repression and which were keeping under repression his sexual feelings toward his mother [p. 27].

evidenced those contradictory meanings whereby libidinal energy was both discharged and disguised. Among other interpretations, he suggested that Little Hans's phobia had the direct result of allowing him to remain physically close to mother, thus enabling him to express indirectly his desire for mother as a libidinal object. Simultaneously, the content of the phobia in the form of the "falling down and biting" horse indirectly expressed both a fear and death wish regarding his rivalrous father. It may thus be seen that here, as in the case of regression, Freud was suggesting that the final form of the symptom was being shaped by qualitatively different activities of the sexual and ego instincts. The symptom was not being understood solely as a form of purposive behavior whereby means were deliberately manipulated toward anticipated ends. Nor was it being understood solely as a form of behavior governed by hydraulic (causal) principles whereby a given action was the result of an antecedent physical event in accordance with deterministic physical laws. In reflecting a compromise between the antagonistic demands of the sexual and ego instincts, symptomatic behavior was being simultaneously directed by hydraulic *and* purposive forces — forces interacting with one another. Thus did this second version culminate in a conception of the symptom that defied easy classification into one or the other of the usual ways of understanding behavior. As a compromise formation, the symptom was, as Peters (1958) has suggested, a unique "admixture" of causal mechanism and purposive intent. And it was precisely because of this, in Peters's view, that this conception represented one of Freud's fundamental contributions to an understanding of psychopathology.

THE FINAL VERSION

I have described this second version in some detail for two reasons: First, many of the views which Freud advanced during this period were retained in his final position. Second, such detail provides a basis for appreciating the serious systematic difficulties which were becoming apparent to Freud and which he attempted to resolve in his final theory. As Freud applied his two-phase conception of symptom formation to various instances of pathological behavior, he found it necessary to further particularize the properties of the sexual and ego instincts. In doing so, he found himself characterizing each instinct in contradictory ways. Thus, in detailing the activity of the sexual instinct, Freud ascribed properties to this organization which seemed to be inconsistent with its basic hydraulic nature. Freud's characterization of libidinal regression, for example, gives the impression that the process is something more than merely an impersonal or causal displacement of energy. There seems to be a purposive quality to the "attraction" which the fixated material holds for libidinal energy by virtue of representing the opportunity for direct libidinal expression.[15] In addition, there was a problem which Freud himself recognized in regard to regression. In accordance with the hydraulic na-

[15] See footnote 12. Indeed, in this regard, Freud would appear to be describing libidinal functioning in an exceedingly slipshod and inconsistent way. For example, in characterizing the libido as being "compelled to take the path of regression and strive to find satisfaction either in one of the organizations which it has already outgrown or from one of the objects which it has earlier abandoned" (p. 359), Freud (1917b) appears to be attributing strategic behavior to the diverted libido and thus to be characterizing libidinal functioning as purposive in nature.

One can, of course, account for such contradictory characterizations in a number of ways. Hartmann, Kris, and Loewenstein (1946), for example, suggest that the purposive quality is a function of Freud's metaphorical writing, serving to communicate his difficult ideas in a direct and relevant way. The metaphorical form, they suggest, "comes closer to our immediate understanding, since the anthropomorphism it introduces corresponds to human experience" (p. 17). I will, in contrast, be interpreting the inconsistency engendered by Freud's metaphors as reflecting the pervasive immutability-discontinuity problem which his formulations encounter.

ture of libido, Freud had posited that the relationship between the component sexual instincts was one of fluid equivalence in that one organization could substitute for another as a mode of discharge. Yet in his description of sexual development, he had also characterized the component sexual instincts as having a hierarchic relationship with respect to one another whereby the more primitive components preceded and were subordinated to a more mature sexual activity. This dual relationship between the components of the sexual instincts, while being necessary to the concept of regression and symptomatic behavior, nevertheless presented Freud with a problem. The difficulty was that each relationship implied opposite qualities. The relationship of fluid equivalence suggested the peremptory quality of libidinal hydraulics, while the hierarchic relationship implied that complete discharge via the more primitive modes was delayed in favor of discharge via the more advanced modes. That Freud recognized and yet was unable to reconcile these contradictory qualities can be seen in the fact that in likening the relationship between the partial instincts to a network of "intercommunicating channels," he was compelled to qualify his metaphor by asserting that this hydraulic equivalence between the component instincts was the case "in spite of" their hierarchic relationship. Moreover, Freud (1917b) could not theoretically account for the dual presence of these properties — it was, he admitted, "a state of affairs that is not at all easily combined in a single picture" (p. 345).

The inconsistencies, however, surfaced most clearly in connection with the functioning of the ego instinct. In an article entitled "Formulations on the Two Principles of Mental Functioning," Freud (1911b) suggested that, as instinctual organizations, the ego instincts as well as the sexual instincts functioned in essentially hydraulic terms, or as he characterized it, in terms of a primitive "pleasure principle." As so governed, instinctual energy was directed toward the immediate, blind discharge of energy with little regard for the consequences of such behavior. However, Freud noted, there was a particular set of circumstances which inevitably served to set the functioning of the ego instinct apart from that of the sexual instincts. To fulfill the aim of discharge, the ego instinct required appropriate external events, such as food, which were beyond the primitive organism's control and which depended for their occurrence on the intervention of others. Accordingly, the primitive apparatus learned to adapt to this contingent reality. Freud (1917b) posited that "under the influence of the instructress Necessity" (p. 357), the primitive pleasure principle was replaced by a modification of it in the form of the "reality principle." The organism, functioning in accordance with the reality principle, anticipated the consequences of an act and delayed its expression if, in balance, the act in the long run brought about a rise in tension that outweighed any immediate gain in tension discharge.[16] This state of affairs was in sharp contrast to that which prevailed in connection with the functioning of the sexual instinct. Rather than being dependent upon a contingent reality, the sexual instincts could easily and immediately be gratified by autoerotic activity, such as thumb sucking and masturbation. Accordingly, the sexual instincts were isolated from the "educative influence" of a contingent reality and continued to function in accordance with the pleasure principle.

Freud was thus suggesting that there were activities of the ego instinct that were derived from an evolutionary in-

[16] As will be elaborated in the next chapter, the immediate satisfaction of the pleasure principle is replaced by the reality principle "only in order to gain along the new path an assured pleasure at a later time" (Freud, 1911b, p. 223). Thus, the reality principle (which I consider equivalent to purposive functioning) and the pleasure principle (which I consider equivalent to hydraulic functioning) are viewed by Freud as being governed by the more basic principle of minimal tension.

heritance and that, in accordance with the pleasure principle, functioned hydraulically to protect the organism. In
this sense, the ego instinct repressed the activity of the sexual instinct in a blind reflexive way. And yet, he was also
suggesting that there were defensive activities of this ego instinct that were derived from experience and that had a purposive quality. In this sense, sexual impulses were being
delayed or disguised by the ego instinct in accordance with
the reality principle, namely, in the light of the organism's
anticipating the negative consequences of immediate or
direct sexual discharge. The clear implication, accordingly,
was that the properties of hydraulics and purpose were both
evidenced in the functioning of the same organization. This
mix of hydraulics and purpose was particularly evident in
the differential contribution of the ego instinct to the two
phases of symptom formation. In the initial phase, symptom formation was a consequence of the ego instinct's built-
in reflexive response of repression to the demands of the sexual instinct, while in the subsequent phase, the form of the
symptom was significantly determined by the strategy of the
ego instinct in permitting the sexual strivings to be expressed
in a concealed way. At the very least, therefore, the two
different properties that Freud had ascribed to the ego instinct begged the question as to the nature of their relationship. At worst, there was a systematic discordance between
the ego instinct's purposive qualities of anticipation and
delay, which were apparently acquired as a function of
experience, and the ego instinct's more fundamental, phylogenetically derived hydraulic quality.

Nevertheless, regardless of how else these qualities of
the ego instinct contradicted one another, they were, at
least, congruent with respect to a basic requirement in
Freud's conception of symptom formation, namely, the antagonism between the sexual and ego instincts. Whether
hydraulic or purposive, and whether innate or acquired, the

protective reaction of the ego instinct to the demands of the sexual instinct was the same: The ego instinct blocked the blind hydraulic expression of the sexual impulse and therefore necessitated an alternative mode of realizing the minimal tension principle. It is within this context that one can appreciate the seriousness of a final discordance which led Freud to reformulate his theory. The problem involved his view that the ego instinct had its own source of energy, and it surfaced when Freud (1914b) extended his theory of symptom expression to narcissistically disordered patients. These patients, Freud observed, were sexually preoccupied with themselves in the broadest and most basic sense. They lovingly ruminated on their own thoughts, on their perceptions, and, indeed, on their very bodily functions. They were, in short, "libidinally cathecting" those functions which Freud had included within the province of the ego instinct as being vital to the individual's survival. If this was the case, Freud reasoned, did this not signify that the energy of the sexual instinct was cathecting structures which he had presumed to be powered by the energy of the ego instinct? And if the energy of the sexual instinct and the nonsexual energy of the ego instinct were being organized by the same structure, how could one legitimately discriminate between such energies (Freud, 1933, p. 103)? Thus Freud came to the realization that if he persisted in interpreting such clinical phenomena in terms of the conception of the sexual and ego instincts, he could do so only at the expense of intermingling the two forms of instinctual energy and thereby dissolving the very antagonism which his theory of neurosis required.[17]

Freud's final version represented his solution to this problem. He maintained the concept of instinctual hydraul-

---

[17] Freud (1933) notes in this regard:

To begin with, the opposition between the ego-instincts and the sexual instincts lay at the base of our libido theory. When later on we belics as well as the view that there was a necessary antagonism to direct libidinal expression. But now he accounted for this antagonism without recourse to a polarity between sexual and ego instincts. Instead he suggested that the antagonism was between the sexual instincts and a punitive reality. Thus, one pole of the antagonism was the internal reality of a constitutionally given organization which Freud designated as the "id." He characterized the id as having a source of physiologically derived libido, as being inherently directed toward sexual objects, and as functioning in accordance with the pleasure principle. Freud (1933) noted in this regard:

> We approach the id with analogies: we call it a chaos, a cauldron full of seething excitations. We picture it as being open at its end to somatic influences, and there taking up into itself instinctual needs.... It is filled with energy reaching it from the instincts, but it has no organization ... but only a striving to bring about the satisfaction of the instinctual needs subject to the observance of the pleasure principle. The logical laws of thought do not apply in the id, and this is true above all of the law of contradiction. Contrary impulses exist side by side, without cancelling each other out or diminishing each other.... Instinctual cathexes seeking discharge—that in our view, is all there is in the id [pp. 73-74].

The other pole of the antagonism was an external reality that included sexual as well as dangerous objects. The primitive organism, governed by the id, was inherently directed toward the sexual objects of this reality (again significantly

gan to study the ego itself more closely and arrived at the conception of narcissism, this distinction itself lost its foundation [p. 102].

including the incestuous object), but blind to those threatening aspects (such as the castrating father) that did not serve as objects of its immediate instinctual desires. How, then, could the id in its "blind efforts for the satisfaction of its instincts" (Freud, 1933, p. 75) escape destruction if the organism was no longer equipped at birth with an instinct that blocked such dangerous impulses from discharge? The answer was given in the form of a purposive organization that was acquired through experience and that mediated between the blind id and the antagonistic reality (e.g., Freud, 1923, p. 25; 1933, p. 75). It was an acquired ego which now functioned in accordance with the reality principle and, accordingly, which assured the long-range rather than the immediate short-lived satisfaction of instinctual need. Freud (1933) noted that the ego, in serving as a mediator between the external reality of satisfactions and dangers and the internal reality of the instinctual needs, represented reality to the id by observing the external world and laying down "an accurate picture of it in the memory traces of its perceptions" (p. 75). Moreover, by virtue of its acquired ability to anticipate the consequences of instinctual action, it coordinated the demands of inner and outer realities by blocking the instinctual impulse from discharge either in action or in conscious thought if it judged that such action would ultimately lead to high states of tension (pp. 75–76).[18]

[18] There are two major omissions in this presentation of Freud's last version. First, I am not distinguishing between the ideational and energy components of the instinctual impulse with respect to their separate fates under the condition of repression. Second, I am not presenting Freud's final polarity between the life and death instincts. In this regard, it should be noted that Freud does not completely give up his view regarding the self-preservative nature of the ego instinct; he retained the notion that certain life-preserving activities, as governed by the life instinct, were natively given. Although these aspects of Freud's theory are important in terms of other issues, such as his treatment of aggression, I do not consider that their omission misrepresents the theory insofar as the continuity-change issue is concerned.

It may be seen, then, that Freud continued to represent the same dimensions of functioning that he had delineated in his prior version, but in a significantly reorganized and ostensibly less contradictory form. On the one hand, Freud (1933) emphasized the hydraulic quality of the sexual instincts even more than in his previous versions. As may be seen in his characterization of id activity, Freud (p. 73) played down the hierarchic organization of the sexual instincts and highlighted their fluid equivalence. Indeed, he did this even to the point of implying that the id had no structure, but only energy.[19] On the other hand, Freud (1933) drastically purified the concept of the ego instinct by divesting it entirely of any quality of instinctual hydraulics. Where he had characterized the defensive activities of the ego instinct in hydraulic terms, now he saw these activities as purposively directed. And where he had attributed these activities to the preformed structures and energy of an instinct, now he attributed these to a "structure" which was devoid of its own source of instinctual energy and which came into existence entirely through experience. Thus, Freud differentiated id functioning, not from an ego instinct which paradoxically had some acquired purposive features, but from a purely acquired, completely purposive organization.[20]

[19] As a number of theorists have noted, in particular Holt (1967), Freud's classic passage (1933, p. 73) in which he characterizes the id as having "no organization" but only libidinal energy, appears to contradict other aspects of his theory in which primitive id functioning is described in terms of both libidinal energetics and structure. Holt's analysis of this passage is in line with my earlier characterization of Freud's metapsychology. We can interpret this passage to mean that Freud is positing here, not pure energy and a lack of structure, but the particular energy-structure relationship embodied in the hydraulic model. In terms of this model, energy activates an otherwise inert structure and is discharged via that structure, thereby taking on the form of its vehicle. Freud's term "no organization" can thus be taken to mean no *hierarchic* organization, rather than to mean no structure.

[20] Note that the distinction here is not between conscious and unconscious behavior, but between hydraulic and purposive functioning. In Freud's view, both purposive and hydraulic functioning could be unconscious.

If this ostensible gain in theoretical coherence was important to Freud, at least of equal importance was the fact that he could now apply these reorganized dimensions of functioning to the narcissistic disorders and yet not undermine the antagonism that was intrinsic to his basic view of psychopathology. For in redefining the antagonism between the sexual and ego instincts as one that existed between the hydraulic id and an external reality, Freud was also transposing this antagonism to one that existed between the hydraulic id and the purposive ego as a *representative* of this external reality. It was in the sense of representing a reality of tension-raising consequences that the ego could be antagonistic to the demands of the id; namely, in accordance with the reality principle, it could block the tendency toward immediate instinctual discharge. Within this context of the ego as a mediator between internal and external realities, the narcissistic disorder, rather than constituting a theoretical problem, was only "an extreme exaggeration of a normal state of affairs" (Freud, 1933, p. 103). As a mediating structure, the ego was *always* being invested (cathected) with libidinal energy from the instincts — energy which was then channelized with respect to the external world. It was no problem now for Freud (1940) to say that the libido "streams to the ego from the various organs and parts of the body" (p. 151), thence to be redirected by the ego toward external events. Thus, when interpreting the narcissistic disorders, Freud was no longer confronted with an intermingling of sexual and nonsexual energies and, accordingly, with an undermining of a theoretically necessary polarity. Instead, Freud could point to the fact that the ego as a structure was merely being cathected with a greater amount of libidinal energy than was usual and, indeed, could derive this "exaggeration of a normal state" from the very polarity itself — that is, from the derived antagonistic function he had ascribed to the ego as a mediator between internal and external realities.

There was, however, a significant ramification of this new antagonism that Freud now posited between the subtly refined hydraulic organization of the id and the drastically purified purposive structure of the ego. In spite of the cognitive and defensive capabilities assigned to it, the ego was now powerless in an energy sense. As an acquired organization, the ego no longer had its own built-in physiological source of energy, but could only direct the blind libido supplied by the id. Thus was Freud (1933) able to say that the ego's relation to the id was like that of a rider to his horse: "The horse supplies the locomotive energy, while the rider has the privilege of deciding on the goal and of guiding the powerful animal's movement" (p. 77). Freud's final view of symptomatic behavior underwent a significant transformation within the context of this view of functioning in which a weak but purposive ego mediated between a powerful but blind id and an antagonistic reality. Although retaining a two-phase conception of symptomatic behavior, he drastically revised his views regarding the process that constituted the initial phase. The extent of this revision can, perhaps, be best appreciated in Freud's (1926) retrospective comments on his earlier formulation of the Little Hans case. Noting that he had repeatedly advanced the thesis that libidinal energy was transformed into anxiety through repression, he felt that he had to say, even though it was unpleasant for him to do so, that his continued study of the phobias contradicted this thesis. Rather, he noted:

> . . . the majority of the phobias go back to an anxiety of this kind felt by the ego in regard to the demands of the libido. It is always the ego's attitude of anxiety which is the primary thing and which sets repression going. Anxiety never arises from the repressed libido [p. 109].

In the previous version, then, repression was followed

by anxiety, while now the reverse was the case: Anxiety was followed by repression. Where anxiety had been converted energy which followed the repression of the blind and powerful sexual instincts by a blind and equally powerful ego instinct, now anxiety was the anticipation of a weak ego that it might not be able to control the libidinal demands of the id.[21] And where repression had been a phylogenetically determined hydraulic response of one powerful instinct to another, repression was now a defensive activity which was instigated by this purposive ego as a reaction to its own anxiety and which was designed to avoid the consequences of an anticipated libidinal discharge. Freud (1926) was thus able to say in regard to this initial phase of symptomatic behavior:

> The conclusion we have come to, then, is this. Anxiety is a reaction to a situation of danger. It is obviated by the ego's doing something to avoid that situation or to withdraw from it. It might be said that symptoms are created so as to avoid the generating of anxiety. But this does not go deep enough. It would be truer to say that symptoms are created so to avoid a *danger-situation* whose presence has been signalled by the generation of anxiety. In the cases that we have discussed, the danger concerned was the danger of castration or of something traceable back to castration [pp. 128–129].

[21] The revised basis for symptomatic anxiety in Freud's (1933) final view is nicely expressed in the following:

> Thus the ego, driven by the id ... repulsed by reality, struggles to master its economic task of bringing about harmony among the forces and influences working in and upon it; and we can understand how it is that so often we cannot suppress a cry: 'Life is not easy!' If the ego is obliged to admit its weakness, it breaks out in anxiety— realistic anxiety regarding the external world ... and neurotic anxiety regarding the strength of the passions in the id [p. 78].

In effect, then, the active purposive quality that had previously been evidenced in the second phase of the symptom, had now been extended to cover the first phase of the symptom process as well. In Freud's final version, the form of the symptom, from the very beginning, reflected the efforts of a weak but purposive ego in mediating between the mutually antagonistic and equally harsh demands of an inner and outer reality.

As might be expected, however, Freud's revision did not evidence itself as dramatically in his conception of the second phase of symptom expression. The essential reason for this was that the final polarity he posited between the id and ego had already been anticipated in his view regarding the interaction between sexual and ego instincts in this second phase. Thus, Freud (1933) reaffirmed his earlier conception of libidinal fixation as well as his view of regression as a hydraulic consequence of repression. And, in particular, he expressed a view that in its essential aspects was the same as his earlier one, namely, that the form of the symptom in this second phase reflected the antagonistic forces of ego and id, but on the new battleground provided by libidinal regression to earlier fixations.

In summary, then, it may be seen that Freud's final version was designed to resolve two problems. The first was the contradictory mix of hydraulic and purposive features that had been evidenced within each of his previously posited instinctual organizations. The second was the undermining of an antagonism between these instinctual domains of personality — an antagonism that Freud had held crucial to his view of psychopathology. In this final version, accordingly, Freud confined the hydraulic and purposive modes of functioning to separate and ostensibly homogeneous organizations. He viewed the id as a relatively pure hydraulic organization of energy and structure, and the ego as a purposive structure devoid of any contamination by the hydraulics of its own instinctual energy. The interactions that Freud posited between these purified dimensions of personality now enabled him to interpret the narcissistic disorders in a less problematic way. He could now interpret these disorders without undermining the new polarity which he had proposed as being critical to the formation of the symptom — a polarity between id and ego derived from the more fundamental antagonism between inner and outer realities.

It may be seen, however, that in proposing interactions between id and ego, Freud was continuing to posit relationships between hydraulic and purposive modes of functioning. Indeed, as the next chapter will attempt to demonstrate, in so conceptualizing behavior, Freud succeeded only in displacing the problem of understanding the relationship between these hydraulic and purposive modes of functioning. He succeeded in displacing the contradictory admixture of hydraulics and purpose from one that occurred within the separate domains of the sexual and ego instincts to one that occurred within the domain of the personality as a whole. The next chapter will focus on the interactions between these modes of functioning in Freud's final version, and on their relationship to the end-state of minimal tension. Specifically, I will attempt to show that it is precisely in regard to the relationship between these hydraulic and purposive modes of functioning that Freud's theory encounters forms of immutability and discontinuity which are identical to those seen in instinct theory and behaviorism and which, in accordance with my thesis, are part of his Cartesian legacy.

4

THE IMMUTABILITY-
DISCONTINUITY PROBLEM
IN FREUD'S APPROACH TO
DEVELOPMENT AND PATHOLOGY

As the basis for my analysis of Freud's theory, two questions can be posed for his final version. The first is relevant to his view of development: If the ego is not an instinctual given, but is acquired through experience, then what is the process involved in its acquisition? In particular, how does the delaying purposive mode of functioning governed by the reality principle develop from the blind hydraulic mode epitomized by the pleasure principle? The second question is relevant to Freud's view of symptomatic behavior: Since the ego is "weak" in the sense that, as an acquired organization, it lacks its own source of instinctual energy, then how can it fulfill the cognitive and defensive functions that have been assigned to it? More specifically, where does the purposive ego get the energy to repress the powerful id impulse hydraulically pressing toward discharge?

FREUD'S "CONFLICT" APPROACH
TO DEVELOPMENT

Freud dealt with the first issue by elaborating on a conception he had already advanced in his earlier versions: The essential basis for the acquisition of purposive functioning was the conflict inherent in the relationship between the hydraulically governed organism and an external contingent reality. In his initial presentation of this view, Freud (1900) had suggested that the organism, in its primitive state, functioned in terms of the minimal tension principle by discharging excitation via reflexive motor activity. This direct and immediate way of maintaining minimal tension was thwarted, however, by the "exigencies of life" which confronted the primitive organism in the form of certain physical needs—notably, the hunger need. In contrast to the "momentary impact" of an external source of stimulation, the pressure of such needs as hunger remained unabated despite the child's cries and helpless struggling, and could only be relieved by contact with an appropriate reality event. In the case of the child, this could only take place with the assistance of others, hence Freud's notion of a fortuitous or contingent reality, that is to say, a reality over which the primitive organism had no control. The experience of satisfaction under these circumstances served to establish a connection between the "memory trace" of the instinctual excitation and the "memory trace" of the satisfying reality event. When the child again became hungry, this connection served as the basis for his "psychic impulse" or wish to re-establish the satisfying event. Given the organism's hydraulic means of reducing tension, this wish-fulfilling activity took immediate and direct expression. Like water flowing along a channel, instinctual energy flowed along the established connection in energizing the memory trace of the satisfying object, thereby re-evoking the former percept as a hallucination:

> Nothing prevents us from assuming that there was a primitive state of the psychical apparatus in which this path was actually traversed, that is, in which wishing ended in hallucinating. Thus the aim of this first psychical activity was to produce a 'perceptual identity' — a repetition of the perception which was linked with the satisfaction of the need [p. 566].

However, Freud (1900) continued, this primitive mental activity could only be modified by "the bitter experience of life." Since the direct discharge onto the memory trace could not possibly produce the same result as discharging such instinctual energy onto the real event, the internal tension persisted. It was this essential *conflict* — this inevitable rise in tension in the absence of the gratifying object — that led to development:

> In order to arrive at a more efficient expenditure of psychical force, it is necessary to bring the regression to a halt before it becomes complete, so that it does not proceed beyond the mnemic image, and is able to seek out other paths which lead eventually to the desired perceptual identity being established from the direction of the external world. This inhibition of the regression and the subsequent diversion of the excitation become the business of a second system, which is in control of voluntary movement — which for the first time, that is, makes use of movement for purposes remembered in advance. But all the complicated thought-activity which is spun out from the mnemic image to the moment at which the perceptual identity is established by the external world — all this activity of thought merely constitutes a roundabout path of wish-fulfillment

which has been made necessary by experience. Thought is after all nothing but a substitute for a hallucinatory wish [pp. 566–567].

The organism under the influence of this second system, then, diverted the energy from hydraulic discharge onto the memory trace as a *hallucination,* and instead merely used a small part of this energy in evoking the "mnemic image" or *memory* of the previous event. The energy saved was now purposively directed toward changing the real world in order to bring about an external event, the perception of which matched the memory of the previously satisfying event — hence "the desired perceptual identity being established from the direction of the external world." Instead of the inadequate discharge via the cathexis of the memory trace as a hallucination, the cathexis of this duplicated external event again served adequately to reduce the instinctual tension.

This conception of development remained essentially unchanged in Freud's (1911b) second version, in which the hydraulic and purposive modes of functioning were represented by the sexual and ego instincts. Both instincts, as we have noted, were seen as functioning initially in accordance with the hydraulic activity of the pleasure principle; that is, the energy of both instincts, when reaching a given level, was seen as being mechanically discharged onto constitutionally determined objects with no regard for the consequences. In contrast to the ego instinct, however, the sexual instinct persisted in functioning in terms of this primitive hydraulic mode. The reason for this, Freud maintained, was that the sexual instinct could be immediately gratified by autoerotic activity and hence was isolated from the "educative influence" of an external contingent reality. This was not the case in regard to the ego instinct. Rather, the survival of the primitive organism, from the very outset, required the intervention of external others. It thus followed that the essential objects of gratification for the ego instinct could not always be immediately available for discharge. Under such circumstances, the primitive organism, governed solely by the pleasure principle of instant gratification, chose the most direct path of wish fulfillment by hallucinating the previously experienced object of satisfaction. But the immediate reduction in tension which resulted was followed by an increase in tension in the long run since this hallucinatory activity could not possibly gratify the steadily mounting instinctual needs. As a consequence of this subsequent rise in tension, the pleasure principle which governed the activity of the ego instinct became modified by the reality principle:

> It was only the non-occurrence of the expected satisfaction, the disappointment experienced, that led to the abandonment of this attempt at satisfaction by means of hallucination. Instead of it, the psychical apparatus had to decide to form a conception of the real circumstances in the external world and to endeavour to make a real alteration in them. A new principle of mental functioning was thus introduced: what was presented in the mind was no longer what was agreeable but what was real, even if it happened to be disagreeable. This setting-up of the reality principle proved to be a momentous step [p. 219].

Accordingly, as in Freud's (1900) initial treatment of the problem, the inherent antagonism between a primitive, ineffectual organism and a contingent reality constituted the condition for development. Where there was instant gratification provided by autoerotic activity—that is, where the organism, so to speak, was "conflict-free"—there was isolation from the educative influence of experience and a lack of development. Where there was a depriving reality upon which the organism depended for its survival, and over which it had no control, there was the development of the pleasure principle into the reality principle: The reality principle came into being as a consequence of the primitive organism's inadequate mechanisms for discharging the rise in tension generated by the absence of the crucial gratifying object. In this second version as well, the essential basis for development was a condition of conflict which Freud characterized as the inevitable rise in tension in an organism whose capacities were inadequate to the demands of a depriving reality.

In his final version, Freud (1933) advanced the same "conflict" conception of development, but now as a process whereby a "portion" of the hydraulic id became modified into a purposive ego by virtue of the "proximity and influence" (p. 75) of an external world of impersonal and interpersonal events. In particular, he derived the ego's characteristics of delay and purpose from the organism's experience with a world made up of significant purposive *others* — a process he termed "identification." In doing so, he distinguished between two aspects of ego functioning:

> We wish to make the ego the matter of our enquiry, our very own ego. But is that possible? After all, the ego is in its very essence a subject; how can it be made into an object? Well, there is no doubt that it can be. The ego can take itself as an object, can treat itself like other objects, can observe itself, criticize itself, and do Heaven knows what with itself [p. 58].

Development in this final version was thus conceptualized as a dual process whereby the id became modified into an ego that was an "object" as well as a "subject" of experience. To that end, Freud (1933) formulated two major types of identification, and proposed that each involved a different type of interaction with an interpersonal other:

> The difference between the two can be expressed in

some such way as this. If a boy identifies himself with his father, he wants to *be like* his father; if he makes him the object of his choice, he wants to *have* him, to possess him [p. 63].

One form of identification, then, involved an interpersonal relationship in which the external other, in being so possessed, served as an object in reducing the individual's instinctual tension. Originally, Freud (1917a) had proposed this form of identification, not as a conception of development, but as a way of accounting for a classic symptom of depressed patients. These patients, in their severe melancholia, typically condemned themselves for possessing a variety of personal attributes which, Freud noted, did not apply to them. These characteristics, rather, applied to a significant other whom the patient had loved and lost. This, in Freud's view, was the key to the clinical picture. The self-reproaches were reproaches that had initially been directed toward the loved other, but that now were shifted onto the patient's own ego so that "the latter could henceforth be judged by a special agency, as though it were an object, the forsaken object" (p. 249). Freud's interpretation of why the patient possessed these criticized attributes paralleled his earlier notion that the infant achieved an "identity" of perception by hallucinating the absent, previously gratifying object. The attributes had originally been those of the loved and lost other—attributes which the patient reproduced as his own and which he criticized in the place of the other now no longer available to him for libidinal discharge. In Freud's (1917b) terms, the patient, in reacting to this loss, had "incorporated" (p. 249) this loved and lost interpersonal object as an aspect of his own ego.

As Freud (1923) subsequently pointed out, however, he had not realized the full significance of this process of introjection. Rather than being confined to the melancholias, this substitution was an activity engaged in by all individuals and was fundamental to building the "character" of the ego. As such, his view of "introjective identification" became a theory of development:

> When it happens that a person has to give up a sexual object, there quite often ensues an alteration of his ego which can only be described as a setting up of the object inside the ego, as it occurs in melancholia; the exact nature of this substitution is as yet unknown to us.... At any rate the process, especially in the early phases of development, is a very frequent one, and it makes it possible to suppose that the character of the ego is a precipitate of abandoned object-cathexes and that it contains the history of those object-choices [p. 29].

For Freud, the significance of this internal substitution was that the individual could protect himself against future increases in instinctual tension when the need-reducing external object was no longer present. The property of the loved one became one's own and hence was always available as an object for tension reduction, albeit in representational form. Thus Freud (1923) noted:

> When the ego assumes the features of the object, it is forcing itself, so to speak, upon the id as a love-object and is trying to make good the id's loss by saying: 'Look, you can love me too—I am so like the object' [p. 30].

Clearly, then, that aspect of the ego which was altered by introjective identification was the ego as the "object" of experience. If, however, the ego-as-object was formed by the acquisition of the lost tension-reducing other, what about the "special agency" which, in the melancholias, criticized this aspect of the ego? What, in other words, was involved in the development of that aspect of the ego which served as subject in taking the criticized aspect of the ego as object? In this regard, Freud (1933) advanced his concept of "identification proper" as a process which involved the individual's wanting to emulate the characteristics of the other.[1] In doing so, Freud focused on characteristics that were also evidenced by the external other, but that were significantly different from those serving directly to satisfy the sexual needs. These were attributes of purpose, integration, power, and control:

> Even if conscience is something 'within us', yet it is not so from the first. In this it is a real contrast to sexual life, which is in fact there from the beginning of life and not only a later addition. But, as is well known, young children are amoral and possess no internal inhibitions against their impulses striving for pleasure. The part which is later taken on by the super-ego is played to begin with by an external power, by parental authority. Parental influence governs the child by offering proofs of love and by threatening punishments. . . . So long as it is dominant there is no need to talk of a super-ego and of a conscience. It is only subsequently that the secondary situation develops . . . where the external restraint is internalized and the super-ego takes the place of the parental agency and observes, directs and threatens the ego in exactly the same way as earlier the parents did with the child [pp. 61–62].

This substitution of the superego for parental authority came about by virtue of a relationship between the child and his parents that epitomized the antagonism between the organism and a contingent reality. Freud designated this relationship as the Oedipus complex and characterized its basic form as one in which the male child wants both to possess mother as the object of the sexual instinct and to get rid of father as a rival. However, because he fears that any

---

[1] The terms "identification proper" and "introjective identification" are taken from Sanford (1955).

expression of his desires will lead to his destruction (castration) by the powerful father, he gives up his erotic attachment to mother by drastically and energetically repressing his libidinal longings. Several possible consequences result from so abandoning the Oedipus complex and thus renouncing the object-cathexis of mother. One is an introjective identification with the "lost mother" whereby her characteristics are represented by that aspect of the ego which serves as object. The other consequence, which Freud considers the normal one for the male child, is an identification proper with father whereby the controlling and punitive characteristics of father become the attributes of the ego-as-subject —an ego which acts toward the ego-as-object "as earlier the parents did with the child." Thus was Freud able to say that the superego was the "heir" to the Oedipus complex.[2]

It may be seen, then, that Freud was suggesting a process that paralleled his earlier formulation that the reality principle came into being in order to prevent an ultimate increase in tension. Direct libidinal expression with respect to

[2] I am not trying here to represent Freud's considerable ambiguity with respect to the process of superego development. At the very least, however, it should be noted that in one account (1933) he seems to attach considerable importance to the role of introjective identification in the resolution of the Oedipus complex, while in another account (1923) he downgrades its importance.

Note, moreover, that I am presuming that Freud, in giving up his view of the ego instinct in favor of an acquired ego, is also giving up his earlier conception that the child instinctively fears castration as a function of the incestuous desire. Instead of being derived from a "phylogenetic history," the child's castration anxiety results from a family history whereby the child, as a function of past experience, comes to fear punishment if he transgresses parental rules (see Fenichel, 1945, for a similar view). This experience, however, finds a fertile soil in a "phylogenetic reinforcement" (Freud, 1933, p. 86). See also Chapter 3, footnote 8.

Finally, it should be noted that, in regard to the issues with which I am concerned, Freud's conception of development in women is the same as his conception of development in men. Since this view is less clearly articulated with respect to women, I am confining myself to an analysis of the Oedipus complex.

mother as a sexual object resulted in tension reduction; but, as in the hallucination of the gratifying object, this was only tension reduction in the short run: The reality of the situation was such that punishment followed and, accordingly, that tension increased. Hence, as a more effective means of realizing the end-state of minimal tension, this immediate hydraulic expression was repressed and the external controlling properties of the punitive father became represented as an inner control of the primitive impulse or, if you will, became represented as the "subject" of experience. In wanting to "be like" the other, the organism in effect wanted to emulate those controlling characteristics of the other which, when so acquired, served to bring about minimal tension levels in the long run.

THE IMMUTABILITY-DISCONTINUITY PROBLEM

Perhaps the most significant reaction to the difficulties inherent in Freud's view of development came from within the psychoanalytic movement itself and, in particular, from Heinz Hartmann (1939, 1956), who can be said to be the initiator of contemporary psychoanalytic ego psychology. White (1963), in his appraisal of this reaction, has observed:

> . . . Hartmann pointed out that Freud's account of the transition from the pleasure principle to the reality principle contained important hidden assumptions. Putting off a present for a future pleasure implies two processes, postponement and anticipation, that cannot be conjured up from the mere fact that an instinctual drive is frustrated [p. 17].

The term "conjured up" has reference to the fact that Freud first suggests that the frustration of instinctual need serves as the necessary condition for the development of the reality principle. And then he seems to give the purposive mode of functioning to the organism with no consideration of any mechanism that could serve to connect this purposive activity to the prior condition of conflict. Freud's (1911b) view is a good case in point. Here, because of the rise in tension, the organism appears simply to abandon the hallucinatory discharge in favor of forming a veridical conception of the real world and of affecting this world in ways that are guided by anticipation and delay. But how does it follow from the prior condition of conflict that the organism blindly pressing toward discharge suddenly acquires the ability to form this veridical conception of the real world and to act in purposive ways? Freud has clearly departed from the continuity given by scientific rules, and has substituted, in its place, a magically produced rabbit-in-the-hat. In a manner reminiscent of Bertocci's criticism of functional autonomy, Hartmann is pointing to the discontinuous appearance of delay and anticipation in an organism that, by definition, has started with only blind instinctual promptings.[3]

If Hartmann's criticism serves to alert us to the discontinuity in Freud's conception of development, where, then, is the immutability problem encountered by this conception? The answer is given in a further examination of Freud's

[3] White (1959) has made a similar point:

In what now looks like an excess of enthusiasm for his own concepts, Freud ... undertook to explain the outgrowing of the pleasure principle and the substituting of the reality principle as a simple and direct consequence of the frustration of instinctual needs [p. 308].

Apparently, White's own concern with the discontinuity of Freud's conception has led him to accentuate this aspect of Hartmann's contribution. In reading White (1963, p. 17), one comes away with the impression that Hartmann's "Notes on the Reality Principle" (1956) focuses sharply on the discontinuity problem—and this is not the case. This is not to say that White has misrepresented Hartmann, for Hartmann does make the point, albeit implicitly, in this article. He has, moreover, clearly articulated this view elsewhere (Hartmann, 1939). However, it should be borne in mind that when I refer to Hartmann's (1956) criticism regarding the discontinuity in Freud's conflict view of development, I am doing so in regard to a view that has been considerably sharpened in White's (1963) analysis.

views. Hartmann's criticism notwithstanding, it may be seen that Freud is not content with merely evoking the reality principle as a simple consequence of frustration. He suggests, at least implicitly, that a series of processes intervenes between the condition of frustration and the emergence of the reality principle. Thus, Freud (1911b) states that "it was only the non-occurrence of the expected satisfaction, the disappointment experienced, that led to the abandonment of this attempt at satisfaction by means of hallucination. Instead of it, the psychical apparatus had to decide to form a conception of the real circumstances in the external world and to endeavour to make a real alteration in them" (p. 219). Now, if it is the case that anticipation and delay are essential qualities of the reality principle, then Freud's conception suggests that these qualities are already being given to the organism in the intervening processes he posits as taking place *before* the formation of the reality principle. The first of these intervening events occurs in connection with the hallucination that follows the initial increase in tension. In suggesting that the hallucination is an "attempt" or a "means" of reducing tension, Freud is implying that this hydraulic discharge is being used in a purposive way—as a means toward an end. The next event in the sequence is the "disappointment" on the part of the organism in the absence of the "expected satisfaction"—qualities that also imply the anticipation of a given end. This, in turn, leads to the organism's "abandonment of" the hallucination—an act that again suggests an ability to delay the peremptory hydraulic discharge of the hallucination. Finally, the organism, in effect, has "to decide" to function in accordance with the reality principle. But, clearly, the act of deciding also suggests anticipation and choice. It is only at this point in the sequence that we have the explicit emergence of the reality principle with its characteristics of anticipation and delay: "A new principle of mental functioning was thus introduced..."

(p. 219). Freud is thus positing a sequence of events, subsequent to the condition of frustration and prior to the emergence of the reality principle, each of which suggests qualities that characterize the functioning of behavior in accordance with the reality principle. Indeed, it can be said that these qualities seem to repeat themselves in a curiously perseverative manner. If this is true, then we can supplement Hartmann's critique in the following way: In having discontinuously conjured up the reality principle as a function of conflict, Freud's conception of development is also evidencing a form of immutability in that it is implicitly assuming, as a prior and necessary condition for the reality principle, the very characteristics that the conception is purporting to explain.

One could object, of course, that my argument capitalizes on an unfortunate use of terms by Freud or, at the very worst, a momentary oversight on his part. I submit that this is not the case, but that we are seeing a *systematic* difficulty — one that is evidenced in other aspects of Freud's theory as well. We have, for example, a variant of the same problem in Freud's (1900) earlier view of development: Given the increase in tension following the hallucination, "it is necessary" (p. 566) that the organism delay the full cathexis of the memory trace so that the energy saved can be used more advantageously. Thereupon, Freud has the organism functioning in accordance with a "second system" that inhibits and deflects this energy so that it can be used in a way that brings about long-term satisfaction. Here, too, attributes are being discontinuously conjured into existence. And here, again, this functioning, like that of the reality principle, presumes itself as a prior condition for its coming into being. Thus, as part of the same conception, we have Freud's notion that the memory trace of the past satisfying event serves as the basis for a veridical match with those external events brought about by the activity of the "second system." To the extent, however, that the memory trace serves as the basis for an "identity of perception" with the real world, to that extent Freud is arbitrarily giving the primitive organism the ability to veridically represent the world as a condition prior to the functioning of the second system—an ability which presumably is an essential characteristic of the second system itself.

Other instances of the same problem are evidenced in Freud's final version. In both concepts of identification, we again see that the relatively primitive subject acquires the more mature attribute as a consequence of conflict. In introjective identification, there is the loss of the gratifying other, a consequent rise in tension, and the "setting up of the object inside the ego." Similarly, in identification proper, there are the successive increases in tension represented respectively by the child's fear of castration and by his giving up the gratifying other, whereupon the subject internalizes the characteristics of the punitive, controlling other. Now, in either case, Freud is unable to provide an explicit connection between such conflict and the consequent identification. For how is it that the organism blindly pressing toward discharge suddenly acquires this ability to take in the representation of the gratifying other, or the attributes of the punitive, controlling other? Indeed, Freud (1923) admits that the nature of the substitution whereby the ego acquires the characteristics of the other is unknown to him. At the same time, these conceptions encounter a problem of immutability that is formally identical to that noted in Freud's earlier versions. This takes a particularly compelling form in the conception of introjective identification. In an explicit extension of Freud's view, Rank and Macnaughton (1950) have proposed that reality testing and the synthesis of functions, as attributes of the mature ego, develop by virtue of a close relationship between the initially fragmented child and a stable, integrated mother. The fragmented child, they suggest, by introjecting a "stable maternal image, conceived as a whole" (p. 56), acquires a stable integrated core that functions in accordance with the reality principle. However, as White (1963) has noted in his critique of Freudian theory, there is a fundamental difficulty in this conception: "Indeed the hypothesized introjection of a whole person implies that the child has already conceived of the mother as a whole person; he already possesses the capacity which the act of introjection is supposed to confer on him" (p. 105). One might restate White's argument and say that if there were no *prior* ability on the part of the primitive organism to selectively organize its experience in accordance with the reality principle, there would be nothing to prevent that organism from incorporating *everything,* including the kitchen sink, along with the mother figure. Accordingly, since the organism has to know *what* to introject, this conception of development must, then, implicitly assume the very characteristic it is directed toward explaining. Thus, introjection, as so formulated, reverses the sequence of events involved in the developmental process. It derives the quality of synthesis from the introjection of an integrated figure when the quality of synthesis has to be present in the first place for such selective introjection to occur. The organism, if you will, has to know in order to know.

One should come away from White's analysis with the unsettled feeling that the very dimension of time itself is out of joint in the Freudian conception of introjection. From a strictly logical viewpoint, the attribute that Freudian theory has conjured up as a consequence of a developmental process requires itself as a precondition for its own emergence! And by virtue of this, the causal sequence of events which Freudian theory posits as a process of development negates itself in the manner, as it were, of a snake swallowing its tail. Thus, even if Freud did use an unfortunate choice of words in describing his conception of development, the dilemma that White has posed for the theory implies that Freud, by virtue of the logic of a situation which he himself has defined, has somehow been forced to presume the very attribute which he intends his model to explain. By virtue of this implicit preformism, accordingly, the Freudian conception is necessarily open to the same criticism which Bertocci directed at Allport's conception of functional autonomy. To paraphrase Bertocci again, we have come full circle to the magical appearance of integration in a fragmented subject. Freudian theory encounters the contradiction of simultaneously characterizing the primitive subject in antithetical ways.[4]*

[4]* Because of its formal significance for my argument, I am focusing on the immutability-discontinuity problem that White's analysis has raised for the concept of introjective identification. I should point out, however, that the notion of identification proper encounters the same form of the problem. We have seen that, as an essential aspect of the resolution of the Oedipus complex, the child in response to his castration anxiety represses his sexual desires for mother, as a result of which he introjectively identifies with the "lost mother" and identifies with the punitive, controlling attributes of father. This latter identification accounts for the formation of the superego. We have already noted the problem of discontinuity encountered by this formulation (see p. 135). But one can ask further, as indeed Freud does, how can we account for such repression on the part of the child? Freud (1933) states in this regard that repressive activity can only be a manifestation of superego functioning:

> Since we have come to assume a special agency in the ego, the superego, which represents demands of a restrictive and rejecting character, we may say that repression is the work of this super-ego and that it is carried out either by itself or by the ego in obedience to its orders [p. 69].

As so characterized, the same repressive activity that is a necessary condition for the resolution of the Oedipus complex and for the acquisition of the superego, is itself a function of the superego. As in his other formulations, then, Freud would appear to be assuming attributes of anticipation and control as a prior and necessary basis for the acquisition of these very same attributes. Now it might be argued that this problem of immutability is dealt with in Freud's (1923) conception, in which he derives repression from an organization that exists prior to the oedipal conflict. In this view, the superego, as the normal outcome of the oedipal conflict, is merely the

White's analysis, then, is obviously relevant to our critique. It suggests that the discontinuity in Freud's conception of how the reality principle is acquired is necessarily connected to the immutability of assuming this principle in order to account for its acquisition. However, to my way of thinking, White's point is intuitively provocative but not formally compelling. In fairness, it should be noted that

---

strengthening of an already present structure. Thus Freud (1923) notes that behind the origin of the superego "lies hidden an individual's first and most important identification, his identification with the father in his own personal prehistory" (p. 31) and, further, that this is "a direct and immediate identification and takes place earlier than any object-cathexis" (p. 31). Accordingly, the outcome of the Oedipus complex is an "intensification of the identifications with his parents which have probably long been present in his ego" (Freud, 1933, p. 64).

But this solution only serves to displace the problem of immutability and discontinuity back in time, in a way that is characteristic of Freud's other formulations. Obviously, there is no problem per se in Freud's attempt to clarify the antecedents of the Oedipus complex. However, Freud seems to be positing, by fiat, this direct and immediate "primary" identification. If this is the case, then Freud is still giving gratuitously to the organism the attributes which his account of the oedipal situation is directed toward explaining and, in doing so, continues to encounter the problem of immutability. Moreover, if we examine the implications of Freud's comment regarding the child's "personal prehistory," a reference to his attempt to account for the phylogenetic origins of the Oedipus complex, we can see yet another backward displacement of the immutability-discontinuity problem. In a continuation of the views expressed in *Totem and Taboo* (1913), Freud (1921) had suggested that the child's primary identification with the father stemmed, in turn, from responses that had been made by his primal forebears, responses that were now represented as predispositions to act in similar ways to similar reality events. Freud had speculated that, in the individual's prehistory, there was a primal horde in which the all-powerful father dominated the sons and monopolized the women for pleasure. The sons, hating the father, united to kill and eat him. Overcome by guilt at their act, they formed a clan with self-imposed taboos against incest. Thus we have the actual prehistoric event in which the son incorporates the father's control—an act which predisposes the modern child toward so identifying with father prior to the oedipal situation. But this portrayal encounters an identical form of the immutability-discontinuity problem. In an analysis that strikingly

White's analysis is but one aspect of a broader, systematic critique of Freud's theory—one that serves as the basis for his own "conflict-free" alternative to Freud's conception. Yet my judgment remains the same in regard to his more elaborated argument as well. Although one does indeed sense that Freud has painted himself into a corner, it is not clear from White's analysis that this is explicitly the case, and certainly it is not clear how this state of affairs has come about. For this reason, White's critique serves as a point of departure for my own thesis which suggests that these forms of immutability and discontinuity are intrinsically connected and can be derived, as such, from Freud's Cartesian epistemology.

THE GUIDING THESIS AS APPLIED
TO FREUD'S THEORY

As detailed in the first chapter, my thesis suggests that cognitive activity is limited to two basic forms in the structuring of temporal events. One form is evidenced when the subject structures such events within the explanatory limits of his available constructs. This form is hierarchic in nature

---

parallels my own, MacIntyre (1970) points out that even if one chooses to interpret Freud's account of the primal horde merely as an illuminating metaphor, it is necessary for the account to be internally coherent. He notes in this regard:

Yet Freud's account is internally incoherent and self-contradictory.... it has to be explained how the transition can have been made from a condition in which the relations between men were purely those of force, in which each sought to impose his own will on others, to a condition in which there were socially established norms and institutions which regulated human behavior in an impersonal fashion. The stages by which this transition was made are not the same as in Hobbes's account; they are guilt, the establishment of taboos, and the making of a social contract. But each one of these presupposes the prior existence and functioning of just those social norms and institutions the origin of which they are to explain [p. 56].

in that the construct which serves to connect the properties of temporal events has a relationship of inclusion with respect to those constructs which serve to distinguish such events. As so structured, the properties of temporal events are, on the one hand, distinguished from each other and, on the other hand, connected to one another as different sequential particulars of a more fundamental realm of being. As so defined, this realm of being is understood as underlying both prior and subsequent events and, accordingly, as existing in invariant form over the span of time represented by these successive events. When temporal events are thus structured, they are further understood as having a relationship of continuity and change. As particulars of an underlying invariant, the difference between prior and subsequent events indicates that a change has occurred with respect to this invariant. By the same token, the presence of this invariant via such different particulars provides the continuity between these successive events.

The other form taken by cognitive activity is evidenced when the subject attempts to solve an unsolvable problem — that is to say, a problem which is beyond the explanatory limits of his available constructs. This "pars pro toto" organization is characterized by an identity relationship between connecting and differentiating constructs. That is, the construct which serves to connect successive temporal events is the same construct which serves to define one of these events as being different from the other. As in my earlier analysis of instinct theory and behaviorism, I will argue that Freud's conception of development takes the form of a pars pro toto in its structuring of temporal events and that it is from this organization that we can systematically derive the problems of immutability and discontinuity which his conception has encountered. Specifically, I will make a case for the following assertions: first, that Freud's conception of development presumes the Cartesian world view; second, that by virtue of this, his conception connects realms of being which are rendered unconnectable by this world view; and third, that in so solving a problem beyond the explanatory limits given in the theory's underlying epistemology, Freud's conception must take the form of a pars pro toto which evidences as its essential properties the attributes of immutability and discontinuity noted in our analysis.

THE CARTESIAN WORLD VIEW
IN FREUD'S THEORY

We have seen that Freud viewed development as the acquisition of purposively directed behavior by a hydraulic subject. For Freud, it was the mark of an acquired maturity that the subject could delay his blind, peremptory impulses in the light of veridically anticipated consequences. It can be shown, in Freud's conception of how such ego activity came into being, that he presumed the Cartesian world view. I mean by this that Freud viewed the purposive, reality-directed qualities of the ego as being acquired from an external world that contained purpose and control as "primary qualities" in the Cartesian sense. And, further, that Freud explicitly characterized the primitive organism as only being able to contribute distorting "secondary qualities" to this independently constituted reality.

My case for this assertion is based on two kinds of evidence. First, there are, in Freud's final version, his wonderfully evocative descriptions of the subject-object relationship. To pick some of the more compelling expressions that suggest the independently constituted nature of external reality: The ego in representing reality to the id "must observe the external world, must lay down an accurate picture of it in the memory traces of its perceptions" (1933, p. 75). In introjective identification, the ego, by virtue of acquired characteristics that mirror the features of the external other, tries "to make good the id's loss by saying: 'Look, you can love me too—I am so like the object'" (1923, p. 30). And in identification proper, the attribute of "external restraint" becomes internalized and functions in "exactly the same way as earlier the parents did with the child" (1933, p. 62). The evidence is intuitively compelling, as well, in regard to Freud's characterization of the id's distortion of this external reality. We have, for example, the striking image of the horse representing the brute force of the id. There is, further, the description of the id's "blind efforts for the satisfaction of its instincts" (1933, p. 75). And we have the id-dominated child represented as having "no internal inhibitions against . . . impulses striving for pleasure" (1933, p. 62).

Such examples of Freud's Cartesian epistemology are not, moreover, confined to his final position, but are evident throughout the various versions of his theory. Thus we have seen that Freud's initial version assumed an external world comprised of real traumas and social constraints which worked their pathological effects upon a malleable, hydraulically organized subject. The trauma, in whatever form it was encountered, literally placed its stamp on behavior in the form of the symptom. It is true, of course, that in this early version Freud had also invested his subject with a more active quality of intentional forgetting and this, as well, served as a determinant of the symptom. But, at best, Freud was merely anticipating the view advanced in his second version that "psychical reality requires to be taken into account alongside practical reality" (Freud, 1914a, p. 52). In no way did the emphasis on what the subject brought to the event change Freud's fundamental notion that this event was an independently constituted one. It only remained for Freud to give this world view its clearest metaphorical expression in his final conception of development. This took the form of the hydraulically organized blind id which interacted with an external, independently constituted reality of purposive, controlling others and which, by virtue of the conflict brought about by this interaction, acquired a delaying purposive ego as the mirror of the outer reality.

The second type of evidence regarding Freud's epistemology requires us to go beyond the literal meaning of such statements and consider the systematic requirements—the internal logic, if you will—of his position. When this is done, it may be seen that it was only by virtue of having assumed a Cartesian view of the relationship between the blind subject and the independently constituted object that Freud was able to conceptualize the process of development in the way that he did. As we have noted, Freud characterized the subject and object as having a particular relationship prior to development. This relationship can be seen most clearly in his final version, although, as our analysis has shown, it is basic to the earlier versions as well. In Freud's final version, the subject-object relationship was one in which id-dominated behavior was directed toward immediate discharge onto the tension-reducing sexual object. In so functioning in accordance with the pleasure principle, the primitive subject was unable to anticipate the tension-raising, life-threatening consequences of his activity. He could not veridically represent those aspects of the other who, as the powerful controlling one in the oedipal triangle, would punish him for his incestuous act. In this sense, Freud conceived of the id-dominated subject as inherently directed toward certain reinforcing properties of the external world, but as blind to other properties—properties of purpose and control—essential to the organism's survival. As so characterized, the subject could only represent the world in terms of his immediate needs and hence could only distort events in this world that were fundamental to his very existence.

This characterization of the subject was essential to

Freud's view of development. To the extent that the powerful id was blindly directed toward immediate satisfaction, and to the extent that the subject did not *yet* have the wherewithal to anticipate, delay, and redirect this instinctual striving into other and more lasting forms of satisfaction, then to that extent, the grounds for development existed. For such blind, peremptory activity led to conflict or a rise in tension. By the same token, if the primitive subject's activity was such that there *was* a lasting satisfaction — if a rise in tension did *not* occur in the long run — then the necessary condition for development did not exist. This implication can be seen clearly in Freud's second version. Freud (1911b, 1917b) noted here that the sexual instinct, in continuing to function in accordance with the natively given pleasure principle, was not subject to development. The reason for this, he indicated, was that the organism was capable of gratifying the demands of the sexual instinct immediately *and* consistently by virtue of autoerotic activity. In contrast, the ego instinct, which also functioned initially in accordance with the pleasure principle, required for its gratification external events that could not be supplied by the primitive organism and that necessitated the intervention of others. Given this relationship between an inadequate organism and a contingent reality, there was the inevitable rise in tension which served as the necessary condition for development.[5]

[5] In further support of my argument, it should be noted that there was an aspect of ego-instinct functioning in this second version that apparently was *not* subject to development, in that it, like the sexual instinct, continued to be governed by the pleasure principle. This was the ego instinct's phylogenetically derived repressive activity. Significantly, the circumstances which prevailed with respect to this aspect of ego-instinct functioning were much the same as those which Freud held responsible for the non-development of the sexual instinct. Freud viewed the ego instinct as natively responding to libidinal strivings continually pressing toward discharge. As so understood, the ego instinct realized its aim by immediately and reflexively blocking the libidinal impulse from expression. As with the gratification afforded by autoerotic activity, so too did the libidinal impulse serve as an

We can say, then, that where Freud conceived of a developmental acquisition, he ascribed this acquisition to an increase in tension (conflict) which, in turn, he derived from the subject's lack of ability to obtain gratification in the long run from a contingent world. Specifically, Freud viewed this inadequacy as the organism's relative lack of those structures that could effectively control and delay its inherently given hydraulic functioning, hence the immediate and blind reaction of the organism to the pressure of instinctual needs with the consequent rise in tension.

It can also be argued from the internal logic of Freud's position that the very properties of purpose and self-control that Freud assumed were lacking in the primitive hydraulic subject were precisely those properties that existed in an independently constituted form in the external, interpersonal world. For if Freud had assumed that the attributes of control and purpose which he ascribed to interpersonal others were not independently constituted, but merely the distorted hallucinatory products of a hydraulic subject who functioned in accordance with the pleasure principle, then he could hardly have suggested that these attributes, when acquired by the organism, would serve to maintain minimal tension in the long run—could serve, that is, as attributes of behavior governed by the reality principle. As hallucinatory products of pleasure-principle functioning, such attributes could only serve to reduce tension in the short run and to engender a *rise* in tension in the long run. We can conclude, then, that when Freud, in his final version, characterized the id as a dumb brute and the ego as mirroring external restraints, the literal intuitive meaning conveyed by this imagery was entirely congruent with the systematic implications of his general view of development: first, that the

---

immediate and readily available "gratifying" stimulus for the repressive activity of the ego instinct. See also Chapter 3, footnote 13.

primitive hydraulic subject lacked the very properties of delay and purpose which the mature other possessed in independently constituted form and, second, that development involved the subject's acquisition of these properties in precisely that form.

THE CONNECTING OF THE UNCONNECTABLE

If this argument regarding Freud's Cartesian assumption is accepted, then the basis is provided for our next assertion. As we have noted, the Cartesian view suggests, on the one hand, the existence of the external, independently constituted object of knowledge in the form of the primary qualities and, on the other hand, a subject of knowledge who, by virtue of the distortion imparted by his material senses, contributes secondary, subjective qualities to this external event. It is within the context of this Cartesian distinction between the primary and secondary qualities that White's (1963) critique of introjection as a conception of development gains its full significance. For clearly the implication of White's analysis is that the "problem of knowledge" which is intrinsic to the Cartesian distinction is also woven into the very fabric of the relationship between the primitive subject and object in Freud's theory. Transposing White's argument to the case of identification proper, we can ask: How does the blind, id-dominated organism, functioning in accordance with the pleasure principle, acquire purpose and control from the external other when, by virtue of its blindness, it cannot distinguish these attributes from the kitchen sink? Is this not another way of stating what necessarily follows from Freud's Cartesian epistemology? Namely, that in his conception of development the primitive subject is being so defined that he can never know the external qualities of purpose and control in their true form, but can only contribute distortion to such properties of the mature other. (That is to say, if the primitive subject cannot anticipate the tension-raising consequences of his libidinal activity, if he cannot veridically represent those qualities of purpose and control the exercise of which will cause him pain, if, in other words, he can know the mature object only to the extent that the object causes either immediate pain or immediate pleasure and cannot know the object in terms of the *subsequent* pain it will cause him, then the primitive subject may be said to "know" the mature object in a distorting way.)[6]

Indeed, the case can be stated in even stronger terms. We have seen that this relationship between the subject and object serves as a *necessary* basis for Freud's conflict conception of development. For it is only from the fact that the subject "lacks" what the other "has" that Freud is able to derive the rise in tension that is the essential condition for development. Accordingly, it is absolutely necessary to Freud's conception of development that the primitive subject be so defined that he can only contribute distortion to the properties of the other and hence be perpetually isolated from this reality. It can thus be said that Freud's conception of development *requires* the subject and object to be bifurcated into alien realms of internal and external being. The hydraulic subject and the external world of purpose and control must, in this conception, occupy "separate but equal" facilities on either side of an unbridgeable gulf.

But there is more to the problem than this. We have

[6] It may be seen that a similar view is implied by Wolff (1967) when he notes that Freud's conception of instinctual drives "does not specify categories of meaning beyond those of pleasure and pain from which we can infer the infant's experience of events" (p. 312).

And although he does not elaborate the point, Rapaport (1951b) is suggesting the same problem of knowledge for Freud's theory in the following passages: "The epistemological paradox of dynamic psychology is: how account for an adequate knowledge of reality when consciousness, the medium for gaining knowledge, is determined by intrapsychic laws?" (p. 519, n. 2); and: "How can the apparatus regulated by the pleasure-principle (drives) be also adapted to reality?" (p. 317, n. 6).

noted that the Cartesian distinction between primary and secondary qualities also implies a relationship between the subject and object of knowledge which is just the opposite of isolation. The very notion of *particular* primary qualities presumes a subject who knows the event *in terms of* these qualities and, accordingly, who is cognitively connected to the event which is so assumed to be independently constituted. This divergent implication of the Cartesian view is also basic to Freud's conception. The perpetual isolation between the primitive subject and object notwithstanding, this same subject and object are, in fact, connected in Freud's conception of development. Evidenced in all three versions, this connection is represented in an especially clear form in Freud's final view of development. As a consequence of the rise in tension which follows the activity of the inadequate subject, the hydraulic id, inherently isolated from the external properties of purpose and control, becomes coordinated to these very same properties by virtue of an ego which mirrors this external reality and which represents this reality to the id. It is thus that we can say that Freud's conception of development "connects the unconnectable." His conception accounts for the acquisition of an ego which, in mediating between the id and reality, connects two realms of being which are required by this very same conception to be intrinsically isolated by an unbridgeable gulf.

My thesis hinges on this paradox of Freud's theory. If there is no more inclusive unity available to the Cartesian world view that can serve to connect the distorting subject with the independently constituted object, and if the argument is granted that Freud's conception of development must presume a subject who is separated by an unbridgeable gulf from an external world, then by that token there is no more inclusive construct available to this conception that can serve to unite inner and outer realms as particulars of an underlying state of being. In this respect, Freud's theory can be said to be facing an unsolvable problem — one that is formally similar to that faced by the child who, in the class inclusion task, is required to unite color groupings which he has distinguished, when he lacks the more inclusive construct for doing so. Just as the child, in spite of lacking the more inclusive construct, solves the problem nevertheless, so too can it be said that Freud's conception of an acquired mediating ego, or, more generally speaking, acquired behavior that functions in accordance with the reality principle, represents his solution to an unsolvable problem. As the child, in place of the inclusive construct which he lacks, uses a construct that has served to distinguish between the beads, so too does Freud use a differentiating construct in the same way that he would have used a more inclusive construct had it been available to him. In connecting the unconnectable realms of inner and outer realities which he has distinguished, he ascribes to the organism characteristics of anticipation and delay that are identical to those of the independently constituted event. And, as we have seen, the independently constituted event is an assumption, or basic construct, which has served in Freud's distinction between inner and outer realms of being in the first place. In my view, therefore, it was neither whim nor creative license that prompted Freud to conceptualize the ego in the way that he did. On the contrary, Freud was forced to connect unconnectable realms of being in terms of an identity relationship between differentiating and connecting constructs, hence an ego which mirrored an external independently constituted reality of purpose and control. My thesis thus suggests that the basic form of Freud's conception of development is that of a pars pro toto. Moreover, it suggests that this form is indicative of the fact that Freud's theory is structuring the problem of development beyond its explanatory limits — limits which I have argued are imposed from the very outset by his Cartesian presumptions.

THE IMMUTABILITY-DISCONTINUITY
PROBLEM REFORMULATED

My third assertion is that the various problems of immutability and discontinuity attributed to Freud's conception of development can be systematically derived from the relationship of identity between differentiating and connecting constructs. In support of this assertion, I will again focus on the sequence of temporal events that Freud posits in his "Formulations on the Two Principles of Mental Functioning" (1911b) and, in particular, on the relationship between the hydraulic and purposive events that make up this sequence. But now I will interpret the sequence in light of the view that Freud is structuring the relationship between such events as a pars pro toto.

We have noted, in this regard, that Freud posits a primitive organism which, at the outset of this sequence, functions solely in terms of the pleasure principle. That is, the organism's activity, prior to development, is represented as a set of hydraulically determined processes in which libidinal energy follows preformed paths of discharge. As we have noted, the essential condition for development in this sequence is a rise in tension; and this occurs precisely as a consequence of the "inadequate" organism's hydraulic functioning in relation to a contingent reality. Up to this point, then, these events are represented as being causally determined. By definition, there is no purpose or anticipation which guides the organism's peremptory blind behavior or its subsequent rise in tension. Such behavior, in Peters's (1958) sense, simply "happens" to the organism. If, now, we skip to the final event of the sequence, we see that behavior has come into being which Freud characterizes as purposively directed and, accordingly, which he clearly distinguishes from the prior hydraulic activity. As a consequence of the rise in tension, the subject is able to delay an act in anticipation of its long-range consequences—the organism functions, that is, in accordance with the reality principle. Now,

I have made the case that in so accounting for the development of the reality principle, Freud has advanced a pars pro toto solution to the problem of connecting realms of inner and outer being that have been isolated by virtue of his underlying epistemology. If this argument is valid, then it follows that this solution can only displace the unsolvable problem of connecting isolated inner and outer realities to the unsolvable problem of connecting isolated aspects of the inner reality itself. For if the organism's blind hydraulic functioning is inherently isolated from the external reality of purposive others, then such functioning must be equally isolated from its own subsequent activity, which, as its essential feature, duplicates such external purpose. And if Freud's theory lacks the inclusive construct that can serve to connect, as particulars, the organism's blind hydraulic functioning with the purposive activity of external others, then his theory must continue to lack the inclusive construct that can serve to connect such prior primitive functioning with the subsequent acquired behavior, namely, behavior that functions in accordance with the reality principle. That is to say, his theory must continue to lack the inclusive construct that can serve to connect the sequence of hypothetical events which comprise his conception of development.

And yet, is this not what Freud has done in his conception of development—namely, connect this sequence of events? For, as we have noted, Freud was not content to account for the development of the reality principle as a bare consequence of frustration. He proposed, albeit implicitly, that a set of processes intervened between the condition of conflict and the subsequent emergence of behavior governed by anticipation and delay. Freud suggested that the hydraulic organism, in consequence of its "disappointment" in an "expected satisfaction," "abandons" the hallucinatory gratification, "decides" to form a veridical conception of the world, and to alter this world so as to obtain long-range satisfaction. Accordingly, it can be said in regard to the intra-psychic domain as well, that Freud is connecting events by an intervening process when he lacks the more inclusive construct for doing so. If this is the case, we can say further that Freud has not only displaced the Cartesian isolation to the intrapsychic realm, but that he has also displaced to this realm his solution to this unsolvable problem. Freud's conception of development, in connecting this sequence of un-connectable intrapsychic events, has assumed a form in which the construct that serves to connect these events is precisely the same construct that serves to define the subsequent event and to distinguish it from the prior event. For the primitive organism to use the hallucination as a "means" of gratification, for it to be "disappointed" in an "expected" satisfaction, for it to "abandon" this "attempt at satisfaction," and for it to "decide" to form a veridical perception of reality—all of those processes that intervene, in other words, between the condition of conflict and the acquisition of the reality principle—imply the very properties of anticipation and delay that characterize functioning in accordance with the reality principle in the first place. In connecting the prior event of hydraulic functioning to the final event of purposive activity, then, each of these intervening processes has a relationship of identity with the subsequent event, namely, each immutably reflects the acquired quality of anticipation and delay.

It is by so interpreting these hypothesized intervening events as reflecting an identity relationship that we can understand the connection between this form of immutability and the discontinuity problem that Hartmann has pointed to in his critique. If each intervening process mirrors the final event of purposive functioning, then each such process must be as isolated from the prior event of hydraulic activity as the final event of purposive functioning and the prior event of hydraulic activity are isolated from each other.

Moreover, it follows from our analysis that if Freud were to try to narrow this gap between a given intervening process and the prior hydraulic activity by positing yet another intervening process, then this additional event, by virtue of the form of immutability that the pars pro toto solution evidences, could only continue to mirror the intervening process that Freud had previously posited. Accordingly, the prior event of hydraulic conflict and the subsequent event of purposive functioning must continue to remain isolated from one another, regardless of how many intervening processes Freud could propose. Indeed, each such successive intervening event could only serve as a successively remote reflection of the final event of purposive functioning which, as we have seen, has itself only served to mirror an external, independently constituted interpersonal reality. In this sense, Freud can only solve the problem of connecting the unconnectable by proposing an infinity of mirrors which, in progressively receding from an external reality, never quite makes the connection with the prior condition of conflict, but only approaches this event in an infinite regress.[7] For this reason, the differences between the prior

[7] Thus can we account for the curiously perseverative quality of Freud's conception. By solving, each time, a problem that remains unsolvable, his solution each time must take the same form of immutability and discontinuity. (See also footnote 4 above in which I argue that Freud's view of identification proper shows a similar perseverative quality.)

The expression "infinity of mirrors" is based on an observation made by Schilder (1920) in his paper "On the Development of Thoughts." In his description of a delusion given by a psychotic woman, what appears to be a thematic progression of ideas—namely, a narrative with a beginning, middle, and end—on further inspection turns out to be an almost endless repetition of the same theme or motif. As Schilder notes:

She gives so many symbol-like pictures of fertilization and birth that the two processes seem to appear in her thinking as often as the picture of a candle in two mirrors at acute angles to each other [p. 512].

The parallel between the perseveration evidenced in this delusion and the perseveration of Freudian thought is consistent with my view that the pars

event of hydraulic functioning and the subsequent event of purposive activity must take the form of discontinuity in the sequence that Freud has proposed. The number of intervening processes notwithstanding, when Freud suggests that the development of the reality principle is a consequence of conflict, then the criticism of Hartmann and White regarding the discontinuity of this sequence of events is applicable, namely, that Freud's conception conjures postponement and delay into existence "from the mere fact that an instinctual drive is frustrated." In a fundamental sense, then, it is precisely *because* each posited intervening process has a relationship of immutability with respect to the final event, that Freud's conception can be criticized for its discontinuity. Freud's conception is discontinuous because he asserts that one event is the consequence of another and yet can offer no convincing mechanism that can serve to tie these different events together. And by "convincing mechanism" I mean a connecting process that derives from a unity more inclusive than the different events it serves to connect.

Our thesis also enables us to understand how the concept of introjective identification in the final version of Freud's theory must encounter the same problem of immutability and discontinuity. I have suggested that when the subject structures temporal events in the form of a pars pro toto, the connecting construct in this organization is "functionally equivalent" to the inclusive construct in a hierarchic form of structuring. By this I mean that the construct in a pars pro toto serves to connect differentiated temporal

---

pro toto is encountered at any level of organization. It is, however, one thing to imply that the immutability of thematic material can be derived from the delusion as a pars pro toto organization and quite another to make the explicit case for it, let alone provide support for the associated notion that the delusion represents the patient's solution to an unsolvable problem.

events in the same way that an inclusive construct does, namely, by implicitly defining a realm of being that underlies both events and that exists as an invariant over the span of time represented by this temporal sequence. At the same time, however, we have seen that this invariant realm of being cannot be particularized in terms of the prior and subsequent events that have been distinguished from one another. Accordingly, rather than engendering a relationship of continuity between temporal events as does an inclusive construct, the connecting construct in a pars pro toto can only serve to distort the temporal sequence in a characteristic way. If the relationship of identity is between the connecting construct and the differentiating construct which defines the subsequent event, then this has the paradoxical effect of turning the subsequent event back upon itself.[8] By virtue of being defined in terms of the same construct, the same essential properties are ascribed to the subsequent event, to the intervening processes, and to the invariant realm of being that implicitly underlies the prior and subsequent events. Hence the properties that have served to distinguish the subsequent event *from* the prior event and that have thus been viewed as *following* the prior event are also implicitly understood as coexisting *with* this prior event. Thus can we interpret the dilemma that White has posed for the Freudian view of introjective identification, in which reality testing and synthesis of functioning, as attributes of a mature ego, develop from the id-dominated, fragmented organism's experience with a mature, integrated mother figure. The child's act of introjecting the independently constituted stable mother is being posited as a

---

[8] As we have seen in other applications of this thesis, the identity relationship can also be one between the connecting construct and the differentiating construct which defines the prior state. This has the seemingly opposite effect of stretching the prior event ahead of itself in time such that it coexists with the subsequent event.

process that intervenes between the prior condition of fragmentation and the subsequent event of integration. Given its underlying epistemological assumption, however, this conception can only serve to connect the unconnectable and, in doing so, must assume the form of an identity relationship — in this case, an identity relationship in which the construct that has served to define the subsequent event of integration also serves to define the intervening process of introjection. Accordingly, the property of integration which is viewed as following from the act of introjection becomes the defining property of the introjective act itself and, in the form of an underlying invariant state, is shifted back in time to coexist discontinuously with the prior event, namely, the child's id-dominated fragmented functioning. The property of integration becomes an essential attribute of the fragmented subject doing the introjecting, and hence a prior and necessary condition for the very act that results in the acquisition of this same property of integration. At the same time, however, if the intervening process of introjection mirrors the final event of ego functioning — as is the case in this identity relationship — then this intervening process must be as isolated from the initial event of id activity as the final event of ego activity and the prior event of id activity are isolated from each other. And if this is so, then the prior event of id activity and the subsequent event of purposive ego activity must continue to remain isolated from one another, regardless of how many intervening processes Freud could propose. Accordingly, the properties of the subsequent event must coexist with the properties of the prior event as antithetical aspects of the same realm of being, and not as connected particulars of a more inclusive unity. Namely, fragmentation and integration must coexist with one another as isolated properties of the child's prior id-dominated functioning. Thus we have the intrinsically connected forms of discontinuity and immutability in the Freudian conception of introjective identification: We have the logical inconsistency or the discontinuity of simultaneously ascribing isolated antithetical properties to the same event and, at the same time, the preformism or the immutability of requiring, as a condition for the process of introjection, the very property that the process is to explain.[9]

In sum, it can be said that even though Freud turned away from an earlier and explicit preformism in rejecting the ego instinct in favor of an ego acquired via the process of identification, he has merely offered in his final view of development an implicit version of the same preformism. And, further, that by virtue of having so assumed the qualities of ego functioning as a condition for their own emergence, Freud's conception necessarily encounters the discontinuity of simultaneously ascribing isolated, antithetical properties to the same event. My thesis has suggested that this intrinsic connection between immutability and discontinuity has a formal basis. I have made the case that Freud's conception of development posits that ego functioning is acquired as a consequence of id-dominated activity that is blind to an independently constituted world of purpose and control. As a mirror of that external reality, the acquired ego can be said to represent an identity solution to the problem of connecting inner and outer realms of being which cannot be connected in terms of a more inclusive construct. As so understood, this solution can only serve to displace the Cartesian isolation between subject and object to an intrapsychic isolation between the prior event of id activity and the subsequent event of ego functioning. Thus, any connection between the id and ego as a sequence of temporal events must duplicate this identity relationship. The forms of immutability and discontinuity attributed to

[9] The reader may want to review the first two chapters for the more extended basis of this analysis.

Freud's theory of ego development can be understood as the logically connected implications of this identity relationship. That is to say, these forms are the hallmark of the pars pro toto organization which cognitive activity must take in structuring events beyond its explanatory limits.

THE IMMUTABILITY-DISCONTINUITY PROBLEM
COMMON TO CARTESIAN CONCEPTIONS
OF DEVELOPMENT

We can now consider Freud's conception of development with respect to the question we have posed for instinct theory and behaviorism: How does his theory understand the nature of the relationship between the subject's behavior as a child and his subsequent behavior as an adult? How does the theory, in other words, distinguish between these events as a temporal sequence of primitive and mature behavior and, at the same time, connect these events such that the child is father to the man? When we focus on Freud's theory in terms of this issue, it may be seen that a case can be made for my earlier assertion that the form of the immutability-discontinuity problem encountered by Freud's theory is identical to that encountered by instinct theory and behaviorism. And this by virtue of the Cartesian view which his theory holds in common with these positions.

In regard to the question of a commonly held epistemology, it is clear that the subject-object relationship which Freud assumes as a necessary condition for ego development is the same relationship which instinct theory and behaviorism assume in their focus on the issue of developmental change. These positions all start with a primitive subject who faces a world of independently constituted properties that are essential to his survival and in relation to which he engages in natively directed, blind activity. This is the case whether the primitive organism's random behavior is directed by the id, by the instinctive propensities, or by the physiologic drives. And it is the case whether the independently constituted world is one of purposive controlling others, or one of escape routes to food.

Given this relationship between the primitive subject and object, all three conceptions understand the differences between the child and adult in the same way. The primitive child becomes the mature adult by virtue of acquiring behaviors which are patterned by these external independently constituted properties and which serve to mediate between the blind native core and external reality. And this, too, is the case whether such mediating activity is designated as an ego, as an acquired instrumentality, or as a habit. When Freud, for example, proclaims as the goal of psychotherapy, "Where id was, there ego shall be," he is saying that this goal is to bring about a state of affairs that normally should have been the result of development: namely, the replacement of peremptory id-dominated behavior by the ability to delay immediate discharge onto sexual objects in the light of veridically perceived consequences. As do instinct doctrine and behaviorism, then, Freud's theory distinguishes between the behavior of the child and that of the adult to the degree that such behaviors are influenced respectively by "inner" and "outer" realms of being. As so understood, various instances of the child's primitive behavior are being unified as particulars of blind hydraulic id functioning and are thus being distinguished from various instances of the adult's mature behavior which, in turn, are being united as particulars of purposive ego activity. It follows from our earlier analysis, therefore, that Freud's conception of development must face the same problem as these other views. If the primitive behavior of the child is distinguished from the mature behavior of the adult by the respective influences of inner nature and external reality, and if, as we have seen, there is no more inclusive construct available to Freud's theory that can serve to connect these inner and outer realms of being, then it follows that there is no more inclusive construct that will serve to connect the sequential events of primitive and mature functioning as so distinguished. It is no accident, therefore, that Freud's theory solves the problem of connecting these events in the same way as instinct theory and behaviorism. A construct that serves to distinguish primitive from mature functioning is the same construct that serves to connect these sequential events.

In this regard, it may be seen that in his conception of development, Freud has proposed two solutions, each of which has been emphasized respectively by behaviorism and instinct theory. On the one hand, he connects the sequential events of primitive and mature activity by the presumption that has defined the prior event and that has thus served to distinguish this event from the subsequent mature behavior. Freud views id activity as being evidenced in its purest form in the child's primitive behavior which is thus distinguished from the adult's reality-oriented ego functioning. At the same time, this native aspect of personality serves as the core of adult functioning and accordingly connects the sequential events of primitive and mature activity by being common to both. Thus it can be said that by virtue of an identical epistemology, Freudian theory and behaviorism are offering an identical solution to the relationship between the primitive activity of the child and the mature activity of the adult. In so defining an underlying immutable state common to both prior and subsequent events, this construct serves to stretch the attributes of primitive functioning forward in time so that these properties coexist with the subsequent characteristics of mature behavior. The primitive characteristics of the child — whether these be the blind activity of a hydraulic id, or random activity instigated by the physiologic drives — persist into adulthood as an immutable core of blind random being. Concomitantly, it is a solution in which the mediating characteristics of mature adulthood —

whether these be the purposive ego, or the habit — are discontinuously juxtaposed upon this core of blind primitivity. This solution is seen most concretely, perhaps, in Freud's (1923, 1933) graphic representation of the "structural" relations between id and ego. In this characterization of the "developed" personality, the ego is portrayed as the outer rind of the id. One need only peel away the ego as "that outer portion of the id which was modified by the proximity of the external world" (1933, p. 75) in order to find the original preserved core of the personality. In Freud's theory, as was the case in behaviorism, the problem of the child as father to the man is solved as the "buried child" — as the child "in" the man.

On the other hand, Freud also connects the sequential events of primitive and mature functioning by the solution exemplified in instinct theory's emphasis on continuity; that is, these events are connected by the presumption of an independently constituted reality that serves to shape random activity into mediating behavior. As we have seen, the prior activity of the id and the subsequent functioning of the ego are connected by a realm of being which has characteristics identical to the ego itself. And by virtue of this identity relationship between connecting and differentiating constructs, the subsequent qualities of ego functioning stretch back in an "infinity of mirrors" to the prior functioning of the id-dominated subject. In this view of development, then, we have an implicit version of the preformist solution advanced by instinct theory. The mediating characteristics of mature functioning are given in identical form in primitive activity and, indeed, require such prior activity as the basis for their subsequent existence.[10]

[10] It should be noted that Freud's implicit preformism has its counterpart in behaviorist doctrine as well. I am referring here to the immutability implied in the behaviorist view that the organism's response repertory contains, at the outset, behaviors which can be connected to the essential event, but which have a low probability of occurrence with respect to these events.

FREUD'S ANXIETY-DEFENSE PARADIGM:
THE LOGICAL PARADOX

I should now like to extend the implications of this analysis to an issue which, for many, lies at the heart of Freud's theory. I am referring to Freud's final view of repression and to a logical contradiction that this view encounters. I will be arguing that this contradiction is yet another manifestation of the immutability-discontinuity problem in Freud's theory and that it can similarly be understood in terms of the theory's Cartesian epistemology. Because of its complexity, I will first present the major lines of this thesis in synoptic form and then elaborate each of its assertions in turn.

Synopsis of Thesis

In rejecting the concept of an ego instinct in favor of an acquired ego structure, Freud not only had to deal with the question of accounting for how this structure was acquired. He also faced the problem that the ego now lacked its own source of instinctual energy. How, then, could the ego fulfill the numerous mediating functions which he had assigned to it? Given Freud's metapsychology, the answer, in formal terms, was clear: The energy for powering the ego structures was ultimately supplied by the sexual instincts. The problem thus became one of accounting for how this transfer of energy was effected. To deal with this problem, Freud posited a process of "neutralization" whereby the energy from the sexual instincts became "desexualized" and, in that form, activated the acquired ego structures. This conception will be considered in the next chapter. The present section is concerned with a major implication of this view—one represented by Freud's (1933) anxiety-defense paradigm of repression.

Consistent with his view of hydraulic functioning,

Freud suggested that unconscious id impulses were continually pressing toward blind discharge into conscious thought. This, Freud (1940) noted, constituted a problem for the organism, particularly if the ego, either because of a failure of development or simply because development had not yet occurred to any significant degree, did not have access to a sufficient amount of neutralized energy whereby it could directly block such discharge from occurring. For, given a conscious awareness of the impulse, the ego would then be "obliged to admit its weakness" in controlling the "strength of the passions in the id" (1933, p. 78) with respect to direct discharge onto the external libidinal object and would thereby be confronted with the possibility of incurring "one of the well-remembered situations of danger" (1933, p. 89). It would thus break out in anxiety. Addressing this problem, Freud posited a particular interaction between the hydraulic id and the purposive ego whereby the ego blocked the id impulse from conscious expression and thereby avoided the anxiety attendant upon such conscious awareness.[11] And this in spite of the fact that the ego lacked sufficient energy resources for doing so directly. As elaborated in his anxiety-defense paradigm of repression, Freud (1933) proposed that the ego accomplished this feat by an unconscious "dodge" (p. 77) or maneuver which, in jujitsu fashion, turned the energy of the id against itself. Because of its importance to my analysis, I am quoting in full the passage describing that interaction:

The next question will be: how do we now picture the

[11] Fenichel (1945) succinctly describes the essence of repression. In his words, repression "consists of an unconsciously purposeful forgetting or not becoming aware of internal impulses or external events which, as a rule, represent possible temptations or punishments for, or mere allusions to, objectionable instinctual demands. The purposeful exclusion of these data from consciousness is obviously intended to hinder their real effects as well as the pain on becoming aware of them" (p. 148).

process of repression under the influence of anxiety? The answer will, I think, be as follows. The ego notices that the satisfaction of an emerging instinctual demand would conjure up one of the well-remembered situations of danger. This instinctual cathexis must therefore be somehow suppressed, stopped, made powerless. We know that the ego succeeds in this task if it is strong and has drawn the instinctual impulse concerned into its organization. But what happens in the case of repression is that the instinctual impulse still belongs to the id and that the ego feels weak. The ego thereupon helps itself by a technique which is at bottom identical with normal thinking. Thinking is an experimental action carried out with small amounts of energy, in the same way as a general shifts small figures about on a map before setting his large bodies of troops in motion. Thus the ego anticipates the satisfaction of the questionable instinctual impulse and permits it to bring about the reproduction of the unpleasurable feelings at the beginning of the feared situation of danger. With this the automatism of the pleasure-unpleasure principle is brought into operation and now carries out the repression of the dangerous instinctual impulse [1933, pp. 89–90].

It may be said, then, that Freud's anxiety-defense paradigm of repression involves the following sequence of purposive and causally determined events. The ego "notices" the hydraulic demand of an unconscious id impulse for immediate discharge into conscious awareness and "anticipates" the satisfaction of the impulse in order to produce a slight increase in tension. This slight increase in tension, or signal of anxiety, in turn, evokes on the part of the id an unconscious reflex action in accordance with the pleasure principle whereby such tension is reduced in the most immediate way. Much like an unthinking withdrawal from the heat of a flame, the id impulse hydraulically "withdraws" from the slight increase in tension represented by the signal of anxiety and, accordingly, is repressed or blocked from attaining conscious expression — a conscious expression that, had it occurred, would have engendered full-blown anxiety.

The problem which this paradigm encounters, and to which our inquiry is directed, can be termed a "logical paradox." Stated in its general form, the paradox involves the fact that primal repression is a defense which the ego sets into motion in order to prevent the anxiety attendant upon the conscious awareness of the dangerous impulse. And yet, in order to generate the signal of anxiety which serves as the necessary condition for the reflexive withdrawal of the id impulse, there first has to be an awareness of the nature of the impulse, its object of satisfaction, and the situation of danger. Namely, Freud posits that the ego engages in a sequence of "knowing" activities as the basis for the blocking or the "not-knowing" of the id impulse: It "notices" that impulse satisfaction will bring about the dangerous consequences, it "anticipates" this satisfaction in order to generate the signal of anxiety, and the anxiety signal itself is a "reproduction of the unpleasurable feelings at the beginning of the feared situation of danger." In short, the ego has to know in order not to know.[12]

Although the logical paradox has been the subject of considerable controversy in the literature, it has not generally been considered in relation to the difficulties attributed to

[12] In its specific, more widely known form, the logical paradox arose in regard to a particular extension of the Freudian view of repression, namely, the concept of perceptual defense. McGinnies (1949), in order to account for his experimental findings that there were differential thresholds of response to the tachistoscopic presentation of neutral versus taboo words, suggested that the higher thresholds for reporting the taboo word reflected a conditioned avoidance to dangerous stimulus objects and served to delay the anxiety that would accompany the recognition of such stimuli. A typical rejoinder to this explanation is Gibson's (1968) comment: "...to state that one can perceive in order not to perceive is a logical contradiction" (p. 291).

Freud's conception of development. Our analysis would suggest, however, that these problems are, indeed, related to one another—that there is more than a surface parallel between the id's knowing in order to know and the ego's knowing in order not to know. I am proposing, in this regard, that the anxiety-defense paradigm, like Freud's conception of development, involves a sequence of hydraulic and purposive events which represent a displaced Cartesian epistemology and which, because of this, cannot be connected to one another in terms of a more inclusive construct. Yet, in spite of this, Freud does connect these events in his paradigm of repression; namely, he posits an interaction between ego and id whereby the ego purposively generates a signal of anxiety which causes the id impulse to withdraw. It follows from our thesis, therefore, that the conception of this interaction must take the form of an identity relationship with its formal characteristics of immutability and discontinuity. As so understood, the logical paradox in Freud's anxiety-defense paradigm and the immutability-discontinuity problem in Freud's conception of development have a common basis. Both reflect the form which cognitive activity must take in solving an unsolvable problem.

These assertions may immediately provoke the objection that they presume something which cannot readily be accepted. Is it really the case, one might ask, that a logical paradox is involved in the anxiety-defense paradigm? Given the past controversy in the literature, it must be admitted that the issue is not all that clear-cut.[13] Nor, in my view, has

[13] For example, Dixon (1971) in his review of the perceptual defense controversy concludes that the problem is really a semantic one, while Howie (1952) takes a position similar to my own regarding the Cartesian basis of the logical paradox. Howie suggests that the logical problem involved in speaking of a perceptual process as "somehow being a process of knowing and a process of avoiding knowing" is attributable to an explanation of behavior "on the basis of organic impulse in fundamental separation from external influences" (p. 311).

the issue been satisfactorily resolved, hence my present concern with it. Accordingly, my argument for these assertions will be directed at the outset toward strengthening my claim that the logical paradox is, indeed, indicative of a real problem in Freud's theory. I will do this first by elaborating my interpretation of the 1933 paradigm in the light of Freud's earlier views regarding repression. In doing so, I will focus on material that I have not previously considered in detail, notably Freud's (1900, 1915b) cathectic view of consciousness and Freud's (1926) concept of anxiety. After elaborating the 1933 paradigm on the basis of these earlier views, I will then consider a major objection that can be raised against my assertion that Freud's paradigm, as so interpreted, encounters the logical paradox. And I will make the case, in this regard, that this objection is not able to eliminate the problem of logical contradiction in the paradigm and, hence, can be rejected.

Freud's Views of Repression Prior to the 1933 Anxiety-Defense Paradigm

Essential to Freud's cathectic view of consciousness was his notion that the organism's experience of external events was mirrored in the form of intrapsychic structures, or "memory traces," which provided a permanent unaltered record of these past events and which were the basis for evoking, in recall, a replica of such events.[14] Freud advanced

[14] As Paul (1967) has noted, Freud accepted a "strong form" of trace theory in which "an experience generates a replica of itself" (p. 221). And Wolff (1967) concludes from his survey of Freud's views that

The passages from Freud that I have quoted [Freud, 1895, pp. 361, 380, 381, 421–422; 1915b, pp. 201–202; 1923, p. 20] either imply or assert a direct correspondence (an isomorphism) between the event as objectively described, the event as registered in memory, and the event as recalled under appropriate dynamic conditions, as if from the start of development, the experience were identical with the physical event [p. 312].

this view as early as 1895 and maintained it, essentially unchanged, in the later versions of his theory.[15] Thus, when Freud (1933) states that the ego, in serving as a mediator between the id and the external reality of satisfactions and dangers, represents this reality to the id by observing the external world and laying down "an accurate picture of it in the memory traces of its perceptions" (p. 75), we can assume that this view of the memory trace was a direct extension of his earlier conception that the memory trace mirrored the experience of the previously satisfying event (Freud, 1900) and that, as an instinct or drive representation (Freud, 1915a, pp. 152–153; Rapaport, 1951b, p. 691), the memory trace served as the basis for a conscious (hallucinatory) image of that experience.

Now our analysis has shown that Freud viewed the functioning of the sexual instinct as causally determined (1900, 1911a, 1917b). As so understood, the sexual instinct was unable to accept partial satisfaction, but was directed toward discharge as long as libidinal energy was not at its lowest possible level (see Chapter 3, footnote 13, for an extended

---

Perhaps the clearest indication of Freud's assumption that the memory trace mirrored the external event is given in his (1925) use of the "mystic writing-pad" as a metaphor for psychological functioning. The external stimuli represented by writing on the plastic surface material of the pad, although vanishing when the covering sheet is lifted, are retained as a permanent trace in the underlying wax slab itself. Freud drew an analogy between the plastic surface and the functioning of conscious perception on the one hand, and, on the other, between the imprint on the underlying wax slab and the unconscious memory trace.

[15] Wolff (1967) has asserted in this regard:

Psychoanalysis has always lacked a theory of learning which is compatible with its developmental principles; the resulting vacuum was tacitly filled by fragments of an outdated association and conditioning theory already implied in Freud's earliest description of the mental apparatus. Inadequate though it has always been, this psychoanalytic learning theory has not essentially changed since then [p. 303].

analysis of this issue). The presence of any sum of libidinal energy, then, was a sufficient condition for the instinctual impulse to be hydraulically directed toward immediate discharge as a peremptory libidinal flow via whatever structures were available for discharge. Given the prior experience of the satisfying event, such structures existed in the form of memory traces or drive representations. Accordingly, it can be said that Freud viewed the libidinal energy of the sexual instinct as continually pressing toward the cathexis of such structures in accordance with the pleasure principle, namely, toward the immediate and blind investment of such structures with libidinal energy. If the memory trace was invested with a sufficient amount of energy, its cathexis resulted in a conscious awareness of the previous experience of instinctual satisfaction (1900, 1915b).

We have seen, moreover, that Freud's early view of repression was advanced within the context of his posited polarity between the sexual and ego instincts (e.g., 1909, 1913, 1915a, 1917b). In this version, Freud ascribed to the ego instinct the function of preserving the individual and, accordingly, the defensive function of repression. As an instinctive response, the act of repression was, like the activity of the sexual instinct, causally determined. Given its phylogenetically derived function of protecting the organism from castration, the ego instinct immediately and reflexively reacted to the push of libidinal energy toward direct discharge into thought or action. Namely, the activity of the ego instinct was hydraulically directed toward the complete reduction of its *own* instinctual energy—toward the complete satisfaction of protecting the individual from any danger of castration, no matter how slight. Accordingly, the response of the ego instinct to the continual demand of the sexual instinct for libidinal discharge via the memory trace elicited an equally indiscriminate and uncompromising blocking of this demand. It followed, then, that if such blocking, or "anticathexis," prevented the memory trace from being cathected with a sufficient amount of energy, then this drive representation remained unconscious.[16]

This early view of repression, then, set the stage for the essential problem that Freud faced in the final version of his theory. Since, in this final version, Freud no longer considered the ego as an instinct with its own source of instinctual energy, but as an acquired structure, he had the problem of accounting for the energy that was used in the anticathexis of primal repression — the energy that, in his final version,

---

[16] We have seen that Freud distinguished between two processes whereby this blocking was effected: repression proper and, of more relevance to our analysis, primal repression. In regard to the latter, Freud (1915b) had this to say:

> What we require, therefore, is another process which maintains the repression in the first case and, in the second, ensures its being established as well as continued. This other process can only be found in the assumption of an *anticathexis,* by means of which the system *Pcs.* protects itself from the pressure upon it of the unconscious idea. We shall see from clinical examples how such an anticathexis, operating in the system *Pcs.,* manifests itself. It is this which represents the permanent expenditure [of energy] of a primal repression, and which also guarantees the permanence of that repression. Anticathexis is the sole mechanism of primal repression... [p. 181].

I am presuming that since Freud advanced this view within the context of his instinct polarity, the energy involved in this anticathexis was the energy of the ego instinct. That is to say, I am assuming that the anticathexis of primal repression involved the energy of the ego instinct which, in its blind protective reaction, reflexively blocked the sexual instinct from its equally blind tendency toward the cathexis of the memory trace as a drive representation.

It should also be emphasized that my critique is confined to Freud's final version of primal repression — or more precisely, the circumstances under which the immature "weak" ego *initially* resorts to repression as a primitive mechanism of defense. Accordingly, I am not representing the subtleties of Freud's (1900, 1915b) cathectic view of repression proper — his concepts of "hypercathexis" and the preconscious, his distinction between ideas and affect, and his distinction between the cathexis of "object" traces and "verbal" traces. For a synopsis of these views, see Rapaport (1951b).

served to block the id impulse from its libidinal cathexis of the memory trace. This problem was particularly salient with respect to Freud's conception of the early stages of ego development. We have noted that Freud, in this final view, dealt with the issue of powering the acquired structures by his conception of neutralization: He posited, concomitant with the development of the ego structures, a progressive desexualization of libidinal energy such that this energy could be used by the acquired structures. As Freud (1940) saw it, however, this process of neutralization lagged behind sexual development, resulting in an imbalance between the amount of neutralized energy that was available to the ego structures and the amount of libidinal energy that, in the form of the id impulses, was pressing toward immediate discharge into conscious thought and action. Thus, simply because neutralization had not yet occurred to a significant degree, the ego did not have access to a sufficient amount of desexualized energy whereby it could directly control this blind hydraulic demand. This "lagging of ego development behind libidinal development" was, in Freud's view, the "essential precondition of neurosis" (1940, p. 200) in that it necessitated the primitive defense of primal repression. For at the same time as the ego was without access to a sufficient amount of neutralized energy for direct anticathexis, it was, in this final version, defined in a structural sense as purposively governed; the ego was, by definition, capable of anticipating the consequences that would occur were libidinal discharge to take place in reality. Accordingly, this "weak" ego would break out in anxiety were it to become consciously aware of the impulse. Namely, the ego would be forced, as it were, to recognize its weakness in regard to the control of the impulse and would fear the consequences of libidinal discharge. In accordance, then, with the reality principle which governed its functioning, the ego was directed toward blocking the id impulse from discharge into conscious awareness. As a means of avoiding the *subsequent rise* in tension represented by anxiety, the ego was directed toward blocking the *immediate reduction* in tension represented by the libidinal discharge into conscious awareness. Given the lag between ego development and libidinal development, however, this blocking could not be accomplished by an ego that lacked a sufficient amount of neutralized energy for direct anticathexis. (Indeed, were a sufficient amount available, the ego, presumably, would not have had to resort to this primitive defense in the first place.) Thus the blocking of libidinal energy had to be accomplished in a different way. This took the form of the maneuver that was central to the anxiety-defense paradigm—a maneuver that Freud proposed initially in "Inhibitions, Symptoms and Anxiety" (1926).

In this initial treatment (and in his subsequent version as well), Freud viewed anxiety as being generated by the ego's recognition of its own weakness in controlling the passions of the id. Given the small amount of neutralized energy at its disposal, the anxious ego felt helpless in the face of massive discharges of libidinal energy. Freud termed a "situation of helplessness of this kind that ha[d] actually been experienced" a "traumatic situation" (1926, p. 166), and went on to distinguish the traumatic situation from a "danger situation," in which the ego, while threatened, had not yet been overwhelmed: "A danger-situation is a recognized, remembered, expected situation of helplessness" (1926, p. 166). To the situation of danger, Freud stated, the ego could respond with either of two forms of anxiety: one that was "paralysing" and "inexpedient" or one that allowed the ego to make use of its small amount of energy in an expedient way, one that was

produced by the ego as soon as a situation of this kind merely threatened to occur, in order to call for its avoidance.... [T]he ego subjects itself to anxiety as a sort of inoculation, submitting to a slight attack of the illness in order to escape its full strength. It vividly imagines the danger-situation, as it were, with the unmistakable purpose of restricting that distressing experience to a mere indication, a signal [1926, p. 162].

Thus, in order to avoid the "paralysing" and "inexpedient" anxiety of the traumatic situation, the signal of anxiety

announces: 'I am expecting a situation of helplessness to set in', or: 'The present situation reminds me of one of the traumatic experiences I have had before. Therefore I will anticipate the trauma and behave as though it had already come, while there is yet time to turn it aside.' Anxiety is therefore on the one hand an expectation of a trauma, and on the other a repetition of it in a mitigated form [1926, p. 166].

In sum, then, Freud's initial anxiety-defense paradigm portrays the ego as "knowing" the signal of anxiety in order not to "know" the full-blown anxiety. That is to say, it is the ego's knowledge of its weakness in the face of massive libidinal discharge that causes the ego to feel anxious. And it is this knowledge of its weakness that the ego seeks to avoid in instituting the process of repression, for it is this knowledge which causes the incapacitating attack of anxiety. And, finally, it is the knowledge of the incipient traumatic situation that results in the generation of the signal of anxiety, which is itself a product of the ego's knowledge of "the slight attack of the illness" it permits itself to experience. We will see that, unless Freud can truly distinguish these forms of knowledge, his paradigm will encounter insuperable logical difficulties.

Elaborated Interpretation of the 1933 Anxiety-Defense Paradigm

With these considerations as a context, we can now return to the question which is at the heart of my analysis. We have seen that Freud (1933) posited a particular interaction between the hydraulic id and the purposive ego whereby the ego "notices" the hydraulic demand of an unconscious id impulse for immediate discharge into conscious awareness and "anticipates" the satisfaction of the impulse in order to produce a slight increase in tension. This slight increase in tension, or signal of anxiety, in turn, evokes the reflexive withdrawal of the id impulse. In this regard, it is important to point out that there is good reason to think that, as far as Freud was concerned, there were essential differences in the sequential events leading to the id's hydraulic withdrawal. When Freud characterizes the ego as "anticipating" the satisfaction of the impulse, he apparently means something quite different from his statement that the ego "notices" that the satisfaction of the instinctual demand will bring about the well-remembered situation of danger.[17] And Freud clearly views such anticipation as different from the ego's *conscious awareness* of the instinctual demand and subsequent danger. In an obvious extension of his 1926 view regarding the ego's submission to a "slight attack of the illness," Freud likens the ego's "anticipation" to an "experimental action," and later speaks of the ego's making use of an "experimental cathexis" (1933, p. 90), by which he apparently means an experimental cathexis of the memory trace of the previously satisfying event. To use Freud's metaphor, as a general shifts small figures about a map, so too is the ego's "anticipation" an active, albeit small-scale, duplication of the actual event. Unlike the unconscious act of passively noticing (which evokes no anxiety), and unlike

[17] Freud's (1933) use of "well-remembered situation of danger" is notably inconsistent with his distinction between traumatic and danger situations in "Inhibitions, Symptoms and Anxiety." I have followed Freud's usage here, but the reader should keep in mind that Freud is undoubtedly referring to a well-remembered *traumatic* situation.

the conscious awareness of the impulse (which evokes full-blown anxiety), the ego unconsciously *simulates* the earlier satisfaction of the impulse. Using the relatively small amount of neutralized energy it has available, the ego "makes believe" that there has, indeed, been a hydraulic satisfaction of the impulse and, hence, that the organism is really about to encounter the well-remembered situation of danger. It is this active, albeit unconscious, simulating activity — as distinguished from the unconscious noticing on the one hand, and the conscious awareness on the other — that evokes the signal of anxiety.[18]

Now it should be noted that Freud was not specific in his 1933 version as to the nature of the experimental cathexis involved in the ego's maneuver of anticipation. Based on our consideration of Freud's earlier views, however, I have presumed the following in my interpretation of the paradigm: First, when taken at face value, Freud's account would suggest that the ego, however weak, does have some energy at its disposal in order to engage in this maneuver. In accordance with Freud's (1926) statements (e.g., p. 161), I am assuming that the ego is functioning here with neutralized energy from the id, however small an amount this might be.[19] Second, I am assuming that the energy which, in the ego's maneuver, cathects the memory trace is not the libidinal energy of the id impulse, but the desexualized energy of the ego. In doing so, I am placing a particular interpretation on

[18] My interpretation of "anticipation" as the simulation of a future event is consistent with the American Heritage Dictionary definition, "to feel or realize beforehand." It should be noted, in this regard, that other meanings of anticipation, especially "having foreknowledge" and "forestalling," are associated but not synonomous with this definition. As part of my analysis, I will distinguish between these various meanings of anticipation.

[19] In the next chapter, it will be seen that the process whereby the ego avails itself of "desexualized" or neutralized energy is itself subject to the immutability-discontinuity problem.

Freud's (1933) statement that "the ego anticipates the satisfaction of the questionable impulse and permits *it* to bring about the reproduction of the unpleasurable feelings at the beginning of the feared situation of danger" (pp. 89–90; italics added). Were one to interpret the term "it" in this passage as referring to the satisfaction of the id impulse itself, then one would have to assume that the experimental cathexis of the memory trace involves libidinal energy and, accordingly, that the ego is manipulating the id impulse directly. We will see that such an interpretation would encounter the logical paradox in an even more direct form than my interpretation. As I see it, "it" refers not to the direct satisfaction of the id impulse (in the sense of libidinal cathexis of the memory trace), but to the *simulated* satisfaction of the impulse — the satisfaction as simulated by the ego. The issue thus becomes one of representing the nature of the energy involved in the ego's simulation of this libidinal cathexis and, in accordance with our previous considerations, I am assuming that Freud views such energy as derived from a prior process of neutralization, now available to the ego as desexualized energy.[20] Third, I am assuming that when Freud refers to an "experimental cathexis," he is referring to the cathexis of the memory trace of the previously satisfying event and, within this context, that the "reproduction of the unpleasurable feelings at the beginning of the feared situation of danger" also involves a cathexis of this same memory trace, but now as the trace mirrors the punishment the organism experienced as a consequence of libidinal

[20] This interpretation is given some support by Freud's renunciation of his earlier "economic" view that anxiety is the result of a hydraulic transformation of libidinal energy (1926, p. 93; 1933, p. 91), and by his alternative conception that anxiety is the reproduction of an "affective state in accordance with an already existing mnemic image" (1926, p. 93), "mnemic image" understood in this context as a memory trace cathected by neutralized energy.

satisfaction.[21] It should be emphasized, however, that my interpretation distinguishes between the cathexis of the memory trace as it mirrors the previously satisfying event and the cathexis of the trace as it mirrors the associated punishment. Although I am assuming that the memory trace in both instances is being cathected with neutralized energy, I am interpreting Freud as saying that the cathexis of the previously satisfying event is an experimental cathexis *purposively* initiated by the ego and that the cathexis of the associated punishment *happens* to the ego as a result of the prior purposive activity. Namely, in my interpretation, the ego, in simulating the satisfaction of the id impulse, allows this experimental cathexis *"to bring about"* (1933, p. 90) the reproduction of the unpleasurable feeling at the beginning of the traumatic event.[22]* Finally, it is unclear as to whether

[21] This assumption is congruent with Rapaport's (1951b) definition of an "idea" as a "drive-cathected memory trace" (p. 691), with the assessments of Paul (1967) and Wolff (1967) regarding the nature of the memory trace in Freud's thinking, and with Freud's (1900, 1915b, 1925) views on the cathectic nature of consciousness. Note also Freud's frequent characterizations of the signal of anxiety as a reproduction of a previously traumatic event (e.g., 1926, pp. 133, 162; 1933, p. 84).

[22]* As I will argue later on, the ego, in so anticipating this previous satisfaction, is thereby simulating a previously experienced hydraulic sequence of events — a sequence in which the traumatic experience *happened* to the organism as a consequence of the blind and immediate satisfaction of its instinctual need. Now the reader may object to this particular interpretation on the grounds that it makes too much of the expression "to bring about." There is no question but that I base my interpretation, in part, on Freud's language. But my interpretation is also influenced by Freud's systematic tendency to view relationships between intrapsychic events as duplicating relationships between the subject and the external world. We have, of course, seen important instances of this tendency in Freud's interpretation of ego development and in his representation of the memory trace. Indeed, Freud (1900) has elevated this quality of his theorizing to a general principle. Characterizing the function of conscious awareness, he states, "The psychical apparatus which is turned toward the external world with its sense-organ of the *Pcpt.* systems, is itself the external world in relation to the sense-organ of the *Cs.*," and then notes, "Here we once more meet the principle of the hierarchy of agencies, which seems

the signal of anxiety involves a nascent conscious awareness or whether we are still dealing at this point with only an unconscious process. Since Freud apparently suggests that the simulation of the satisfying event is an unconscious form of knowing, I am assuming that the recall of the associated danger is similarly unconscious.

It should be emphasized, however, that my case for the logical paradox in Freud's paradigm does not depend on my particular interpretation. Indeed, as I will attempt to show, the paradigm will encounter the paradox in an even more direct and blatant form if any of the following are assumed: (1) that there is a conscious recall, however nascent, of either the earlier satisfaction or the earlier punishment; (2) that the energy involved in the experimental cathexis of the memory trace is the libidinal energy of the id impulse; or (3) that the ego is experimentally cathecting the memory trace as it mirrors both the previously experienced satisfaction *and* the previously experienced punishment. My critique is thus directed at what I consider to be the strongest, most defensible view of the paradigm, and is based on the strategy that if I can make the case in regard to this interpretation, then it will hold all the more in regard to the other interpretations that can be made. Where relevant, I will note these other interpretations and the form of the paradox they encounter.

Given this elaboration, we can now consider a major objection to my view regarding the logical paradox encountered by the anxiety-defense paradigm. This objection hinges on the argument that if the ego activities discussed above do, in fact, differ from one another, then they can be

---

to govern the structure of the apparatus" (p. 616). I will be arguing, then, that the ego's simulation in the anxiety-defense paradigm represents another instance of this principle — one in which the original hydraulic sequence of events leading to the development of the purposive ego is now purposively duplicated by the ego itself.

characterized in antithetical ways with no paradox. Namely, this position would argue that just as there is no contradiction in the fact that someone can open one door while simultaneously closing another, so too there is no contradiction in characterizing one form of knowing as existing, and another essentially different form of knowing as simultaneously not existing. It is only when the same knowing activity is characterized as existing and not existing at the same time — when, so to speak, the same door is opened and closed simultaneously — that we have the logical paradox. Thus, this objection would note that my analysis has not really addressed the implications of Freud's comment that the ego's maneuver is a process that "is neither conscious nor preconscious" but one that takes place "between quotas of energy in some unimaginable substratum" (1933, p. 90). And it would point out that it is only by so failing to acknowledge Freud's notion of unconscious awareness that I am able to pose the logical problem for his paradigm. As this viewpoint would have it, it is precisely because the id impulse withdraws from the signal of anxiety that there is only the minimal cathexis of the memory trace by means of neutralized energy rather than the stronger cathexis of the memory trace by means of libidinal energy. Hence, there is only the signal of anxiety and not the full-blown anxiety that would have resulted from the libidinal cathexis — that is to say, from the conscious awareness of the impulse and the situation of danger. From this viewpoint, then, it is an *unconscious* knowing which generates the signal of anxiety and thereby serves to prevent the *conscious* knowing from coming into being. Accordingly, there is no paradox, for we would merely have two forms of knowing which, being different, can be characterized in terms of the antithetical properties of existence and nonexistence with no contradiction. There is no paradox, in other words, in the ego's knowing unconsciously as the basis for not knowing consciously.

Further consideration, however, suggests that the logical contradiction in Freud's conception cannot be avoided by so distinguishing between levels of awareness, at least not as these levels are represented in the anxiety-defense paradigm. My case for rejecting this attempt to rescue the paradigm can be synoptically stated as follows: If we accept the interpretation that the ego's maneuver is purposive (namely, that this activity is guided by the reality principle), then we have to assume that the ego has initiated this maneuver by virtue of its foreknowledge of the consequences of libidinal discharge. But if we also grant that this maneuver serves to generate only a *signal* of anxiety, then we must also have to assume that the ego simultaneously has *no* foreknowledge of these consequences for if it did, the full-blown, albeit unconscious, affect would be reproduced. Hence, in so attempting to rescue the paradigm, this interpretation would have the ego's unconscious knowing (its foreknowledge of the consequences) serve as the basis for its unconscious not-knowing (its lack of foreknowledge of the consequences). The anxiety-defense paradigm, in other words, would continue to encounter the paradox of knowing in order not to know, but now at an unconscious level of awareness.

In elaborating this argument, let us grant Freud's explanation that an unconscious ego activity can anticipate the satisfaction of the id impulse and can, accordingly, bring about a signal of anxiety—that is to say, a reproduction of the unpleasurable feelings at the beginning of the well-remembered situation of danger. It may be seen that in so accounting for the signal of anxiety, Freud is also, by that token, assuming a number of other events as necessary aspects of his paradigm. He is assuming, first of all, that the organism, at a prior time, had expressed the forbidden impulse in actuality and, as a consequence, had experienced the unpleasurable feeling of really being punished. It is this prior experience of libidinal gratification and subsequent punishment that is now being represented intrapsychically "in some unimaginable substratum" as a memory trace. Second, it is clear in Freud's account that unconscious as well as conscious functioning is governed by the minimal tension principle. The maneuver of the ego in provoking the signal of anxiety, and the withdrawal of the id impulse in response to this signal, are only understandable in terms of this minimal tension principle — and, as Freud has emphasized, these activities take place at the unconscious level of awareness. Third, it is equally clear that the operative aspect of the anxiety-defense paradigm is an unconscious purposive activity on the part of the ego, namely, activity in accordance with the reality principle of maintaining minimal tension in the long run. Now it is true that Freud does imply the existence of a hydraulic transaction when he notes, in describing the ego's maneuver, that he is merely translating into the "language of our normal thinking" a process that takes place between "quotas of energy" (p. 90) at a deeply unconscious level. This account notwithstanding, however, there is no getting around the fact that, in this final version, Freud has explicitly rejected (1926, p. 140) his earlier view that anxiety is hydraulically transformed libido. Anxiety is now the inexpedient response on the part of the ego to its conscious awareness of a possible future danger, and the ego's "dodge" is precisely what the term implies: Even though unconscious, it is a pre-emptive maneuver, an act designed to prevent such full-blown anxiety and to bring about in its place a desired alternative — the signal of anxiety and, thereby, the id's hydraulic withdrawal. It is, in short, an ongoing act prompted and guided by a foreknowledge of its consequences. Thus, Freud's remark concerning an underlying energy transaction is essentially gratuitous, for he makes no systematic connection between such a hydraulic process and the explanatory significance he ascribes to the ego's defensive purposive activity.

Given these considerations, we can raise the following problem for Freud's conception: Why does the unconscious anticipation of satisfaction serve to reproduce only the *signal* of anxiety? Why does it not serve, as well, to reproduce the full-blown affect that was also experienced in the previous punishment and that is now *also* being represented in the unconscious memory trace? If such unconscious knowing is capable of reproducing the one affect, then why not the other? The answer, as we have seen, is clear in Freud's paradigm. Only a signal is being generated because the reproduction of the unpleasurable feelings is a restricted one—it is limited to the *beginning* of the feared situation of danger. Clearly, this answer confines the sequence of events in the anxiety-defense paradigm to a relationship of causal determinism, a relationship that could be represented, essentially, by the hydraulic metaphor of flood waters pressing toward discharge. Thus, the demand of the id impulse would correspond to the pressure of the flood waters, the signal of anxiety to a leak in the dam, and the withdrawal of the impulse to the repair of the leak. As the repair of the leak prevents the subsequent flood, so too does the hydraulic withdrawal of the id from the signal of anxiety prevent libidinal cathexis and the generation of full-blown anxiety.

But, as I have argued, one cannot accept such a narrow hydraulic interpretation of the anxiety-defense paradigm since this would simply contradict the operative aspect of Freud's conception, namely, that the ego's maneuver is *purposive*—that there is a deliberate anticipation of impulse satisfaction as a means toward the intended end of impulse withdrawal. In effect, Freud's final view has inserted a far-sighted engineer into the causal sequence of events represented by the pressure of the flood waters, the leak, and the subsequent non-occurrence of the disaster. This engineer, as it were, fearing that the dam will not hold back the flood waters, not having the resources on his own to shore up the dam, and facing the problem of a short-sighted townspeople who will not help him, deliberately makes the leak occur so as to arouse the people and generate the help that he so desperately needs. To repeat, the signal of anxiety is not simply one of a sequence of causally determined events but is also the result of a purposively initiated action of "anticipation," designed to prevent the situation of danger that will occur if no such forestalling action is undertaken. If it is the case, then, that the ego simulates the satisfaction of the impulse in order to provoke a signal of anxiety—if, in other words, it unconsciously undertakes this "play-acting" as a forestalling activity—then this must imply that the ego has an unconscious foreknowledge of the consequences that would ensue were this activity *not* to be undertaken; and this, in turn, implies that the ego, at this unconscious level, must also know the remainder of the well-remembered situation of danger. But if the anticipation of impulse satisfaction is capable of engendering a signal of anxiety at this unconscious level, by virtue of reproducing the "beginning" of the feared situation of danger, then it should follow that the unconscious foreknowledge of the remainder of the dangerous consequences should be equally capable of engendering the full-blown affect.[23]* Accordingly, if we accept Freud's account that the ego's unconscious maneuver *only* serves to produce a signal of anxiety, then we must also have to assume that this maneuver has somehow been successful in

[23]* One might possibly counter this argument by saying that there is no full-blown affect under these circumstances for one or all of the following reasons: (1) because the knowing of the consequences *is* unconscious; (2) because the ego "knows" that the maneuver will be successful; or (3) because the energy that is involved in the cathexis is not the libidinal energy of the id impulse but neutralized energy. These explanations, however, would have to face the other side of the question which I have posed for the paradigm: On what basis could one then account for *even* the signal of anxiety? If such knowing does not serve to engender the full-blown affect, then it would follow that such knowing should not be capable of engendering the signal of anxiety as well.

erasing the pre-existing unconscious knowing of the remainder of the well-remembered situation of danger without which the maneuver could not have been undertaken in the first place. Thus we again encounter the logical paradox of knowing in order not to know, but now at an unconscious level of awareness. That is, in order not to know unconsciously the tension-raising consequences of cathecting the remainder of the memory trace, the ego must already know unconsciously the consequences of cathecting the *entire* memory trace.

Essentially, then, in regard to the argument that these knowing events are different from one another, and that the logical paradox is thereby avoided, my rejoinder is that "a rose by any other name...." Even if one distinguishes between forms of ego activity in terms of levels of conscious awareness, and even if one represents the unconscious anticipation of the ego as an active simulation rather than a passive noticing, this does not do away with the logical paradox if such activities are understood as being purposive in nature and as functioning in accordance with the minimal tension principle. The paradigm merely encounters the paradox at the unconscious level.[24*]

Having thus made the case that the logical paradox is

[24*] It may be seen, moreover, that if the attempt is made to avoid the paradox by positing still more unconscious levels of knowing, this can only serve to generate an infinite regress whereby the paradox is shifted to these more unconscious levels. By the same token, any further attempt to avoid the paradox by confining the cathexis of neutralized energy to the reproduction of even smaller parts of the danger situation, and hence to even more nascent signals of anxiety, can only condemn the paradigm to the infinite regress whereby the knowing of successively smaller parts implies the knowing of successively larger remainders of the danger situation.

Finally, it may be seen that my critique applies even more directly to those interpretations of the anxiety-defense paradigm which assume (1) that the signal of anxiety is being produced by a nascent conscious awareness of the dangerous consequences; (2) that the ego is experimentally cathecting that aspect of the memory trace which mirrors the beginning of

indicative of a real problem in Freud's theory, I can now argue for my assertion regarding the *form* taken by this paradox. In doing so, I will first contrast the anxiety-defense paradigm with two other temporal sequences. My intent

---

the subsequent danger situation as well as that aspect of the trace which mirrors the previously satisfying event; or (3) that the experimental cathexis of the memory trace involves the libidinal energy of the id impulse.

In regard to the first alternative: If one assumes that a state of conscious awareness, however nascent, is producing the signal of anxiety, then the paradigm cannot even retreat, as it were, to its first line of defense: It immediately encounters the paradox of knowing *consciously* in order not to know consciously.

In regard to the second alternative: Given the purposive nature of the ego's activity in experimentally cathecting the memory trace, it would follow that the experimental cathexis of any *part* of the memory trace must also be purposively directed, including, of course, the cathexis of that part of the memory trace which mirrors the beginning of the danger situation. It would thus follow that the ego's cathexis is deliberately selective — that is, that the ego is purposively avoiding the cathexis of that part of the trace which mirrors the remainder of the danger situation. In accordance with my earlier argument, then, the success of this maneuver in generating only a signal of anxiety would imply that the ego unconsciously knows the entire situation of danger as a basis for not knowing the remainder of the danger situation.

In regard to the third alternative: The assumption that the experimental cathexis of the memory trace involves libidinal energy implies the very event which the defense of repression is designed to prevent — the conscious awareness of the impulse. The only alternative to this contradiction, as I see it, is to assume that the amount of libidinal energy involved in this experimental cathexis is somehow reduced. But this solution is equally problematic. If we accept a drastic form of this solution — namely, a reduction of libidinal energy so extreme that the cathexis results in only an unconscious awareness of the impulse — then the paradigm becomes redundant; that is to say, there is no longer any necessity to posit the defense of repression. Three variations of this solution can be suggested, each of which encounters the immutability problem in this blatant form. The first variation, and the least defensible in my view, would assume that there is only a minimal amount of energy at the very outset — that the id impulse, blindly pressing toward discharge, carries only a minimal energy charge. But, clearly, if this were the case, then there would be no reason to posit a defense of repression in the first place, for there would be no danger of conscious awareness.

here is to show that the events in these two sequences, although similar in certain respects to the events which comprise the anxiety-defense paradigm, do not encounter the logical paradox but, on the contrary, have a continuity-

---

The second variation would make the more reasonable assumption that the id impulse does indeed carry a full libidinal charge. But if one then posits that only a minimal amount of energy is subsequently involved in cathecting the memory trace, this would imply that the full energy charge of the impulse is now being limited — and that it is precisely the ego which is doing the limiting. Thus, this interpretation would suggest that the ego's maneuver, in generating only a signal of anxiety, requires the very capacity for repression which the maneuver is designed to produce. The ego, if you will, is repressing in order to repress. And by virtue of this problem of immutability, the anxiety-defense paradigm would negate itself in the most fundamental way. For this interpretation would give the "weak" ego the very resources the *lack* of which constitutes the essential condition for repression. The anxiety-defense paradigm, as so interpreted, would self-destruct, even before it got off the ground.

The third variation — and one that might seem to avoid this difficulty — would be based on a particular interpretation of Freud's (1933) statement that "the ego anticipates the satisfaction of the questionable impulse and permits it to bring about the reproduction of the unpleasurable feelings at the beginning of the feared situation of danger" (pp. 89–90). This view would have it that the ego "permits" the fully charged id impulse to cathect the memory trace because it "knows" that this cathexis can succeed only up to a point, after which point the signal of anxiety will automatically be generated, thereby bringing about the withdrawal of the impulse. The libidinal cathexis of the memory trace would thus be kept to a minimum, not by virtue of its being directly contained by the ego, but because the id's withdrawal in response to the automatic anxiety signal occurs before the libidinal energy of the impulse can be fully discharged. But this interpretation would encounter an obvious problem: The foreknowledge that would justify the ego's "permitting" the experimental cathexis would, by that same token, justify the ego's complete inaction. Namely, the ego would know that *any* libidinal cathexis — experimental or otherwise — would have to result in the automatic generation of the signal of anxiety and, hence, that even if it did nothing, the withdrawal of the id impulse would take place. In this interpretation of the paradigm, then, there is no reason why the purposive ego would even bother to engage in its maneuver of "permitting" the experimental cathexis. The paradigm, in other words, would be rendered superfluous. (See also footnote 23 above.)

change relationship with respect to one another. In contrasting these sequences, then, I hope to show that the essential form taken by the logical paradox is one that is identical to that of the immutability-discontinuity problem encountered in Freud's conception of development.

In the first of our examples, we have two cars, one following the other.[25] The lead car hits a pothole, and the car in the rear moves to the side, thus bypassing the pothole. Now, it is apparent that one can understand the movements of the rear car as being purposively governed with respect to the activity of the car in the lead and, when so considered, as being similar to the sequence of events in the anxiety-defense paradigm. One can posit a state of knowing (the fore-knowledge of hitting a pothole), followed by a maneuver which is guided by that foreknowledge and which results in a state of "not-knowing" (the absence of the experience of hitting the pothole).[26] That is to say, the driver's foreknowledge of hitting the pothole has led to a defensive activity — one that is designed to negate and, indeed, does negate the actual experience of the event. However, it is intuitively obvious that in spite of this similarity, no paradox is involved

---

Nor will compromise afford a way out of the dilemma faced by these interpretations. If one takes the middle road by assuming that the amount of libidinal energy is merely diminished to the point of producing a nascent conscious awareness, then the solution faces the problem encountered by the first alternative we have considered. In assuming such a state of awareness, the paradigm would again encounter the paradox of knowing consciously in order not to know consciously.

[25] The examples have been influenced by Peters's (1958) analysis of the purposive and causal-deterministic models of interpretation.

[26] There are, of course, a number of ways in which the sequence can be characterized. For example, one could describe the driver's behavior in terms of a sequence of cognitive events in which a state of knowing (the anticipation of a possible crash) precedes a second state of knowing (the experience of the crash *not* having occurred). As will be seen, however, this would not provide the formal counterpart to the anxiety-defense paradigm and, accordingly, would not highlight the nature of the logical paradox.

in this sequence of "knowing in order not to know." And the reason for this, it can be suggested, is that this sequence of events is being hierarchically structured in terms of a model of explanation whereby initial and subsequent events have been distinguished from one another in terms of their antithetical properties and, at the same time, have been connected to one another as different particulars of a more inclusive unity. This unity is the goal we have imputed to the driver whereby his various activities are particularized as different means. The activity of steering the car in the light of anticipating the pothole and the subsequent lack of experience of hitting the pothole can be understood as means that serve to realize a more encompassing goal of the driver, whether it be that of avoiding the cost of a broken axle, getting to dinner on time, etc. By that token, the antithetical properties of these events can be taken as signifying that a change has occurred with respect to this more encompassing invariant intent. Correlatively, these antithetical events have a continuity with respect to one another by virtue of their serving, each time, to particularize this goal. In common sense terms, we represent this continuity-change relationship by saying that the individual has progressed toward his goal via these different means. As so structured, then, the antithetical properties of "knowing" and "not-knowing" apply to different events separated over time. More specifically, the anticipation of a future state of knowing (the experience of hitting the pothole) is understood, not as bringing about the negation of the state of knowing that is doing the anticipating, but rather as bringing about the negation of the state of knowing that is being anticipated. Since these antithetical properties serve to distinguish different events over time, this sequence involves no more logical contradiction than would be involved in characterizing a door as being open and that same door, at a subsequent time, as being shut.

The second sequence of events is that of a flame burning itself out. It may be seen that here, too, the sequence is analogous to the anxiety-defense paradigm. An initial event has been followed by a state of affairs in which there is an absence of the properties that characterized this initial event. Again, however, there need be no logical difficulty in so understanding this sequence, and for the same formal reason. This sequence can be structured in terms of a causal-deterministic model of explanation whereby initial and subsequent events are differentiated from one another in terms of antithetical properties and, simultaneously, connected to one another as particulars of a more inclusive unity. Thus, a connection between these events can be provided by a principle of conservation whereby the earlier existence of the flame and the subsequent nonexistence of the flame are understood as different manifestations of the same underlying realm of being. Within this context, the antithetical properties of the flame's existence and nonexistence signify that a change has occurred with respect to this underlying realm of being, which is thereby understood as having continuity precisely by virtue of being evidenced through these different, antithetical states. Here too, then, the antithetical properties apply to separate events over time and hence involve no contradiction. As so understood, the dying of the flame, rather than negating the fact that the flame had existed earlier, on the contrary, requires this earlier existence.

In contrast to these examples of a continuity-change relationship, the antithetical properties in the anxiety-defense paradigm follow one another, and yet exist as attributes of the same event in time—hence the contradictory or paradoxical nature of the conception. A sequence of events is being posited in which an initial state of knowing (the foreknowledge of the consequences of satisfying the instinctual impulse) gives rise to a subsequent activity (the hydraulic withdrawal of the id impulse) which prevents that initial state of knowing from coming into being (primal repression). A given event has to exist as a necessary basis for that very same event not to have existed in the first place. And, as we have seen, this contradiction cannot be avoided by the major argument that can be raised against my position. In considering this counterargument, my analysis has indicated that the unconscious maneuver of anticipation implies that the subject knows the consequences of impulse satisfaction. And yet, in producing only a signal of anxiety, this same maneuver also implies that the subject simultaneously *cannot* know the same content. That is to say, the success of the ego's anticipation in only eliciting a signal of anxiety presumes the very event (the not-knowing) which this anticipation is designed to bring about, thereby contradicting the foreknowledge that is implied when we view the act of anticipation as a purposive defensive maneuver. In short, the ego's act of anticipation negates itself in Freud's anxiety-defense paradigm of repression. It is as though the second driver in my example, in avoiding the pothole by virtue of having anticipated it, thereby erases, at the outset, the foreknowledge that was intrinsic to this anticipation.

A clear parallel thus exists between the form taken by the logical paradox and that taken by the immutability-discontinuity problem encountered in Freud's conception of development. As in the conception of development, so too has the sequence of temporal events in the anxiety-defense paradigm doubled back on itself such that the final event becomes a necessary condition for its own emergence. Namely, the event which follows the ego's forestalling maneuver of anticipation — the event of not-knowing — refuses, as it were, to stay in its place and insists, instead, on becoming an intrinsic part of the prior act itself. Thus, where the conception of development encounters the immutability of giving the primitive organism the attribute of "knowing" as the basis for acquiring that same property via identification, the anxiety-defense paradigm encounters the immutability of giving the mature organism the attribute of "not-knowing" as the precondition for that same "not-knowing" to be produced via the act of anticipation. By the same token, moreover, both conceptions encounter an identical form of discontinuity; namely, both imply the simultaneous presence of antithetical properties—in the case of development, the blind id's knowing, in the case of repression, the knowing ego's not-knowing.

It is my contention that Freud's conception of development and his anxiety-defense paradigm evidence the same form of the immutability-discontinuity problem because both conceptions represent the same solution to an unsolvable problem. Namely, both conceptions serve to connect, in terms of an identity relationship, purposive and hydraulic modes of functioning that have been rendered unconnectable by a Cartesian isolation of the subject and object of knowledge. In making this case, one can point to a direct parallel between the sequence of events which Freud posits as leading to development and the sequence of events which he posits as leading to repression. As we have seen, Freud's final conception of development presumes a subject-object relationship in which the primitive subject, in accordance with the pleasure principle, is hydraulically directed toward immediate discharge onto the external gratifying object and is unable to represent veridically those aspects of the external other who, as the powerful, controlling one in the oedipal triangle, will punish him for his libidinal act. In this sense, Freud has so defined the id-dominated subject that he can only know external events in terms of his immediate needs and wants. He is governed solely by the pleasure principle and is thus directed toward certain immediate reinforcing properties of the external world, while blind to other properties—properties of purpose and control—that in the long run will serve to raise his level of tension. The very same subject-object relationship is presumed in the anxiety-defense paradigm of repression, but now within the intrapsychic realm. We have an unconscious id impulse blindly pressing toward immediate libidinal discharge, but now onto a *memory trace* of the external gratifying other and, when so discharged, entering conscious awareness. And here, too, such discharge, although immediately gratifying, results in a subsequent rise in tension — the full-blown anxiety on the part of an ego which now represents the external purposive other intrapsychically and yet recognizes its own powerlessness in controlling the behavioral expression of the conscious impulse.

We can see, then, that Freud faces the same problem in his anxiety-defense paradigm that he faces in his conception of development — that of connecting isolated realms of inner and outer being, represented now as isolated realms of an intrapsychic reality. Just as the primitive id impulse is natively directed toward libidinal objects and inherently isolated from the external properties of purpose and control, the exercise of which will cause the organism a future rise in tension, so too is it isolated from these properties as they are mirrored intrapsychically in the form of the acquired ego structure and the memory trace of the previously traumatic event. That is to say, the primitive id impulse knows these qualities only to the extent that they cause the organism immediate pleasure and immediate pain and, by that token, not in terms of their potential to bring the organism future pain. Specifically, the id impulse cannot anticipate the tension-raising consequences of libidinal cathexis of the memory trace of the gratifying other, namely, the ego's capacity to react with full-blown anxiety to the conscious awareness of the impulse. Accordingly, the problem of knowledge which surfaces in Freud's view of development applies, as well, to the anxiety-defense paradigm. The id impulse is so defined that it can never know and, in this sense, is irrevocably isolated from, the essential aspects of an independently constituted reality, now as intrapsychically represented.[27]

And yet we have seen that, in spite of this gulf, Freud posits a connection between these realms of intrapsychic being—a connection which, in fact, constitutes the central process in his anxiety-defense paradigm. The ego, functioning in accordance with the reality principle, simulates the satisfaction of the impulse by using whatever neutralized energy it has at its disposal to cathect the memory trace of the previously satisfying event, thereby generating a signal of anxiety from which the id reflexively withdraws in accordance with the pleasure principle. It can thus be said that the anxiety-defense paradigm, like the conception of development, is connecting purposive and hydraulic modes of activity which, by virtue of being defined in terms of a Cartesian world view, cannot be connected as particulars of a more inclusive construct. And, in accordance with our thesis, it follows that the anxiety-defense paradigm, like the conception of development, must take the form evidenced by cognitive activity when structuring a problem beyond its explanatory limits, namely, that of an identity relationship whereby the process that serves to connect the hydraulic and purposive events is being defined in terms of a construct that

---

[27] Although this is not his intent, and although he places a different interpretation on the material, Paul (1967) nicely portrays the problem of knowledge inherent in the relationship between the id impulse and the memory trace. In noting that the psychoanalytic conception of memory parallels Bartlett's (1932) view of memory as a "reconstruction," Paul states:

> Freud originally dealt with memory by means of a two-factor trace theory (e.g., Freud, 1895, 1900); one factor is the structure of the trace, and the second factor is the process, the way cathectic energy is used. The basic formula is: Remembering consists of the cathectic "innervation" of traces. The trace remains permanent and unaltered; it is the processes of reactivation that bring about the form of the recall, the distortions and condensations, the elaborations and modifications, and the forgetting [p. 229].

has served to distinguish between these events in the first place.

Thus can we understand the formal parallel between the logical paradox and the immutability-discontinuity problem encountered by Freud's conception of development. The logical paradox evidenced by the ego's activity of mediating between the id impulse and the memory trace can be derived as a problem of immutability and discontinuity from an identity relationship between hydraulic and purposive events. More precisely, we can understand the ego's transaction between the id impulse and the memory trace in terms of *two* identity relationships — one in which a *purposive* ego knows the essential attributes of the memory trace as these mirror the experience of the previously traumatic event, and the other in which a *hydraulic* ego simulates the blind functioning of the id.

The former of these identity relationships has its roots in Freud's conception of development. We have seen that the anxiety-defense paradigm requires the presence of an acquired purposive ego; that is to say, the maneuver which constitutes the central feature of the paradigm is only possible given an organism that can act in the light of an intended outcome. And in Freud's final view of personality, this mode of activity is acquired as a function of experience. We have also seen, however, that Freud's conception of ego development itself represents an identity relationship between differentiating and connecting constructs. In positing an acquired ego that mediates between the id and the external independently constituted world, Freud can only connect these unconnectable events in terms of a construct that has served to distinguish between these realms in the first place. Thus, the acquired purposive ego mirrors the attributes of the external event. It is this same identity relationship that is replicated in the anxiety-defense paradigm, but now in the form of a purposive ego that mediates between the id impulse and the memory trace. For if we accept Freud's view that the memory trace is a mirror of external reality, then the presumption of an independently constituted reality of essential properties serves to define the memory trace, thereby distinguishing the trace from the distorting id, and also serves to define the construct that connects these differentiated events, namely, the mediating activity of the ego as a purposive mode of functioning. As so defined, the ego's response to the emerging id impulse is represented as an initial sequence of purposively governed events: The ego's noticing of the id impulse, its foreknowledge of the consequences of libidinal expression, its implied ability to distinguish between the essential and unessential aspects of the memory trace, and its maneuver to forestall the possible anxiety attack are all related to one another as a means toward the end of maintaining minimal tension in the long run.

But as our analysis of Freud's conception of development has indicated, this identity relationship can only serve to displace the Cartesian isolation between the subject and object of knowledge. For now this isolation exists between the hydraulic id impulse and the purposive ego: If the id is so characterized that it can only distort the essential aspects of an independently constituted reality, and if it is, by that token, isolated from that independently constituted reality, then it is similarly isolated from an ego which mirrors this reality—from an ego, in other words, that has the foreknowledge of the consequences of libidinal expression and that can distinguish the essential from the unessential aspects of the memory trace. It follows, therefore, that the sequence of events that next occurs in the anxiety-defense paradigm—namely, the activity of the ego that affords the *connection* between the unconnectable id and ego—must similarly take the form of an identity relationship between differentiating and connecting constructs. And in the sequence of events that is elicited by the ego's maneuver, this is precisely what we have.

Indeed, this sequence of events is but an attenuated version of the hydraulic sequence that Freud posited originally in his conception of development and, again, in his conception of anxiety. Thus, in Freud's conception of *development,* the id, blind to the consequences of its actions, libidinally cathects the external satisfying object and subsequently encounters punishment. This same sequence, but now as intrapsychically represented, is replicated in Freud's view of *anxiety:* The id impulse blindly presses toward the libidinal cathexis of the external satisfying event as mirrored in the memory trace, and cannot anticipate the rise in tension that will befall it as a consequence of the conscious awareness that results. In the *anxiety-defense paradigm* of repression, we have yet another replication of this hydraulic sequence, and in a still more remote form: The ego, by its experimental action, simulates the id's libidinal cathexis of the memory trace and thereby sets into motion a repetition of the trauma in "mitigated" form (1926, p. 166), thereby producing a mere signal of anxiety. It can be said, then, that the ego's maneuver in the anxiety-defense paradigm serves to pre-empt the "real" sequence of hydraulic events — the events leading to full-blown anxiety — by substituting, at a critical point, a pale reflection of this hydraulic sequence. Namely, the ego's experimental cathexis of the memory trace as it mirrors the satisfying experience serves to elicit, in turn, a neutralized cathexis of the memory trace as it mirrors the associated pain that occurred at the beginning of the traumatic event. Thus, the ego's activity, in simulating the hydraulic satisfaction, serves to "bring about" the signal of anxiety: Just as the full-blown anxiety "happened" to the id as an unanticipated consequence of the libidinal cathexis of the memory trace, so too does the signal of anxiety "happen" to the "hydraulic ego" as an "unanticipated" consequence of simulating this libidinal cathexis. In effect, then, Freud has connected the id impulse to the ego and thence, via the ego, to the essential aspects of the memory trace. But he has done so in terms of a second identity relationship—one in which the presumption of a distorting inner nature has not only served to define the id impulse, thereby distinguishing it from the memory trace, but has also served to define the construct that connects these differentiated events, namely, the ego's mediating activity as a hydraulic form of behavior.

Now there is no question but that the connection between the id impulse and the memory trace so afforded by the ego's mediating activity represents an ingenious solution to the problem of knowledge that besets Freud's theory. Indeed, in a sense, this connection solves the problem in a radically different way from that represented by Freud's conception of development and, in particular, his concept of introjective identification. For instead of implicitly giving attributes to the distorting id whereby it can know the qualities of a reality to which it is inherently blind, Freud has posited a reality that *can be known* by the distorting id. He has so characterized the ego that it has the ability to produce, as an attribute of itself, an intrapsychic reality of heightened tension to which the id can directly respond. By its signal of anxiety, the ego has rendered immediate the tension-raising consequences of which it has foreknowledge and, accordingly, has represented itself in a way that corresponds to the id's distorted conception of the world as immediately gratifying or immediately punitive. In effect, the *future* tension-raising consequences of the id's activities— and, by that token, the essential aspects of the previously experienced event as mirrored in the memory trace—have, as it were, been pre-digested by the ego and rendered *immediate* for the id's consumption.

In the final analysis, however, the implications of so

connecting the unconnectable in terms of an identity relationship are the same, and this is the case regardless of how
many identity relationships are involved. Rather than
resolving the dilemma represented by the Cartesian problem
of knowledge, Freud's solution further displaces the dilemma to yet another domain, namely, to the ego itself. More
precisely, the dilemma emerges as a contradictory relationship between two faces of ego activity. When the ego faces
in one direction—when its activity is characterized as
discriminating between the essential and unessential aspects
of the memory trace—such activity is being defined by the
presumption of an independently constituted reality. And
when the ego faces in the other direction—when its activity
is characterized as simulating the id—such activity is being
defined by the presumption of a blind subject that can only
contribute distortion to this independently constituted event.
Accordingly, in connecting the id impulse to the memory
trace, the ego's mediating activity is being characterized as a
contradictory admixture of hydraulics and purpose—an admixture of modes of functioning that have been rendered
unconnectable by the Cartesian isolation between the subject and object of knowledge. In being so displaced, then,
the Cartesian problem of knowledge has re-emerged as the
classic dichotomy between mind and body, but now in the
functioning of the ego itself.

It is by thus understanding the anxiety-defense paradigm as a juxtaposition of two identity relationships that we
can derive the logical paradox as a form of the immutability-
discontinuity problem. When its activities are defined as a
sequence of hydraulic events, the organism cannot know the
consequences of its acts. It can only move blindly from act
to consequence, thereby finding itself in a state of not-
knowing (the withdrawal of the id impulse in response to the
signal of anxiety). And when its activities are defined as a
sequence of purposively governed events, the organism *must*

know the consequences of its actions since these are now being posited as a means toward an intended end. Accordingly, when the organism is characterized in terms of both models of explanation *simultaneously*—as acting from the outset in the light of its foreknowledge of the essential aspects of the memory trace and, at the same time, as blindly impelled from one act to another, finally to a state of not-knowing that reflects its original blindness—its original *lack* of foreknowledge—it is then that the organism's knowing is negated, at the outset, by its not-knowing. It is then that the organism is characterized as having foreknowledge of the consequences of its acts and, simultaneously, as lacking foreknowledge of these very same consequences.[28*]

More particularly, by understanding the anxiety-defense paradigm as a juxtaposition of identity relationships we can formally account for the "time-out-of-joint" phenomenon whereby the subsequent event of not-knowing turns back on itself to become part of the prior event of knowing. In connecting the purposive mediating activity of the ego with the

[28*] It is no accident in this regard that I selected for comparison with the anxiety-defense paradigm the sequence of one car following the other and the sequence of the flame burning itself out. These were chosen because in my view they differed from the anxiety-defense paradigm in an essential respect. Instead of representing an interaction between hydraulic and purposive events, each of these sequences can be interpreted in terms of a single or homogeneous model of explanation. That is, the sequence of activity evidenced by the rear car can be interpreted solely in terms of a purposive model, while the sequence of the flame burning itself out can be interpreted solely in terms of a deterministic or hydraulic model of explanation. And it can be seen that, under these circumstances, no logical paradox is encountered. On the contrary, these events are hierarchically structured in terms of a continuity-change relationship. Now this is not to imply that hydraulic and purposive explanations, when taken separately, *never* encounter contradiction, only that they need not necessarily do so. I am asserting, however, that the anxiety-defense paradigm does, of necessity, encounter the logical paradox because the paradigm—like Freud's conception of development—involves a sequence of both purposive and causal models of explanation, or what amounts to the same thing, an interaction of purposive and hydraulic events.

hydraulic activity of the id by implicitly redefining this mediating activity in terms of the presumption of a distorting inner nature, Freud is positing an initial sequence of purposive events (the ego's noticing of the impulse and its foreknowledge of the consequences of libidinal satisfaction) as being followed by a sequence of hydraulic events (the simulated satisfaction, the reproduction of the anxiety signal, and the withdrawal of the id impulse). But by virtue of this same presumption, he is also positing, albeit implicitly, an invariant realm of distorting inner nature — one that underlies both the prior purposive activity of the ego as well as the subsequent sequence of hydraulic events. Accordingly, the final state of hydraulic not-knowing in this sequence turns back on itself, via the underlying invariant of blind distortion, to coexist with the prior event of the purposive ego's foreknowledge, thereby negating this prior state of knowing.[29] Hence the logical paradox encountered in the ego's knowing in order not to know.

We can say, then, that while Freud's conception of development solves the problem of connecting the id and the independently constituted event by an identity relationship whereby the blind hydraulic id is implicitly given the attribute of purposive knowing, the anxiety-defense paradigm solves the problem of connecting the id and the independently constituted event (as mirrored in the memory trace) by the additional identity relationship whereby the purposive knowing ego is given the attribute of hydraulic blindness or lack of knowing. In short, instead of solving the problem of knowledge in the way that he has in his conception of devel-

---

[29] We can also view the connection between ego and id as being mediated by an identity relationship between the connecting construct and the differentiating construct that defines the prior event. Under these circumstances, the purposive knowing, or foreknowledge, stretches forward in time to coexist with the subsequent hydraulic lack of foreknowledge, leaving us with the same logical paradox — the same collapsing of time — whereby the ego's knowing and not-knowing negate each other.

opment, namely, by giving the antithetical properties of knowing and not-knowing—of purpose and hydraulics—to the id, Freud has solved the problem in the anxiety-defense paradigm by giving these antithetical properties to the ego.

In conclusion, our analysis of Freud's final version has pointed to various problems of discontinuity and immutability encountered in the relationship between hydraulic and purposive dimensions of functioning. Our thesis has suggested that these problems can be understood as the surfacing of a fundamental paradox that Freud's theory encounters by virtue of defining the subject and object in Cartesian terms. His theoretical constructs create an isolation between a distorting subject and the essential life-involving event—an isolation that cannot be bridged by a more inclusive construct. In this light, Freud's conceptions of development and repression have been viewed as a form of organization evidenced by refined cognition in solving an unsolvable problem, that is to say, a pars pro toto solution to the problem of connecting events that cannot be connected. The forms of immutability and discontinuity attributed to Freud's theory of personality can be derived from the various solutions of identity which Freud proposed in so connecting the distorting subject to the independently constituted event. As one solution, he structured the temporal events of personality development in terms of an identity relationship between a connecting construct and the differentiating construct which defined the *prior primitive* state. As so understood, the prior event was perpetuated in immutable form as a distorting primitive core upon which mature functioning was discontinuously juxtaposed. In this respect, Freud's solution evidenced a form of immutability and discontinuity identical to that encountered by behaviorist doctrine in its focus on the problem of developmental change. As a second solution, Freud structured the temporal events of personality development in terms of an identity relationship between a connecting construct and the differentiating construct which defined the *subsequent* event of *mature* functioning. As so understood, mature activity stretched back in time such that it coexisted with the antithetical properties of the primitive state and, indeed, required itself as a precondition for its own existence. This form of the immutability-discontinuity problem, typically characterized as preformism, is identical to that encountered by instinct theory in its focus on the issue of developmental continuity.

We can say, then, that one identity relationship proposed by Freud with respect to the problem of personality development solves the problem as a discontinuous acquisition of anticipation and delay by the primitive hydraulic subject. The other identity relationship that he proposed solves the problem by implicitly redefining the hydraulic subject in such a way that the coordination between the subject and object is given from the very start. There is yet a third solution that Freud proposed in connecting the unconnectable—one that, of necessity, also takes the form of an identity relationship. This is represented by his anxiety-defense paradigm of repression. Rather than redefining the hydraulic subject so that its activity is natively coordinated to the essential object, Freud leaves the hydraulic subject intact and redefines the object as the basis for this coordination. It is clear, however, that this solution, as well, cannot resolve the fundamental paradox of Freud's theory. For, as we have seen, when Freud connects the subject and object from one side of the void by implicitly redefining the hydraulic subject, then the paradox surfaces as a contradiction in his approach to development, namely, he assigns antithetical properties to the id. And when Freud connects these isolated realms of being from the other side of the void by implicitly redefining the object (as now represented by the ego), then the paradox surfaces as a contradiction in his anxiety-defense paradigm, namely, he assigns antithetical properties to the ego.

It is ironic, then, that the very movement in Freud's thinking—the evolution of his theory—is attributable, in part, to his efforts at solving the contradictory mix of hydraulics and purpose in his earlier versions. His final version separated these dimensions and confined them to the isolated and purified organizations of the id and ego. Yet, in this final version, the interaction between id and ego only served to reinstate the contradictory relationship between hydraulics and purpose. As my thesis has suggested, the persistence of the problem throughout Freud's revisions can only be attributed to his continuing Cartesian assumption. His conceptions served to bring together the divergent implications of a Cartesian epistemology which assumes a subject who knows, and yet who can never know. In this sense, it can be said that Freud's conceptions of development and pathology have all served to connect the mind and body as defined in Cartesian terms. In whatever form they take, then, Freud's theoretical explanations have thus connected the unconnectable, and therein lies the basis for the various problems of immutability and discontinuity which these explanations encounter.

5

CONFLICT-FREE CONCEPTIONS OF
PERSONALITY DEVELOPMENT

This chapter focuses on the conflict-free conceptions of development advanced by Heinz Hartmann, David Rapaport, and Robert White. Two goals guide my analysis of these contemporary psychoanalytic views. First, I want to show that in spite of any shift in emphasis that these positions might represent with respect to Freud's classical view of development, they nevertheless encounter the same form of the immutability-discontinuity problem, and for the same reason: Namely, they share the same Cartesian epistemology. Second, a number of psychoanalytically oriented theorists (most systematically represented, in my view, by Robert White) have suggested that there is another basis in Freud's theory for those difficulties that I have characterized as problems of immutability and discontinuity. This view would have it that these problems are a function of Freud's "metapsychological" dichotomy between energy and structure. I intend to show that this interpretation, although valid as far as it goes, can be derived, in turn, from my own thesis regarding Freud's epistemology. My second goal, then, is to show that this Cartesian epistemology is the more basic determinant of the immutability-discontinuity problem encountered by Freudian theory.[1]

THE CONCEPTS OF CONTEMPORARY PSYCHOANALYTIC EGO PSYCHOLOGY

We have seen that Freud's conception of symptomatic behavior culminated in a view of the subject-object relationship in which the ego, as a knowing, purposive organization, mediated between a blind, hydraulic id and an external antagonistic reality. In this final version, Freud's view of the id as functioning in accordance with hydraulic principles did not, of course, signify any dramatic change in an approach that had started with the constancy principle and had subsequently delineated the vicissitudes of the sexual instinct. An important shift in emphasis, however, was represented by the notion that the purposive mediation of the ego was, in itself, a fundamental constituent of symptomatic behavior. The concept of a "defensive" ego, purposively directed toward the organism's survival — even at the expense of symptomatic behavior — provides what is commonly accepted as the defining characteristic of Freud's final "ego psychology." More than anyone else, the contemporary theorist most closely identified with Freud's final emphasis on the adaptive functioning of the ego is Heinz Hartmann. In part, Hartmann's (1956) position has already been discussed. It will be recalled that his criticism of Freud's "Formulations on the

[1] I am grouping White with Hartmann and Rapaport, not only because of a common epistemology, but also because White's conflict-free position has been directly and significantly influenced by many of Freud's tenets, including his anxiety-defense paradigm of symptom expression (see White, 1972). It will be seen, however, that Hartmann and Rapaport accept Freud's dichotomy between energy and structure, in contrast to White, who explicitly rejects this dichotomy. Accordingly, while all three can be characterized as contemporary psychoanalytic theorists, Hartmann and Rapaport can be further distinguished from White as Freudian ego psychologists.

Two Principles of Mental Functioning" (1911b) served to alert us to the discontinuity involved in the classic conflict conception of development. In considering ego psychology in its own right, we can now focus on a related implication of this criticism, namely, that it served as the basis for Hartmann's own *conflict-free* version of ego development. For, as White (1963) has noted, Hartmann took the position that postponement and anticipation could not be conjured up from the mere fact of frustration, but rather that the very presence of such delaying activity—crude and elementary though it was—demonstrated that "some preparedness for dealing with reality" (Hartmann, 1956, p. 35) *preceded* the experience of conflict.[2] Thus, Hartmann concerned himself with adaptive ego functioning within a context very different from that of conflict and the defensive maneuvers of symptomatic behavior. His criticism of the discontinuity in Freud's conception led him to what was essentially a revision of Freud's final approach, a revision in which the ego's self-preserving qualities were neither activated nor acquired solely as a function of conflict. Rather, adaptive forms of ego activity were evidenced prior to the onset of any significant conflict and, indeed, were given at the very outset of life.

In this attempt to turn the discontinuity in Freud's conception to theoretical advantage, Hartmann's (1956) analysis extended a line of reasoning he had proposed in an earlier paper (Hartmann, 1939). In this prior paper, Hartmann first noted the same trend in Freud's thinking that I have described in our earlier consideration of Freud's revisions. He suggested that Freud's initial focus on hydraulic drives became increasingly supplemented in his successive versions by a "structural" consideration of those defensive and purposive aspects of functioning which secure the organism's survival. He further noted that Freud's pervasive concern

[2] See Chapter 4, footnote 3 on White's analysis of Hartmann (1956).

with the dynamic conflicts involved in symptomatic behavior and psychotherapy had led him to conceptualize such adaptive ego functioning as being mobilized and, indeed, created in order to reduce tension or to avoid an increase in tension. Hartmann's reaction to this view of adaptive functioning was the same as in his later paper: He objected that such conflict could not be considered a sufficient condition for ego development. In addressing himself to Freud's view of the development of the reality principle, Hartmann asserted: "How this modification into the reality-principle could, so to speak, be foisted upon the pleasure-principle has still not been answered unequivocally" (1939, p. 381). And in elaborating upon the discontinuity implied by his analysis, he noted further that the renunciation of immediate gratification for future satisfaction could not "be derived from the pleasure-principle alone; not even memories of pain experiences suffice to explain it" (1939, p. 381).

Hartmann suggested, then, that even when the development of adaptive functioning was based on conflict, conflict alone was not a sufficient condition for such development. In this sense, the discontinuity in Freud's conception was due to the fact that it left out important determinants of ego development. And, significantly, it is at this point in his exposition that Hartmann advanced the major line of his proposed revision. In order to understand such development, one had to assume that the organism came to the conflict situation with adaptive "precursors" to delay. These precursors were the "inborn conflict-free apparatuses" which, by virtue of their built-in coordination to the external world, constituted the organism's primary guarantee of survival. These inborn apparatuses were designated as the structures of "primary autonomy" (Hartmann, 1952) and were viewed as serving "motility, perception, and certain thought processes" (Hartmann, Kris, and Loewenstein, 1946). So named because they were independent of the vicissitudes of the sexual instincts from the very outset, these adaptive precursors of ego functioning, together with analogous precursors of id activity, constituted a "common root" (Hartmann, 1939), or a primitive "undifferentiated phase" (Hartmann, Kris, and Loewenstein, 1946).

In this view, then, development involved not the modification of id into ego, but a process whereby both the ego's means of reality testing as well as the id's primary process functioning became differentiated from this common matrix of built-in coordinations to external reality. As a function of this differentiation, Hartmann (1939) proposed that the developed ego structures took over "on a higher level, functions which were originally carried out by more primitive regulations..." (p. 384). In so delineating development as a process of increasing hierarchization, Hartmann not only suggested that primitive and advanced activity had functional characteristics in common, but also that there were qualitative differences between primitive and mature behavior. For example, he distinguished between the peremptory qualities of earlier diffuse functioning and the delaying qualities of later integrated behavior. Ego development, in his view, involved the increasing elaboration of an inner world of thought which freed man from the demands of the immediate perceptual situation. This inner world of thought, by enabling man to take himself as an object, liberated him "from his slavery to the stimulus-reaction compulsion of the immediate here and now" (Hartmann, 1939, p. 388).

Hartmann proposed two processes in accounting for development as so characterized. His more radical conception was that of "conflict-free" development. Hartmann (1939) noted in this regard:

> Not every adaptation to the environment, not every learning and maturation process arises from a conflict. I refer to the *conflict-free* development of perception, intention, object-comprehension, thinking, language,

recall phenomena, and productivity; to that of the well-known phases of motor development, grasping, crawling, and walking; and to the maturation and learning processes implicit in all these and many others... [p. 365].

Hartmann thus suggested that a realm of adaptive functioning came into being on the basis of determinants other than those involving an increase and reduction of instinctual tension. The antecedent of conflict, as posited by Freud, simply was not involved in such development. This realm of adaptive functioning, moreover, was an exceedingly broad one indeed. It is all the more striking, therefore, given the radical nature of his conception and its breadth of application, that Hartmann's various accounts of conflict-free development were quite deficient in delineating the process involved. Fortunately, however, Rapaport has attempted to make this process explicit, and it is to his treatment of conflict-free development that we can turn. Rapaport (1951a) asserted in this regard:

> We must remember that the motor, perceptual, and memory apparatuses, as well as other inborn apparatuses such as those of affect expression, stimulus barrier, etc., have definite thresholds which are their *structural characteristics*. These *structural characteristics* will set limits to the discharge of drive tension, that is, to the pleasure principle, even when the need-satisfying object is present, and even before drive discharge is prevented by the absence of the need-satisfying object. The very nature of structure will always prevent total discharge of tension. The existence of inborn structural elements in the undifferentiated phase may be what precipitates developmentally the differentiation of it into the ego and the id. The developing ego then integrates these structural apparatuses and re-represents their dis-

charge-limiting and -regulating function in forms usually described as defenses. These are the foundations of the primary autonomy of the ego...[pp. 362–363].

Rapaport argued, then, that the primary autonomous structures, simply by virtue of their existence, acted to prevent the complete and immediate discharge of instinctual energy and thereby provided the essential condition for their own development. His reasoning was that, given the threshold of discharge which defined any structure, there must be a preliminary build-up of tension before discharge can occur. Therefore, there can never be a complete and immediate discharge of instinctual energy by means of structure. It is in this sense that the "very nature of structure will always prevent total discharge of tension." Rapaport used a revealing metaphor in attempting to clarify how this characteristic of structure served as the essential condition for its own development. In describing the sources of the "countercathexes" that correspond to the defense mechanisms of the ego ("each of these [defense mechanisms] is a new apparatus of the ego, added to the already discussed inborn ego apparatus" [Rapaport, 1951a, p. 363]), Rapaport (1951b) stated:

> What are the sources of these countercathexes? The analogy of a river, which where it is slowed down builds up sand bars to slow it further, may help us to visualize what the evidence seems to suggest: the countercathexes seem to be derived from the drive which they repress. We may assume that in their genesis the structural limitations of discharge ... play the role of initial obstruction. A "need is made into a virtue": the organization of the energy which is denied discharge so changes as to prevent future discharge [p. 695].

Note that here Rapaport was clearly referring to the same limitations of discharge we have referred to above, namely, those of the primary autonomous structures. If we liken the primary autonomous structure to a sand bar, and libidinal energy to the flow of a stream, we can analogize the process involved in ego development to the slowing down of the current by the sand bar, thereby promoting the precipitation of sand particles and adding to the height of the bar. Given this increased height, the flow of the stream is slowed down even more, more sand is deposited, etc.[3] The essential basis for conflict-free development, then, was the prior existence of inborn structures that inherently prevented complete and immediate discharge of energy; this condition, like the progressive build-up of the sand bar, gave rise to additional delaying structures, and so on, to a progressively developed hierarchy of controlling structures.

The second process which Hartmann posited was, for all intents and purposes, a direct extension of Freud's conflict model. Given the nature of Hartmann's critique, this of course is not surprising. Rather than totally rejecting conflict as a determinant, Hartmann had merely said that conflict was not the *only* source of development. Thus, the notions of primary autonomy and conflict-free development were advanced, not to supplant Freud's conflict model, but to supplement it within the overall framework of Freud's theory. Hartmann's version of the conflict model did, however, take on additional features as a function of his emphasis on conflict-free development. As in Freud's conflict model, Hartmann continued to account for new structures by virtue of the relative inadequacy of the more

[3] It should be acknowledged that the terms of Rapaport's metaphor are to a degree ambiguous. It might be argued, for example, that Rapaport was not analogizing the primary autonomous structures to a sand bar, but merely to that point in the river where it was "slowed down"—a narrows perhaps. This reading would have the advantage of better conveying his notion of structure as inherently "discharge-limiting." On the other hand, it would seem to contradict his later characterization of the structural limitations of discharge as "playing the role of initial obstruction." In any event, the distinction between these readings does not have theoretical significance.

primitive structures in reducing tension. But these primitive structures, instead of being those of a non-delaying id, were the adaptive precursors of the ego, namely, the primary autonomous structures. Hartmann stressed, moreover, that the activity of the acquired ego structures — whether acquired as a function of conflict or not — differed qualitatively from the rhythmic ebb and flow of primitive behavior, revealing a greater independence of the tumescence and detumescence of instinctual activity than did primitive behavior (1939, p. 388). Such activity, we might say, has a sustained and modulated quality that is absent in primitive behavior. These additional structures, once they were acquired as a function of conflict, in turn, became "conflict-free." They became autonomous of the conflict situation that had produced them. These new structures, accordingly, were the apparatuses of "secondary autonomy" as differentiated from those of primary autonomy (Hartmann, 1952).

It may be seen, however, that in spite of whatever changes were implied in Hartmann's view of development, this view was nevertheless couched in terms of the energy-structure dichotomy that had characterized Freud's classical conflict model. Regardless of how Hartmann otherwise understood the primary and secondary autonomous structures, he understood them as being powered by psychic energy, as giving form to psychic energy, and as discharging such energy.[4] Accordingly, having proposed his alternatives to ego development, Hartmann had to deal with the same problem that Freud had faced in his final conception of the

---

[4] As Hartmann (1939) has stated: "It is obvious that the apparatuses, both congenital and acquired, need a driving force in order to function" (p. 395). Ego psychology's acceptance of Freud's metapsychology is further indicated by Rapaport's (1959) view that even though the ego apparatuses of primary autonomy may be conflict-free with regard to development, "this does not imply that they have no relation to the drives. They are part and parcel of the apparatus which executes drive actions" (p. 96).

ego and the mechanisms of defense. Just as Freud had to provide an energy source for the repressing activity of a weak acquired ego, so too did Hartmann have to provide an energy source for the functioning of the autonomous structures. And having posed the problem in a similar way, it is not surprising that Hartmann also accepted Freud's solution. Such energy was seen as ultimately supplied by the instincts. The manifest form of this solution, however, was quite different from that evidenced by Freud's anxiety-defense paradigm. The reason for this had to do with the very different nature of the activities involved. The activity of the developed structures — whether these structures were a result of conflict-free or conflict development — was sustained and modulated. As such, this activity was of a quality very different from the intense, desperate, and unconscious activity of repression as a defense of the weak ego. It followed that the nature of the energy required for such activity was very different from that involved in repression. And this, in turn, called for a different conception of how such energy was acquired from the instincts. Rather than making use of the anxiety-defense paradigm in which the ego capitalized on the primitive aim of the instincts by its dodge of turning the highly charged libidinal energy against itself, Hartmann (1955) exploited Freud's concept of "neutralization." In this conception, libidinal energy became completely detached from its original instinctual aims and hence "desexualized" with respect to its highly charged initial state. Libido, as so neutralized, formed a "reservoir" of free energy which contrasted with the pulsating ebb and flow of instinctual energy and which thereby served as a constant source of power for the modulated and sustained activity of the developed structures, including the secondary autonomous structures, in their adaptive relationship to the world.

THE IMMUTABILITY-DISCONTINUITY PROBLEM IN EGO PSYCHOLOGY'S APPROACH TO DEVELOPMENT

Although brief, this review provides evidence for two conclusions. The first is that the relationship between ego psychology and Freud's classical theory is the same as the relationship between instinct theory and behaviorism. As we have seen, Hartmann objected to Freud's conception that development occurred solely as a function of conflict. Even under those circumstances where conflict was a necessary condition for development, it was not a sufficient condition in Hartmann's view—hence the theoretical discontinuity of foisting the delaying function of the ego upon the blind immediacy of the id. As Bertocci had pointed to the "magical" discontinuity of functional autonomy, so was Hartmann pointing to the discontinuous appearance of delay in the classical model of conflict. And as Bertocci had corrected for the discontinuity of functional autonomy by proposing that the purposive propensities were there "in the first place," so too was Hartmann correcting for the discontinuity of Freud's model by explicitly building into the model the preformed adaptive precursors of the ego. In this sense, Hartmann was reverting to Freud's earlier, discarded notion of the ego instincts and, in doing so, was again making explicit an immutability which, in the course of Freud's revisions, had become implicit.

Our second conclusion is closely related to the first. Just as instinct theory represents no real alternative to the immutability-discontinuity problem encountered by behaviorism, the concepts being proposed by ego psychology provide no real alternative to the immutability-discontinuity problem encountered by Freud's classical model. Consider, first, Rapaport's view regarding the primary autonomous struc-

ture and its role in conflict-free development. Even though
the "discharge-limiting" qualities that Rapaport ascribes to
the primary structures might appear to be different from acquired delay, his metaphor of the process involved in this
acquisition suggests otherwise. If one assumes that the original sand bar stands for prior structures and that the stream
stands for the primitive ebb and flow of instinctual energy,
then it can be said that the *acquired* structures, as
represented by the *build-up* of the sand bar, are somehow
already contained in this instinctual energy in the form of
the sand particles being carried by the stream.[5] Indeed, this
is but a slightly different version of a criticism of Rapaport's
paradigm that was first made by White. Addressing the question as to how the countercathexes could be derived from
the drive cathexes, White (1963) stated:

> The weak spot with respect to energy is the assumption
> that instinctual energies can be split and thrown into an
> opposition of cathexis and anticathexis when circum-
> stances present an obstacle to the original cathexis. If
> we take this literally, we have to imagine that "wanting
> food" and "wanting food" can stand in conflict so that
> one "wanting food" inhibits the other and causes it to
> send out a more realistic derivative. Such a feat on the
> part of energies is not made more plausible by the
> analogy of sand bars in a river unless one is prepared to
> suppose that instinctual energy contains silt which is
> deposited when the flow is made slower. Of course,
> Rapaport did not intend any of this to be taken quite
> literally. He was aware of the dangers in the metaphors
> he employed, but he did not attempt a more explicit

---

[5] This implication is consistent with Rapaport's (1958) suggestion
that there is no essential difference between energy and structure—that
structure is merely a slow rate of change, while energy is a more rapid rate
of change.

solution for the mysterious splitting of one stream of energy into two opposing forces [p. 57].

Of course, White capitalizes here on the problem I have represented in terms of acquired ego structures metaphorically present as sand particles in the stream of instinctual energy. But whether the problem is represented in terms of sand particles or different kinds of streams, the criticism is essentially the same: The countercathexes—as a function of the acquired structures of the ego—are somehow already present in the flow of instinctual energy from the start.

Now it might be objected that neither interpretation does justice to Rapaport's more formal conceptualization of the process in which "the organization of the energy which is denied discharge [by the structural limitations of discharge] so changes as to prevent future discharge" (1951b, p. 695). In this conceptualization, the inborn "discharge-limiting" structures would seem to "convert" libidinal energy into a structure that, in turn, prevents further libidinal discharge. But this conceptualization would suggest that there is in fact no qualitative difference between the primary autonomous structure and the acquired structure. That is to say, the acquired ego's function of delay would be viewed merely as a further elaboration of the "discharge-limiting" quality of *any* structure. Its ability to control the discharge of energy would merely be a consequence of the build-up of originally given structures, now with ever-increasing structural thresholds. The delaying, purposive character of the acquired ego's activity would thus be reduced to a form of activity of the inborn autonomous structures. (Indeed, Rapaport's [1951a] view that the structural characteristics of the inborn apparatuses set limits to discharge "even when the need-satisfying object *is present*" [p. 363; italics added] would imply that this acquisition is fundamentally independent of experience.) That this preformist solution to the problem of the development of acquired ego structures is essential to Rapaport's conceptualization of the process follows necessarily from White's analysis as stated above. That is to say, Rapaport's treatment of the primary autonomous structures can be seen as an attempt to avoid a conceptualization of change in which there is a magical discontinuous appearance of acquired ego structures from the mere fact of libidinal energy — or, to add yet another metaphor, a change in which water is transformed into sand. Thus the construct of the primary autonomous structures serves in Rapaport's conception to mediate between the prior event of libidinal energy pressing toward discharge and the subsequent event of an acquired ego structure. And yet, we have seen that this same construct, in so serving to connect these discontinuous events, is itself identical with the subsequent event of the acquired structures. In sum, Rapaport's model, like Freud's, accounts for the development of an attribute by assuming its prior existence in nascent form.[6]

Moreover, if we can say that the immutability of

---

[6] Rapaport's statement that the "developing ego then integrates these structural apparatuses and re-represents their discharge-limiting and -regulating function" (1951a, p. 363) only accentuates the problem. For by what means does the ego, defined solely in terms of its discharge-limiting precursors, acquire the ability to "integrate" and "re-represent?"

It should be noted, moreover, that Rapaport offered his paradigm as a way of resolving a fundamental question which he had posed in regard to the relationship between the conflict-free and the classical conflict conceptions of development:

> If the ego grows on conflict, how are we to conceive of the participants of this original conflict? Note the circularity: The ego is both born out of the conflict, and party to the conflict. How can we explain this seeming contradiction? [1951a, p. 361].

Thus it may be seen that the immutability-discontinuity problem encountered by Rapaport's paradigm is the very problem he intended his paradigm to solve.

Freud's view finds its counterpart in ego psychology's concept of primary autonomy and conflict-free development, so too can we say that the discontinuity of Freud's view finds its counterpart in ego psychology's concept of secondary autonomy and the neutralization of instinctual energy. It is clear, in this regard, that even though Hartmann views conflict as being neither a necessary nor sufficient determinant of development, his concept of secondary autonomy implies that conflict can serve as a determinant under certain conditions. It follows, then, that under these conditions, the primary autonomous structures must be viewed by Hartmann as being "inadequate" with respect to reducing instinctual tension in the long run. For if Hartmann were to assume that such adaptive precursors to delay were completely adequate to the task, then there would be no basis for the generation of conflict in the first place. But this raises a fundamental problem for the concept of secondary autonomy. To the extent that these prior structures are viewed as being inadequate to the task of securing long-term gratification, then they are functionally equivalent to the non-delaying id, regardless of how they might otherwise be characterized. In effect, the concept of secondary autonomy must nullify the primary autonomous structure as an adaptive precursor to delay. And since the primary autonomous structure is thereby being negated as a determinant of development — a determinant which Hartmann had added to Freud's conflict model in order to deal with the problem of discontinuity — the concept of secondary autonomy is open to Hartmann's own criticism that discontinuity is involved in deriving delay from the mere fact of frustration.[7]

---

[7] The problem would be the same were one to counter my criticism by suggesting that the conditions for development lie in the fact of frustration *plus* the primary autonomous structures: namely, that given a condition of conflict, the secondary autonomous structures develop from pri-

Finally, we should note that another analysis — that of Robert White (1963) — has also critically evaluated the notion of secondary autonomy and the related concept of neutralized energy. Although White's critique is governed by a perspective different from mine, the problems which he articulates in regard to Hartmann's views are strikingly similar to those we have focused on in the present inquiry. These problems are most clearly brought out in White's analysis of the notion that the energy used to power the secondary autonomous structures is derived from a reservoir of free libidinal energy that is detached from its original instinctual aims. White points out, in this regard, that this process of neutralization involves a temporal sequence of energy states that Freudian theory cannot connect in any reasonable or convincing way. Thus, he asks: If such libidinal energy is originally bound to organic structures and is initially pressing toward instinctual aims, how can one account for the drastic change that must take place if, as the concept of neutralization implies, the instinctual drives "release a part of their force from all connection with original aims?" (p. 170). Under such circumstances, White points out, the concept of neutralization "refers to what is, when we stop to think of it, a pretty drastic change in energy. The concept can hardly advance from being a magic word unless the conditions and processes of this change can be specified" (p. 170). And significantly, it is precisely when White examines the "conditions and processes" which Freudian theory *does* posit to account for neu-

---

mary autonomous structures. For now this conception would encounter the discontinuity of being unable to provide a convincing mechanism by which acquired secondary structures, adequate to the task of delay, are derived from primary autonomous structures which, by definition, are inadequate to the task of delay. Thus, the discontinuity encountered by this conception is the same as the discontinuity involved in Freud's view whereby purposive ego functioning is derived from the conflict engendered by blind id activity.

tralized libido that he is able to show the systematically linked problems of discontinuity and immutability that our own analysis has shown to be so characteristic of Freud's approach to development. Thus White suggests that the explanations advanced by both Freud and Rapaport magically bring structural characteristics into existence, while simultaneously involving the "chronological trap" (p. 171) of requiring the very existence of such structural characteristics as a precondition for their own emergence.[8]

THE CARTESIAN EPISTEMOLOGY UNDERLYING CONFLICT-FREE DEVELOPMENT

In accordance with our guiding thesis, the problems so encountered by ego psychology lend themselves to a particular interpretation: Even though ego psychology is proposing conflict-free development as an alternative to the discontinuity of the classical Freudian model, this alternative is itself being governed by the same Cartesian epistemology that led to this discontinuity in the first place; hence the forms of immutability and discontinuity that are evidenced in the conceptions advanced by this contemporary Freudian position. Unfortunately, however, when it comes to providing support for my interpretation, the proponents of ego psychology are not as obliging as Freud in elaborating upon their conceptions, particularly in regard to conflict-free development. It is difficult to provide direct evidence for their Cartesian presumptions, let alone evidence for the connection between this epistemology and the immutability-discontinuity problem. Of course, it can be reasoned that since ego psychology has, in part, accepted Freud's conflict approach to development, then to that extent this view also

---

[8] Specifically, White addresses himself to the processes posited in Freud's concept of identification and Rapaport's "sand bar" model of neutralization. I am not elaborating his critique here because it closely parallels my own analysis of these particular conceptions of development.

accepts the epistemology that governs Freud's conflict model. But this reasoning, whether justified or not, does not serve to further particularize my thesis with respect to the conflict-free aspects of this position.

There is, however, a source of support for so extending my thesis, unlikely though it may first appear. This support is provided by an alternative formulation regarding the root of the difficulties in Freudian theory—one that seemingly conflicts with my own. Suggested by a number of contemporary psychoanalytic theorists, and perhaps most systematically by White (1959, 1963), it holds that the formal difficulties encountered by both the classical and contemporary Freudian positions stem from the dichotomy between energy and structure that is inherent in Freud's assumption that instinctual energy is organized, directed, and discharged by psychic structure. Now, I think that there is much to be said for this alternative formulation, in particular, as it is advanced by White. First of all, the case for the existence of a fundamental dichotomy between energy and structure in Freudian theory is a compelling one, whether as presented by those who advance the thesis or as derived from my own analysis guided as it is by a different point of view. That is to say, while ego psychology's conception of conflict-free development may be vague and unelaborated with respect to its Cartesian presumptions, there is no doubt that this conception entails a dichotomy between energy and structure: The autonomous ego structures, however they are conceived as coming into being, are powered by a separate energy source and, in particular, by neutralized energy. Thus White's alternative formulation has the advantage over mine of applying directly to the conception of conflict-free development advanced by ego psychology. Second, we have seen that the systematic difficulties encountered by classical Freudian theory and contemporary ego psychology do, indeed, surface in a particularly clear way in association with energy and structure concepts. To mention but a few of the more striking examples, there are the contradictions raised by the intermingling of instinctual energies in Freud's view of the narcissistic disorders; there is the logical paradox involved in the energy transactions of the anxiety-defense paradigm; and there is the immutability encountered by Rapaport's "sand bar" metaphor of conflict-free development. Third, we will see that White (1963) does make a good case for a systematic connection between the energy-structure dichotomy and the immutability-discontinuity problem. However, the persuasiveness and direct applicability of this alternative formulation, rather than raising a problem for my own thesis, is all to the good. And this is so with particular regard to the problem of extending my thesis to ego psychology's conception of conflict-free development. For, in my view, the systematic connection between the energy-structure dichotomy and the immutability-discontinuity problem can be accounted for by a more fundamental Cartesian dichotomy between the subject and object of knowledge. If this is the case, then the more persuasive the alternative formulation, the stronger the support for my contention that ego psychology encounters the immutability-discontinuity problem in its conception of conflict-free development by virtue of its implicit acceptance of Freud's Cartesian assumptions. Thus, in extending my thesis to ego psychology, I am accepting the position that the difficulties which this contemporary Freudian viewpoint encounters are systematically connected to a dichotomy between energy and structure. And I am asserting that this connection, in turn, is derivable from a Cartesian epistemology that is basic to this viewpoint.

Three lines of argument can be presented in support of my assertion. While none of these taken separately is compelling, I believe that their conjunction is persuasive.[9] The

[9] The most persuasive argument, of course, would derive the energy-structure dichotomy directly from the Cartesian isolation between the sub-

first argument is that Freud, at times, viewed the relationship between energy and structure as equivalent to the relationship between id and ego. At various points in his exposition (notably in his characterization of the id as a "chaos
of seething excitations," and his portrayal of the ego's relation to the id as one of a rider to his horse), Freud pictured
the ego as a powerless structure giving form to, and being
powered by, the id as pure but formless energy. To the
extent that the energy-structure dichotomy and the id-ego
dichotomy are so equivalent in Freud's thinking, then one
can, in accordance with my earlier analysis, derive the
separate dimensions of energy and structure from Freud's
Cartesian definition of the subject-object relationship. From
this viewpoint, the inchoate, power-giving dimension of
energy would be inherent in the original core of a distorting
subject, while the organizing structural dimension would be
acquired from an independently constituted world of primary structural properties. Under such circumstances, it
would follow that the argument I have advanced for the
id-ego relationship could also be advanced for the energy-
structure dichotomy. Namely, that the discontinuity involved in the various "intrapsychic" transactions between
energy and structure (in particular, those posited in the
process of neutralization) merely represents a "displacement" of the more fundamental paradox inherent in the
original Cartesian dichotomy between subject and object.
And, indeed, one might be tempted to exploit this argument
by citing instances in which the energy and structure dimensions are apparently being connected by "identity solutions"
that parallel those advanced by Freud in connecting id and
ego functioning—Rapaport's conception of conflict-free

ject and the independently constituted event. Freud, however, did not
describe his theory in terms that permit such a derivation. Hence my
alternative strategy, which is reconstructive and inferential.

development, for example, as discussed above. This argument, however, is inadequate when taken by itself. Clearly, Freud portrayed the id as more than just a series of chaotic energy displacements, and he portrayed the ego as more than just pure structure. As both White (1963) and Holt (1967) have pointed out, and as my own analysis indicates, Freud more often than not explicitly conceived of the id as having the characteristics of instinctual organization in addition to libidinal energetics. And, as the analysis of the anxiety-defense paradigm has stressed, Freud conceived of the ego as mirroring an external other who embodied more than impersonal structural properties. The ego mirrored an other who displayed the purposive qualities of goals, anticipations, and intentions. Accordingly, this argument, taken by itself, distorts Freud's position by oversimplifying it.

The second line of evidence is based on White's critique of Freudian theory. I will argue that when White is able to show that the energy-structure dichotomy is at the root of the systematic difficulties in Freudian theory, it is precisely at these times that this dichotomy can be reinterpreted as an isolation between hydraulic and purposive modes of functioning. Specifically, I am asserting that Freud's concept of neutralization involves a state of instinctually bound libido followed by a state of free desexualized libido, and that this sequence can be reinterpreted as one in which hydraulic functioning is followed by purposive activity. If this can be shown, then it would follow from my thesis that the systematic difficulties noted by White can also be derived from the paradox of connecting modes of hydraulic and purposive functioning that are inherently unconnectable. And this, in turn, can be understood in terms of the Cartesian epistemology that is fundamental to this paradox. The next section, accordingly, is devoted to this reinterpretation of White's thesis as exemplified in his analysis of neutralization.[10]

[10] The Freudian dichotomy between energy and structure exemplifies

WHITE'S THESIS REINTERPRETED

In arguing that the problems of immutability and discontinuity stem from the energy-structure dichotomy, White notes first of all that this dichotomy is represented by Freud's view that libidinal energy functions independently of neural structure and serves to electrify otherwise dead neural connections. He points out, however, that such a view is fundamentally incompatible with our current knowledge of brain functioning. The research of contemporary neurophysiology has resulted in a conception of the nervous system in which energy is *intrinsic* to a given structure. It is a conception, as White (1963) states, in which "the 'apparatus' is alive . . . composed of living cells rather than inert wires, [which] contain the energy that makes the system operate" (p. 178). In the light of this contemporary conception, White asserts, the energy changes that Freudian theory posits in the neutralization process are absurd. The energy intrinsic to the organic structures which make up the primitive instinctual pattern cannot be "plucked out" (p. 179) of these structures as a disembodied force, only to be further deposited in the autonomous ego structures. These transformations, White states, are "simply not possible in the system as we have come to know it" (p. 179).

Moreover, White notes, these transformations are impossible not only in terms of our current view of nervous-system functioning. They are also metaphorically absurd. They cannot be represented by Freud's own hydraulic metaphor — that is, the hydraulic model that Freud uses to portray the nature of libidinal transformations in general. The

---

the "machine theory" of functioning as this has been characterized by Köhler (1947). Accordingly, a significant similarity exists between White's critique of Freudian theory and Asch's analysis of instinct theory and behaviorism, based as it is on Köhler's Gestalt formulations (see Chapter 2, footnote 7).

point is well made in the following:

> The absurdities arise largely from the use of an unfortunate metaphor, that of a flowing liquid. It was Freud who introduced the hydraulic analogy, and it continues in Rapaport's references to flowing streams and Hartmann's image of a reservoir. If we were dealing with one energy, one water that tends to flow downhill, the trouble would be less, but when we start with two streams representing different *kinds* of energy—a distinction "which presupposes physiological processes running in opposite directions" (Freud, 1923, p. 43)— when we let them flow together and become one kind in a reservoir of neutralized energy, and when we add the proviso that they can flow out again and resume their original characters, our imagery begins to dance like that of a delirium. Once the waters of the White Nile and the Blue Nile have joined in a common stream, is there any way to draw them out and conduct them back to their original beds, taking care that no blue is sent back to the white or white to the blue...? [p. 176].[11]

It will be argued here that when White notes that the different energy states in the neutralization process are discontinuous with respect to one another, and when he derives this discontinuity from Freud's separation of energy and structure (see pp. 220-221 above), one can also derive this discontinuity from an isolation between hydraulic and purposive modes of functioning. My argument exploits White's contention that the energy transformations involved in neutralization are absurd with respect to Freud's hydrau-

---

[11] In the "two streams representing different kinds of energy," White is referring to the energies of the sexual and aggressive instincts. As may be seen by White's comments, a consideration of the aggressive instinct would serve to compound Freud's problems. However, it is not necessary that I include this concept in my analysis in order to reinterpret White's argument in accordance with my thesis.

lic model. I am suggesting that these energy transformations are absurd because the hydraulic model is being implicitly tailored to conform to the requirements of purposive activity, and that, given Freud's Cartesian assumptions, this is impossible to do without encountering the immutability-discontinuity problem.

In support of this argument, we have noted that Freud's dichotomy between energy and structure implies that he is viewing these dimensions as separate or independent realms of being, each possessing qualities that the other realm lacks, and each impressing these qualities upon the other. Moreover, we have seen that throughout the various versions of his theory, Freud represented this separation between energy and structure as a hydraulic metaphor. Energy was viewed as having formless fluid properties which activated an otherwise inert structure, was discharged via this structure, and took the form of its vehicle. In particular, our analysis stressed the fact that in so representing this dichotomy between energy and structure, the hydraulic model served as the basis for Freud's conception of primitive, instinct-dominated behavior. Indeed, it is for this reason that I designated such behavior as "hydraulic." The blind ebb and flow of energy along the interconnected channels represented the highly charged rhythms of primitive behavior — the tumescence and detumescence of instinctual activity. Equally important, the separation between energy and structure given in the hydraulic metaphor enabled Freud to represent a concept that was central to his interpretation of the symptom, namely, that the structures of the component sexual instincts served as equivalent modes of libidinal discharge.

It should be noted, however, that when the energy-structure dichotomy is so represented in hydraulic terms, the properties that are ascribed respectively to energy and structure are independent of one another only in a *limited,* concrete sense. These dimensions are independent of one another only in the sense that a river, in overflowing its banks, is no longer dependent upon its prior structure—the river is no longer being contained and given form by the banks along which it had previously flowed. In a more *general* or formal sense, however, the dimensions of energy and structure are inextricably intertwined. They presuppose one another. By this I mean that the river's overflow has merely taken a different form—one that is successively imposed on it, first, by the structural characteristics of the river bank over which the water escapes, and then by the structural constraints of the surrounding terrain. By the same token, in being displaced from one "channel" to another, libidinal energy may thereby be independent of the prior mode of discharge, but such energy is necessarily tied to another instinctual structure that now serves as the equivalent mode of discharge. Necessarily implied, as well, are the concrete structural arrangements along which libidinal energy flows from one discharge mode to another. Thus it can be said that when the energy-structure dichotomy is understood in terms of the hydraulic model, certain constraints are imposed on these concepts by virtue of the systematic requirements of the model. When libido is interpreted as a flowing, displaceable liquid that activates structure, then this conception must imply the concrete and immediate presence of some kind of structure as a passive vehicle which gives form to such flowing energy. To otherwise characterize the relationship between libidinal energy and psychic structure would not fulfill the systematic requirements of the hydraulic model. Put more specifically: To characterize libidinal energy as being completely free of *any* structural constraint (or to omit consideration of such constraint) would contradict the properties of fluidity and displaceability that have been attributed to libido in terms of the hydraulic metaphor.[12]

[12] Holt (1967) advances the same argument when he states that, given

It is clear, then, that when White characterizes the organization of libido as a "distinctively bound instinctual force" (p. 177), he is referring to primitive functioning as understood in terms of the energy-structure dichotomy, and as concretely represented by the hydraulic metaphor. Now, one could conceivably argue that under these conditions the systematic requirements of the metaphor are being met — namely, that when primitive functioning is thus represented by the hydraulic metaphor, we have the concrete presence of passive structure which gives form to flowing libido. However, regardless of the position one takes on this issue, the same cannot be said with respect to neutralized energy. As White's analysis suggests, neutralized energy is a formless reservoir of force, a disembodied free agent completely independent of any structural constraint, to be used when and where necessary as a source of power for the secondary autonomous structures. And yet, this liberation notwithstanding, neutralized energy is still being defined in terms of the hydraulic model. In the free as well as the bound states, libido is characterized as a fluid energy which has the properties of displaceability, of activating otherwise inert structure, and of being organized by such structure. We can say, then, that when Freud characterizes neutralized libido as being free of any structural constraints, he is characterizing libido in a way that is inconsistent with its hydraulic properties — properties which, I have suggested, systematically require the immediate presence of some kind of organizing structure. By that token, when White states that the libidi-

---

the physicalistic model upon which Freud bases his metapsychology, one cannot conceive of function without structure, of energy without form. If Freud's metapsychology is to be consistently interpreted, Holt suggests, even the concept of the id as a seething cauldron of chaotic energy displacements requires, however implicitly, that one assume structural arrangements along which such energy is displaced. See also Chapter 3, footnote 19.

nal transformations given in the neutralization process are "simply not possible in the system as we have come to know it," his assessment applies equally well to *two* systems. Such transformations are impossible not only in the system of intrinsically energized structures that has been suggested by the findings of contemporary neurophysiology. They are impossible, as well, for the waters of the White and Blue Nile. The transformation of libido from bound energy to a disembodied force is absurd because it violates the requirements of a hydraulic model of explanation. More particularly, in pointing to the "drastic" magical changes from an instinctual state of bound energy to the non-instinctual state of free energy, White is necessarily referring to a transformation that makes no sense in regard to such properties as the fluid displaceability of libidinal energy—properties that have been assigned to libido in terms of the hydraulic model.

But, then, one can raise the question: If the "structureless" quality of energy is absurd in terms of a hydraulic system, is there any system within which it *does* make sense? My argument would have it that the disembodied quality of free energy makes sense—but only in terms of a purposive model of explanation. We have seen, in this regard, how neutralized energy meets the requirements of mature purposive functioning as distinguished from primitive activity. Desexualized energy serves as the power source for sustained, modulated functioning whereby the individual puts aside his immediate wants and pleasures and engages in a variety of different "means" behaviors directed toward long-range goals. The image of the reservoir, with its back-up supply of free energy, no longer evidencing the ebb and flow of instinctual libido, and on tap for a variety of different occasions, clearly corresponds to this behavioral quality of mature, sustained effort. I would attribute a particular significance to the fact that certain properties of neutralized libido are congruent with the hydraulic model, while other properties of neutralized libido, which are incompatible with this model, are congruent with the properties of mature, purposive functioning. I would suggest that Freud, rather than adhering to the systematic implications of the hydraulic model, used it opportunistically. Rather than always translating his observations of behavior in accordance with the requirements of the model, he "stretched" the model—implicitly tailored it—to fit behaviors he understood as being purposively directed.[13] In order, then, to represent the sustained energy requirements of long-term purposive behavior, Freud derived "free" energy by exploiting the *limited* independence of energy and structure that is implied in the hydraulic model. But, in so representing this property of energy, Freud had to negate the more *general* implication of the relationship between energy and structure as represented by this same hydraulic model. He was forced to disregard the systematic requirement that energy, when viewed as having such hydraulic qualities as fluid displaceability, can never be free of some structural constraint.

We can thus agree with White's analysis as far as it goes: Because of the way in which Freud dichotomized

[13] I am not alone in this assessment of Freud's use of the energy-structure dichotomy. White (1963) has criticized Freud's "abiding uncertainty" in his treatment of libido, and noted that Freud gave libido the attributes of either bound or free energy "as occasion demanded" (p. 177). In a more positive vein, Holt (1967) has suggested that three dimensions of the energy concept, i.e., "inhibited" versus "uninhibited," "free" versus "bound," and "not neutralized" versus "neutralized," allow the theory to "more closely approximate the great variety of empirically observable cognitions" (p. 347).

Thee is some evidence that Freud was aware of the difficulties involved in his use of the hydraulic metaphor. It will be recalled that in characterizing libidinal energy as being both displaceable as well as hierarchically organized, Freud (1917b) implied that these dual properties could not be adequately represented by the hydraulic metaphor—they could not, in effect, be "easily combined in a single picture" (p. 345).

energy and structure in his concept of neutralization, we are left with a metaphorical absurdity. But our analysis goes further in suggesting that the connection between this absurdity and the energy-structure dichotomy can be attributed to a more basic source. I have argued that the hydraulic and purposive modes of functioning are isolated from one another by virtue of representing a displacement of a Cartesian epistemology to the intrapsychic realm. If this is true, then no amount of cutting and fitting can make the hydraulic model an appropriate metaphor for the purposive event. On the contrary, stretching the hydraulic metaphor to fit purposive activity can only result in yet a further transposition of the Cartesian isolation between the subject and object: The lack of fit between the hydraulic model and the purposive event can only be transposed to a discordance within the frame of the hydraulic metaphor itself. It can be suggested, therefore, that Freud was stretching the hydraulic model to conform to an event in relation to which the model was fundamentally incompatible. And this was the reason why Freud was forced to depart from the systematic requirements of the model—the reason why he posited an energy state the structureless quality of which contradicted its fluid displaceability. My reinterpretation of White's critique therefore can be summed up in the following way: When White refers to the discontinuity between the energy states involved in neutralization, he is pointing to a transformation that is impossible from the vantage point of the hydraulic model. In doing so, he makes the case that this metaphorical absurdity is due to Freud's separation of energy and structure. And yet, there is a more basic reason for this absurdity: namely, that Freud exploited the energy-structure dichotomy to the end of tailoring the hydraulic model to fit purposive behavior. Given Freud's Cartesian presumptions, however, this could only result in a mixed metaphor—in an admixture of activities that is impossible within a hydraulic system. Accordingly, while it can be said that the magical discontinuity that White ascribes to the transformation of bound to free energy is a function of the energy-structure dichotomy, this discontinuity more fundamentally reflects an isolation between successive states of hydraulic and purposive behavior. And this isolation, in turn, derives from the fact that such behaviors have been defined in terms of a Cartesian epistemology.[14]

The third line of evidence for the priority of Freud's Cartesian epistemology over his energy-structure dichotomy comes from a critique of White's own conflict-free alternative to the Freudian conception of development. In this alternative, White explicitly rejects the energy-structure dichotomy in favor of the notion that energy is intrinsic to adaptive structures—that it cannot be separated from such structures. It can be argued, however, that instead of similarly rejecting Freud's Cartesian view, White implicitly perpetuates this epistemology as the basis for his concept of intrinsically energized adaptive structures. If, then, White's conflict-free alternative encounters the immutability-discontinuity problem in the same form as the Freudian conception, we can infer that this problem is due to the epistemology that he is implicitly assuming, rather than the energy-structure dichotomy that he is explicitly rejecting. This

---

[14] I have previously noted that the hydraulic model, in serving as a metaphor for the metapsychological constructs of energy and structure, represents Freud's view of the causal-deterministic mode of functioning. Thus, libidinal energy is viewed as providing the immediate, prior cause of function by virtue of activating otherwise inert structure and thereby taking the form of this now activated vehicle. As so understood, energy, even in its neutralized state, is the immediate cause of the activation of the secondary autonomous structures. Accordingly, it may be seen that the metaphorical inconsistency of characterizing neutralized energy as having the property of fluid displaceability, while yet being "structureless," is reflected in the formal inconsistency of Freud's admixture of hydraulics (the activation of the secondary autonomous structures by neutralized energy) and purpose (the means-end functioning of such autonomous structures when so hydraulically activated).

demonstration, moreover, would have all the more force for my thesis if White's approach represents, as I believe it does, one of the more persuasive and systematic of the contemporary conflict-free conceptions of development.

CONFLICT-FREE DEVELOPMENT FROM WHITE'S VIEWPOINT

We have seen that Hartmann proposed the primary autonomous, or conflict-free, structures as a correction for the discontinuity of Freud's conflict model, only to face, in turn, White's criticism regarding the discontinuity in the various accounts of the development of these structures and, in particular, the discontinuity involved in powering these developed structures with neutralized energy. It may now be seen that just as Hartmann's criticism of the conflict model served as the basis for contemporary ego psychology's alternative account of development, so too does White's criticism of neutralization serve as a basis for his own conflict-free approach to development — one that is founded upon the conception that neutral energy is intrinsic to adaptive structures. Now it is true, of course, that White's alternative is based on more than a formal analysis of Freudian theory. His argument makes significant use, for example, of current research findings in neurophysiology, learning theory, and child development. Thus he argues that since such research has pushed back the presence of nonsexual, intrinsically energized adaptive activity to progressively earlier periods of functioning, the energy transformations posited in neutralization turn out to be redundant: Neutralization of erotic energy is being posited to account for a form of energy that is already present at the very beginnings of life. At the same time, however, it is obvious that White's formal analysis of the systematic problems involved in the neutralization concept is intended to clear the way for a more coherent conceptualization of development. After having noted the discontinuity of neutralization, White (1963) raises this question:

> ... is it more valuable to assume that neutral energies are there from the start, as part of the natural endowment of the living being, or is it more valuable to assume that only the two classes of instinctual energy are there from the start, and that they can be transformed later into neutral energies? [p. 166].

And he provides this answer:

> ... my main hypothesis equips the infant from the start with a kind of energy and with a kind of structure that dispose him to construct a stable, objective, real world [p. 60].

The fundamental tenet of White's alternative, then, is that the autonomous structures posited by ego psychology are intrinsically powered by neutral energy from the very outset, rather than being powered by a separate instinctually derived libido. Even in primitive functioning, White suggests, such energy is neutral to begin with, rather than being initially libidinal and then becoming neutral in the discontinuous way posited by Freud and accepted by Hartmann. It may be seen, however, that just as White is able to point to the immutability-discontinuity problem in Hartmann's conflict-free alternative to the classical Freudian model of development, so too can one point to this same problem in White's alternative. And for the same reason — namely, that in the final analysis, his conception accepts Freud's Cartesian epistemology.

My argument for this assertion is based, in part, on the way in which White exploits the immutability-discontinuity problem in Freudian theory in order to make the case for his own position regarding prior intrinsically energized structures. This strategy can be seen clearly in his analysis of introjective identification as a process of development. It will be recalled that the process of introjection involved the child's acquiring attributes which he lacked, such as integration and control, from the mother who possessed these qualities in independently constituted form. White pointed out, however, that when Freudian theorists interpreted the child's development in terms of this process, their conception necessarily implied that the subject had these qualities in the first place. Namely, it followed from the "hypothesized introjection of the whole person" that the child "already possessed the capacity which the act of introjection was supposed to confer on him" (p. 105). And it was precisely at this point in his exposition that White advanced the basic line of his own alternative: One would get a less "jumbled" sequence of events, he stated, if the child were characterized as discovering "the boundaries of and relations among things" (p. 105) by virtue of actively manipulating his world — an activity that, as we will see in White's alternative, is mediated by already given adaptive structures.

Now there is no question but that there are significant points of correspondence between this analysis and my own critique. It should be emphasized, however, that White was not suggesting here — as I have — that the problem encountered by introjection is indicative of an unsolvable dilemma stemming from a Cartesian definition of the subject-object relationship. White was not arguing, in other words, that the Freudian conception of introjection, by virtue of presuming this subject-object relationship, necessarily serves to collapse the temporal events of development such that the subsequent event coexists with the prior event. Rather, White reverses the very temporal sequence posited by Freud in order to support his own alternative that the child comes to the conflict situation with *already formed* adaptive structures. White's strategy, then, is to derive from Freud's definition of the subject-object relationship an implication that can be used as positive evidence for his own alternative. But if this is the case, then it follows that White is also accepting as valid the presumption that serves logically to generate this implication. For it is precisely by virtue of the Cartesian definition of the subject-object relationship that White is *able* to reverse the sequence of events in the Freudian conception of introjection in favor of his own alternative; just as it is precisely by virtue of my *rejection* of that definition of the subject-object relationship—or, more precisely, my acceptance of the constructionist presumption in terms of which I critically evaluate this subject-object relationship— that I am able to derive the implication essential to my own project: that the Freudian conception of introjection serves to connect a sequence of temporal events in terms of an identity relationship, and thereby collapses this sequence as a form of immutability and discontinuity.

If my analysis is correct, White does not reject the Cartesian view in rejecting Freud's dichotomy between energy and structure, but—as my position would have it—merely rejects a derivative of this view. Accordingly, we should expect White to encounter the immutability-discontinuity problem in the same form as that evidenced in classical and contemporary Freudian theory. That this is indeed the case is indicated by the problem of immutability and discontinuity encountered by White's alternative to the Freudian conception. White provides the context for this alternative by first considering the process of imitation in general, thereby noting the importance of understanding this process in terms of what the child brings to the external situation:

> Imitation, then, even in its simplest forms cannot be conceived of as an abrupt act of copying another's behavior. Imitation can occur only in an organism that has already elaborated a sufficient matrix of actions so that it can produce something resembling the act to be

copied. The child can imitate when he is, so to speak, already almost there, when manageable variations of his existing repertory will produce behavior similar to the model [p. 111].

He then extends these considerations to the concept of identification as a process of development or, if you will, to the imitation of important interpersonal others:

> Our definition implies that identifications will not occur until a certain level of ego development has been reached. This is consistent with deriving identification from imitation, in which the imitated acts must be already approximately formed in the child's repertory [pp. 112–113].

He then concludes:

> The child, in short, reaches a point in his repertory of behavior and comprehension which permits him to act a little like an adult, and he then begins to use identification as a means of becoming more like one [p. 114].

Clearly, were the notion of prior structures to constitute White's sole conception of imitative identification, then his formulation would encounter an obvious problem: White would find himself perpetually frozen into assuming explicitly what Freud had assumed implicitly. His conception of development would gratuitously give to the organism attributes that continuously preshadow the characteristics evidenced by the external world. But I would be doing a disservice to his thinking were I to suggest that such a simplistic preformist solution constitutes the sum and substance of White's approach to the problem of development. It is clear that White does not view these prior structures as fully formed, as merely duplicating the external event. These structures, rather, *approximate* the event, hence the terms "almost there," "approximately formed," and "a little like an adult." The question one must ask, then, is: How does White conceive of the process whereby the child moves from being a little like an adult to being more like one? And, in this regard, it can be said that White advances two quite different and, in my view, unconnected conceptions of this process.[15] One is his notion of change as a function of action and its consequences. In this conception of change, White evokes an image of the organism that is in sharp contrast to that of Freud's theory. Instead of the inadequate, passive subject at the mercy of a contingent world, White portrays a competent organism that actively manipulates a responsive reality in accordance with its approximate, intrinsically energized structures and thereby discovers the differential consequences of its actions. In order to dramatize how his conception differs from the classical Freudian approach to change, White (1963) recasts into his own formulation of action and its consequences Freud's account of the development of the reality principle:

> Frustrated need constitutes a call to action; more specifically, to restless action beyond the preparation and performance of consummatory responses. In the young infant this action may consist of little more than squirming, thrashing, and emitting cries, but the cries at least are likely to have a decided effect on a properly tuned environment. If the cries are soon answered in a way that brings gratification, a basis is laid for the future anticipation that will make it possible to tolerate delay. What the child learns is what he can expect to happen as a consequence of his cries [p. 46].

[15] Note that White does not distinguish between these conceptions as separate processes, nor does he designate them by the terms I will be using — namely, that of "competence-action" and "imaginative synthesis." I am so representing White's view of development, first, because I believe that these processes *can* be distinguished in his presentation and, second, in order to provide a context for the related concepts of "consolidation" and "developmental reorganization" which I will be advancing in the constructionist alternative outlined in the last chapter.

White goes on to stress that acquiring a knowledge of the world is equivalent to the "knowledge of the effects that can be produced by action" (p. 47). More particularly, the child comes to know about the world by testing "the feedback from his repertory of acts" (p. 61). It is this "competence-action" approach to development that he presents as a specific alternative to Freud's problematic concept of introjection. Instead of a sequence in which the mature attribute of synthesis is acquired as a consequence of introjecting an integrated mother figure, White suggests that

We get a less jumbled sequence of events if we suppose that the infant, through active exploration and manipulation, and with the probable assistance of maturation, discovers progressively the boundaries of and relations among things [p. 105].

White is thus proposing that the infant, by acting on a "properly tuned" world in terms of intrinsically energized approximate structures, literally changes the properties of this world and acquires, via feedback, a knowledge of the relationship between his action and its consequences. The knowledge of the relationship between frustration, cry, and gratification, or, more generally, the knowledge of his own activity as related to changes in external reality, is the "basis" for the movement to a relatively mature form of functioning, namely, the "future anticipation that will make it possible to tolerate delay." The clear implication, then, is that the knowledge of such relationships, when added to the prior approximate structures that are "almost there," enables the subject to move from being a little like an adult to being more like one.

Now it might appear that this view of the relationship between a competent organism and a properly tuned reality provides a clear alternative to Freud's assumption of an inadequate organism and a reality over which the organism has no control. As I see it, however, this recasting of the subject-object relationship is based on the same epistemological assumption as Freud's. White's view of development continues to be predicated on a relationship between the subject and object in which the subject lacks "something" which is contained in the external world in independently constituted form. But now this "something" is not an essential property of the external other such as integration or purpose. Rather, the subject lacks the knowledge of the changes in external reality that can be brought about by his activity. And just as development for Freud is the subject's acquisition of such external properties as integration and purpose, so is development for White the subject's acquired knowledge of this relationship between his actions and their consequences. In sum, instead of assuming the primary qualities of an independently constituted reality, White's conception of development assumes that the child's actions have consequences in a properly tuned world, and that these actions *as so connected* to these consequences are independently constituted; independently constituted in the sense that the relationship of the child's actions to the consequences of those actions cannot be known by the subject in terms of his available cognitive structures. Rather, this relationship can only be known by means of structures which the child acquires by virtue of his transaction with the properly tuned world and which mirror this very transaction.

If this is so, if White's conception of development is predicated on the fact that the subject has yet to know this independently constituted relationship between his actions and their consequences — if his conception, in other words, presumes that the subject lacks something that he acquires in kind from an external reality — then it can be said that his conception imports developmental change from the same foreign soil as does Freud's and should therefore encounter the problem of knowledge that we have seen to be intrinsic to Freud's theory.[16] In this regard, the question can be raised: Given that in White's conception the subject's prior approximate structures enable him to act on reality and to bring about changes in this reality, how does he *acquire* the further knowledge of the independently constituted event that he has brought about, namely, his actions as related to their consequences? To paraphrase White, this problem cannot be "conjured away" by saying that the child tests the feedback from his action on the object. For then the problem merely shifts to one of understanding how such feedback is known. And here White's own critique of Freud's theory can only consign the subject to a magic circle of knowing those relationships between his actions and their consequences that he is capable of knowing in the first place. For it follows from White's own critique that if the subject can profit from such feedback, then he must already possess those structures that enable him to distinguish this feedback from other stimuli — from the kitchen sink, as it were. In addition to the approximate structures that he has explicitly assumed, White would thus be assuming implicitly these additional structures as well.[17] Accordingly, not only would White face the net result of a full-blown problem of preformist immutability, but this implicit assumption would negate the very presumption upon which his conception of development is based, namely, that the subject lacks the knowledge of the connection between his actions and their consequences.

White's conception thus faces the same unsolvable dilemma that he has posed for Freud. This conception, in presuming a subject who lacks an attribute that exists in

[16] Kelly (1955) has similarly characterized the contemporary scientific outlook in his tongue-in-cheek description of the "kick the bottle" fallacy.

[17] If it were to be replied that these additional structures *are* the prior structures, then, clearly, development could not be said to occur — the child would already "be there."

external, independently constituted form, is so defining the subject that he can never know this attribute. And this is the case even if one were to extrapolate White's conception of approximate structures to make them increasingly more and more like the external event, and were thus progressively to narrow the gap between the subject and object to an infinitesimal degree. Developmental change would still be seen as the subject's lacking something, however minute, which he acquires in kind from an independently constituted reality. Accordingly, the essential isolation between the subject and object would remain in that the subject would continue to lack the structures needed in order to acquire that extra something, however small, from the object. White's formulation, as so extrapolated, would merely condemn his subject to the fate of an Achilles who, with each successive action, halves the distance to a goal that continues to remain perversely just out of reach. It can be said, therefore, that White's formulation faces the same immutability-discontinuity problem as does Freudian theory, and for the same reason: By virtue of his Cartesian presumption, he has been able to distinguish between primitive and mature functioning when, by virtue of this same presumption, he is unable to posit a convincing construct which can serve to connect these sequential events.

The second process of developmental change evidenced in White's alternative differs significantly from his first. This is his view that identification serves as "an imaginative short cut to the mastery of complex adult patterns of behavior" (p. 114). It will be seen that White is implying here that developmental change is a function of a cognitive reorganization — a restructuring in terms of imaginative activity whereby less mature behaviors are integrated into mature "patterns as wholes." In this respect as well, White takes pains to distinguish his view from Freud's classical account of identification. He does this, in part, by pointing out that there has been an implicit distinction in the literature that parallels his own distinction between what we can term "imaginative synthesis" and Freud's conflict conception of development. Thus, he refers to an analysis presented by Sanford (1955) which suggests that the term "identification" has been used to cover two very different processes. Citing the therapy relation as a case in point, Sanford notes that when one says that the patient has "identified" with the therapist, one is usually referring to behavior of the patient that is an exaggerated, "slavish" imitation of a superficial, isolated attribute of the therapist, such as his manner of speaking or mode of dressing. This activity, Sanford maintains, can be readily interpreted in terms of Freud's conflict conception of the identification process. It can be seen as a "taking on" of the attributes of the other in order to maintain a minimal tension state of instinctual need or anxiety. It is a process

> ... unconscious and unrealistic, with a patient who is unsure of himself and, at the moment at least, unconcerned about other people; in desperation he adopts a piece of poor economy as a means of escape from a critical situation [Sanford, p. 108].

However, Sanford continues, when one says that the therapist has "identified" with the patient, one is usually referring to behavior of a qualitatively different order — behavior that simply does not lend itself well to the classical Freudian interpretation. The therapist is not primarily concerned with himself but is freely empathizing with the characteristics and feelings of the patient. In contrast to the desperation and instability of the patient, the therapist is "conflict-free," that is, free of anxiety and of primitive sexual need. It is a therapist, moreover, who enters into the world of the patient and yet is not overwhelmed by the experience; who retains all the while a sense of who and what he is. Accordingly, this kind of identification refers to behavior that is governed by an integration of the experience of the other with a solid sense of one's own identity. Clearly, this organization should be distinguished, Sanford emphasizes, from the inner emptiness evidenced in the patient's narrow caricature of the other. As he notes, "it is stretching the term identification too much to apply it both to what happens in the therapist—when he is functioning well—and to what happens in the patient" (p. 108).

White further underscores the difference between imaginative synthesis and classical identification by noting the similarity between his view and Erikson's concept of synthesis. To this end, he quotes Erikson's (1959) statement:

> ... none of the identifications of childhood (which in our patients stand out in such morbid elaboration and mutual contradiction) could, if merely added up, result in a functioning personality.... The fact is that identification as a mechanism is of limited usefulness. Children, at different stages of their development, identify with those *part aspects* of people by which they themselves are most immediately affected.... Their identifications with parents, for example, center in certain overvalued and ill-understood body parts, capacities, and role appearances.... The final identity, then, as fixed at the end of adolescence is superordinated to any single identification with individuals of the past: it includes all significant identifications, but it also alters them in order to make a unique and a reasonably coherent whole of them [1959, pp. 112–113].

White, then, distinguishes between the Freudian view of identification and his own concept of imaginative synthesis by suggesting that they serve to denote significantly different processes—processes that occur under different conditions and that lead to essentially different forms of personality organization. In Freud's view of identification, the acquisition of the other's characteristics takes place under conditions of conflict and serves to maintain a minimal level of tension. As our analysis has indicated, this acquisition implies the perpetuation of prior, fully formed structures which provide the basis for a rote imitation of the external other and which, in so doing, result in an isolated juxtaposition of unstable, contradictory elements. In White's concept of imaginative restructuring, change takes place under conflict-free conditions. This change involves an active, internal synthesis on the part of the knower of patterns as wholes—a reorganization which, in Erikson's terms, is an integration of more primitive "part" identifications into a stable, coherent sense of identity. Now, if these two forms of change are so different—if White's concept of imaginative synthesis differs so radically from the Cartesian view of development represented by the Freudian concept of identification—then what is my justification for saying that White's approach to development offers no fundamental alternative to the Cartesian view? My assertion is based, in part, on the fact that the concept of imaginative synthesis receives relatively little emphasis in White's exposition and, as such, apparently has little significance in regard to his overall approach. The more significant reason for my assertion is that an examination of White's position will reveal that he offers no theoretical constructs that can serve to connect the concept of imaginative synthesis with the concept of competence-action. And this is the case even though he posits that both forms of change are produced by the same activity of knowing, namely, the activity of approximate, intrinsically energized structures. Indeed, in the light of my analysis, one is justified in asking whether such a connection is possible in White's formulation. For, if my argument regarding White's Cartesian epistemology is valid, then this would imply that these forms of change are derived from isolated, mutually alien realms of subjective and objective being. That is to say, White, on the one hand, views the form of change we have termed "imaginative synthesis" as an "imaginative short cut" to the mastery of adult behavior patterns, and as a cognitive reorganization or "imaginative restructuring"—that is, as a form of change that results solely from knowing activity itself. And, on the other hand, White views the form of change we have termed "competence-action" as a "knowledge of the effects that can be produced by action"—by testing "the feedback from one's repertory of acts" on a responsive reality. The concepts of imaginative synthesis and competence-action, then, refer to forms of change which are based, respectively, on the subject's knowing activity and the effects of this knowing activity on the object. But, as I have argued, White's Cartesian epistemology necessarily isolates the subject's knowing activity from the changes in the object that result from such knowing activity.[18] Accordingly, even though White may posit that the same activity of knowing can lead to these two forms of change, his epistemology consigns the consequences of such knowing activity to mutually exclusive realms of being and, hence, serves to isolate irrevocably the two forms of change from each other. We can conclude, therefore, that White's notion of imaginative synthesis is, of necessity, an isolated one in his position on development and hence cannot affect the nature of the immutability-discontinuity problem encountered by his conception of action and its consequences.[19]

In sum, it can be said that in his conception of develop-

[18] My point is similar to that made by Piaget (1952) in his analysis of the empiricist hypothesis of trials and errors:

... instead of acknowledging, as we shall do, an indissoluble relation between subject and object, the hypothesis of trials and errors makes distinction between two terms: the production of trials which are due to the subject since they are fortuitous in relation to the object, and their selection, due to the object alone [p. 395].

[19] It could conceivably be argued that the attribute of synthesis—the

ment, White's implicit acceptance of a Cartesian epistemology leads him to the same form of the immutability-discontinuity problem as that encountered by classical Freudian theory and ego psychology. And this, in spite of his clear rejection of Freud's energy-structure dichotomy. This conclusion, in conjunction with my first two arguments, permits me to say that the Freudian dichotomy between the subject and object is the more fundamental determinant of the immutability-discontinuity problem encountered by psychoanalytic theory. It follows, then, that when ego psychology's conception of conflict-free development encounters the immutability-discontinuity problem, and when this is linked to the energy-structure dichotomy, this connection can, in turn, be ascribed to the Cartesian assumptions of the theory.[20]

THE MINIMAL TENSION PRINCIPLE: AN INCLUSIVE CONSTRUCT?

The analysis of White's alternative essentially completes my critique of the Freudian position. One final issue,

---

integration of patterns as wholes—results from the child's discovery, by virtue of competence-action, of "the boundaries of and relations among things" (p. 105), and that the concepts of imaginative synthesis and competence-action are thereby connected. If, however, such a connection is implied in White's approach, it is clearly not explicated. Moreover, the case can be made that if one does equate the quality of synthesis with the discovery of the "relations among things," and derives this from acting on a properly tuned world, this conception itself encounters the immutability-discontinuity problem. As a product of competence-action, the quality of synthesis would have the same formal status as that of the subject's acquisition of the knowledge of the relationship between action and its consequences. This conception, accordingly, would be subject to the difficulties pointed to in my analysis of competence-action.

[20] It may be unnecessary, perhaps, to add that I would account for the connection between this inferred Cartesian epistemology and the immutability-discontinuity problem in terms of my thesis regarding the two forms of cognitive organization. It should again be noted, however, that, in my view, ego psychology has not elaborated its formulations such that they can provide direct evidence for this extension of my thesis.

however, remains to be considered. I have proposed that the Freudian approach to development, because of its Cartesian presumptions, distinguishes between hydraulic and purposive modes of functioning in such a way that any attempt to connect these activities does so in terms of an identity relationship and hence encounters the problem of immutability and discontinuity. What, then, is the status of that very principle which Freud *expressly* proposed as the basis for connecting these modes of functioning? Freud, it will be recalled, held that the behavior of the organism was governed at all times by the principle of minimal tension. This was the case whether such behavior was causally determined or purposive. As so interpreted, behavior was directed toward an end-state that Freud typically characterized in equilibrium terms. When the organism's level of tension deviated too far from this optimal state of minimal tension, then this discrepancy was the antecedent condition for causally determined and/or purposive behavior that served to restore this end-state. Now, if my thesis is valid that the hydraulic and purposive functioning of the Freudian subject are separated by a Cartesian gulf, then it would follow that the minimal tension principle cannot be inclusive of such functioning, but rather can only serve to connect these modes of activity in terms of an identity relationship. Namely, the principle of minimal tension must serve to define a realm of being that is identical to either the hydraulic or the purposive modes of functioning. I believe that my analysis of the Freudian position provides support for this inference. We have seen that Freud represented the minimal tension principle, in its most general or formal sense, in his metapsychological constructs of energy and structure. It was in this form that the minimal tension principle was advanced as being inclusive of both the hydraulic and the purposive modes of behavior. Thus, primitive hydraulic functioning was portrayed as libidinal energy that stemmed from somatic sources, ebbed and flowed along the instinctual structures of the id, and was directed toward immediate discharge onto appropriate objects in accordance with the pleasure principle. And in the same formal sense, mature purposive activity was understood in terms of desexualized energy that provided modulated power for the structures of the ego, and was directed toward discharge onto appropriate events in accordance with the reality principle — toward tension reduction in the long run. As White's analysis has shown, however, it is precisely when primitive and mature behaviors are so represented in terms of this formal energy-structure dichotomy that the Freudian position encounters the problem of immutability and discontinuity. Furthermore, as our reinterpretation of White's analysis has suggested, in so representing primitive and mature events in terms of the energy-structure dichotomy, Freud implicitly stretched the hydraulic metaphor to accommodate purposive activity, thereby importing the isolation between these modes of behavior into the frame of the metaphor itself. It can thus be said that the minimal tension principle, when represented in its most general metapsychological terms to cover both hydraulic and purposive events, reduces itself to a problematic admixture of such modes of functioning — an admixture that our analysis has shown to be intrinsically connected to the problem of immutability and discontinuity and that our thesis derives, in turn, from an identity relationship between differentiating and connecting constructs.[21]

[21] Peters (1958) has documented a similar point in his analysis of Freudian theory. He notes that Freud has attempted to unite the hydraulic and purposive modes of functioning under an all-embracing pleasure principle as a model of minimal tension. But in the final analysis, as Peters demonstrates, this attempt fails. Instead of an inclusive principle, Freud ends up talking about two isolated principles — the pleasure principle that governs hydraulic functioning *and* the reality principle that governs mature purposive behavior.

6

A SUMMING UP: THE TASK FOR A
CONSTRUCTIONIST ALTERNATIVE

Two goals — one immediate and the other long-range — have guided my inquiry into Freudian theory. My immediate goal has been to reformulate and thereby connect two common criticisms of the Freudian position. I have argued that the problems of preformism and logical inconsistency attributed to Freudian theory can be understood as characteristic of the cognitive functioning of a subject who, in understanding the nature of personality development in terms of Freudian theory, imposes a pars pro toto organization on a sequence of events. As the formal basis for this thesis, I have proposed that, whatever his level of maturity, a subject is limited to two forms of organization in understanding the relationship between sequential events. He can structure such events into a hierarchic relationship of continuity and change, or he can structure such events into a pars pro toto relationship of immutability and discontinuity. I have further proposed that these organizations are evidenced when the subject structures sequential events within his explanatory limits in the case of the hierarchic organization, and beyond his explanatory limits in the case of the pars pro toto organization. These assertions have permitted me to interpret the problems of preformism and logical inconsistency as forms of immutability and discontinuity that occur in a pars pro toto structuring of sequential events beyond the explanatory limits of the Freudian position.

In elaborating this argument, I have noted that the immutability-discontinuity problem encountered by Freudian theory is characteristic and pervasive, evidenced in contemporary conflict-free versions of the Freudian position as well as in Freud's classical approach to development and pathology. Our inquiry has thus indicated that the immutability-discontinuity problem arises in connection with a wide variety of polar concepts that Freudian theory advances in its view of personality functioning. These include the constructs of hydraulic (causally determined) activity versus purposive behavior; the pleasure principle versus the reality principle; id versus ego; and instinctually bound libido versus neutralized energy. No one of these dichotomies, I have argued, is more fundamental than another in generating the immutability-discontinuity problem. Rather, they all have the same functional significance in that each forces the subject to impose an organization on sequential events beyond his explanatory limits — to solve, if you will, an unsolvable problem. Thus, any one of these dichotomies permits us to distinguish behavior in terms of primitive and mature modes of functioning. We are able to do this by virtue of characterizing each mode as possessing attributes that are defined by one of the constructs of a given dichotomy, and as lacking those attributes that are defined by the other, polar construct of the dichotomy. In terms of the polarity between hydraulic and purposive behavior, for example, we are able to characterize primitive functioning as hydraulic and non-purposive, thereby distinguishing such behavior from mature functioning, which we characterize as purposive and non-hydraulic. In the final analysis, however, each dichotomy represents a Cartesian isolation between a distorting subject of knowledge and an independently constituted object of knowledge. Hence, while primitive and mature behavior can be distinguished in terms of these dichotomous constructs, there can be no more inclusive construct whereby these sequential events can be connected. By virtue of the Cartesian presumption, then, a fundamental discontinuity exists between primitive and mature behavior when understood in terms of these Freudian dichotomies. Yet, this isolation notwithstanding, Freudian theory provides us with a basis for unifying these very same behaviors. And this, in terms of one or the other of the polar constructs that has served to distinguish between these behaviors in the first place. Accordingly, it can be said that in understanding the nature of development in terms of Freudian theory, the subject is connecting events that in a fundamental sense cannot be connected. And he is doing so by using as a substitute for the inclusive construct which the theory lacks, a construct that has served to define a part, namely, one of the events in the sequence as distinguished from the other.

It is from this pars pro toto organization that I have formally derived the problems of preformism and logical contradiction. I have argued that when a Freudian construct serves to unify primitive and mature modes of functioning, it does so by defining a realm of being which underlies this temporal sequence of events and which is, hence, immutable over the time span represented by this sequence. If, then, any event in this sequence is also defined by this connecting construct, the attributes of this event must be identical to those of the underlying immutable realm of being. Accordingly, in so structuring development in terms of an identity relationship between differentiating and connecting constructs, the subject is connecting primitive and mature modes of functioning by perpetuating one of these modes over time. As a result, this form of organization encounters the problem of immutability and, when the connecting construct defines the subsequent mode of functioning, the more specific problem of preformism. Moreover, it follows that in being so perpetuated, the attributes of this event must, paradoxically, coexist with those of the event that has been explicitly defined as *lacking* such attributes and, indeed, as possessing the opposite attributes. Thus, we have seen that in its conception of development, Freudian theory implicitly gives to the primitive hydraulic state (the id) purposive qualities that are only to be acquired in the course of development, while in its conception of repression, the theory gives to the mature purposive state (the ego) hydraulic qualities that define the primitive state from which the ego is supposed to have developed. It can be said, then, that the fundamental discontinuity between the sequential events of primitive and advanced functioning has been further compounded. These isolated events are being connected by means of a logical contradiction: Namely, a state that is being explicitly characterized as possessing a given attribute and as lacking its polar opposite, is at the same time being implicitly characterized as having this "absent" polar opposite.

Thus has our inquiry served to integrate what I believe to be the two fundamental problems attributed to the Freudian position. Preformism and logical contradiction are the only ways in which a Freudian theory of development can bridge the gap that its own Cartesian assumption has created between primitive and mature functioning. Essentially, one can say that in so connecting the prior functioning of the hydraulic id to the subsequent functioning of the purposive ego, Freud's conception of development has united the classical Cartesian realms of mind and body. In the terms provided by our constructionist assertions, the problems of preformism and logical contradiction are the formal properties of this pars pro toto organization. They represent the intrinsically connected forms of immutability and discontinuity that refined Freudian thought is forced to assume in connecting the unconnectable—in structuring the sequential events of development beyond the explanatory limits set by its Cartesian epistemology.

If this critique has been persuasive, then it constitutes an initial step toward my second, longer-range goal of advancing a formulation that can serve to organize in a more coherent way those events of personality development that have been so structured in terms of Freudian theory. This should not be taken to mean that my proposed alternative will somehow magically supply the more inclusive construct that is lacking in Freudian theory and that would serve to connect in a relationship of continuity and change the isolated sequential events defined by the Freudian polarities. My alternative does not presume, in other words, to solve the mind-body problem as this is defined by the Cartesian world view. In a sense, a more drastic solution is required. If this critique has any merit, it suggests that the difficulties encountered by the Freudian polarities derive from explanatory limits that are fixed by the epistemology of the theory. Accordingly, if I am to advance a more coherent alternative, then I must start with an epistemology that differs essentially from that of the Cartesian presumption—an epistemology that provides the basis for redefining the Freudian polarities into a radically different form. In my view, this epistemology is given in the two propositions that are basic to my thesis and that have served to guide my inquiry from the very outset. Thus, in the remainder of the chapter, I will again consider the constructionist and orthogenetic propositions, but now with respect to their implications for my proposed alternative to the nature of personality development.

THE BASIS FOR A CONSTRUCTIONIST ALTERNATIVE TO FREUDIAN THEORY

In terms of the constructionist proposition, my critique has presumed that the object of knowledge does not exist apart from the knower in the form of independently constituted primary qualities such as motion, number, and extension, but is actively constructed by the knower—is known by virtue of the way in which the subject is organized. The object has the properties of being graspable, suckable, and biteable, as it were, by virtue of the fact that this object can be grasped, sucked, and bitten by the subject. By the same token, an object is understood as having such "primary qualities" as extension and width to the extent that relevant cognitive structures are available to the subject that he can impose upon a "properly tuned" event—an event that can be organized in terms of these relevant cognitive structures. The subject, in other words, knows the object insofar as it can be organized in accordance with patterns of activity that are available to him—in accordance with those functional characteristics of mental organization that he is able to impose on his experience. The constructionist assumption, accordingly, can be said to posit a unity between the subject and object that stands in essential contrast to the isolation engendered by a Cartesian epistemology. Since objective reality, in order to be known, must conform to the essential structure of the mind, its known properties are intrinsically connected to mental activity, instead of being separated from it by the unbridgeable void represented by the Cartesian problem of knowledge.

The constructionist assumption has two significant implications for my alternative to the Freudian conception of development. First, it provides the basis for reconceptualizing the dichotomy between primitive and mature functioning that has been engendered by the Freudian polarities. The

primitive functioning of the child and the mature functioning of the adult, instead of representing a transposed relationship between a distorting subject and the independently
constituted object, can be interpreted as different forms of
constructive activity that serve to structure a properly tuned
reality. This implication of the constructionist assumption,
in turn, serves to define the task for the proposed alternative: If the Freudian polarities create a gulf between primitive and advanced functioning that can only be spanned by
means of preformism and logical contradiction, then my
task is to show that these sequential events, when reinterpreted as different forms of constructive activity, can be
connected in a more coherent way.

But therein lies a problem—one that is raised by the
very unity presumed by the constructionist position. If the
subject imposes his organization on whatever in reality can
be so organized—if the properly tuned event then resonates,
as it were, at the subject's frequency—does it not follow that
the subject can only encounter the vibrations of his own organization in the object? And if this is the case, then how
can the subject know anything that he does not already
know—how can he know anything new? For to know something new would imply the presence of an already given
structure of knowing and, hence, would imply that this
"something" is already known. It can be said, therefore, that
the very nature of its root assumption creates a fundamental
tension for my constructionist alternative: In presuming
that the object, as known, is formed by the activity of an
already given structure, my alternative has an inherent and
systematic tendency toward preformism. And yet, I cannot
solve this problem by deriving developmental change from
the "naked thing in itself," for to do so—however implicitly—would simply contradict my very starting point. The
problem, then, for my alternative is this: If we interpret the
sequential events of primitive and advanced functioning as

different forms of constructive activity, how can we account for the developmental movement from one form of constructive activity to another without, on the one hand, negating the constructionist assumption or, on the other hand, gratuitously giving these forms of activity to the subject? How can we, in other words, connect these forms of constructive activity as sequential events and yet avoid the very problems of logical inconsistency and preformism that we have criticized in the Freudian position? In short, it is all very well to posit a unity between the constructing subject and a properly tuned reality. And, further, to set this unity against a Cartesian alienation of subject and object. But could it not be contended that I am encountering these very same problems, only now as transposed to the domain of constructive activity itself?

If this dilemma is created for the proposed conception of development by virtue of its constructionist presumption, a way of resolving it is afforded by the second proposition that has guided my inquiry. I refer to Werner's (1957) orthogenetic principle which defines development in terms of increasing differentiation and hierarchic integration and which, accordingly, restricts the domain of my inquiry to the pars pro toto and hierarchic forms of constructive activity.[1] Here, as well, two significant implications follow when constructive activity is so understood. The first and more critical implication of the orthogenetic principle is that it affords a particular solution to the constructionist dilemma. When constructive activity is understood as taking the pars pro toto and hierarchic forms of organization, the developmental movement from one form of functioning to another can be derived, not from the independently constituted object, nor from preformed structures that exist prior to experience, but

---

[1] The reader may want to review Chapter 1 with respect to the relationship between the orthogenetic principle and the formal assertions that have served to guide my critique of the Freudian position.

from the organization that characterizes the very activity of knowing—that is to say, from constructive activity itself. More precisely, I am suggesting that the very problem that is evidenced in the pars pro toto structuring of an event—the immutability-discontinuity problem—constitutes the essential condition for development. Namely, the immutability-discontinuity problem can be seen as constituting the condition for the movement from the pars pro toto form of constructive activity to a more hierarchically organized form of behavior.

Moreover—and this is the second implication that follows from understanding constructive activity in terms of the orthogenetic principle—the case can be made that the Freudian polarities that have served to distinguish the primitive and advanced modes of functioning can be reinterpreted respectively as pars pro toto and hierarchic forms of constructive activity. To list some of the polarities that lend themselves to such redefinition, we have blind hydraulic functioning versus purposive means-end behavior; primary versus secondary process thinking; and defensive, fragmented identification versus conflict-free "superordinated" identification.[2] It follows that if the primitive and advanced poles of the Freudian dichotomy can be so reinterpreted, then these sequential modes of functioning can be connected to one another in terms of the proposed solution to the constructionist dilemma. One can view behavior that has been characterized in terms of the primitive pole of a Freudian dichotomy as a pars pro toto form of activity and,

[2] The idea that primitive and advanced functioning, as interpreted by Freudian theory, can be characterized respectively as pars pro toto and hierarchic forms of organization is, of course, not original. This correspondence has been suggested by Freud and highlighted by such theorists as Arieti (1959) and Von Domarus (1944) in their formal analyses of symptomatic behavior. Indeed, in focusing on the dream and symptom expression in terms of such formal characteristics as condensation and displacement, Freud has provided us with a classic description of the pars pro toto.

accordingly, as providing in and of itself the essential condition for its own development into behavior that has been characterized in terms of the mature pole of the Freudian dichotomy or, if you will, the hierarchic form of activity.

Thus do our two propositions, taken in conjunction with one another, provide the basis for reinterpreting the Freudian polarities and thereby connecting them in a more coherent way than that afforded by the Freudian position. More specifically, the solution I am proposing would distinguish the movement from one form of constructive activity to another in terms of two separate but interdependent processes: *consolidation* and *developmental reorganization.* The first is similar to the process posited in White's view of competence-action: The subject is seen as actively forming his object of knowledge in accordance with already given cognitive structures and capable of changing this object of knowledge in the process of so constructing it. My alternative would further characterize such consolidative activity in terms of the assertions that have been advanced in elaborating the two forms of cognitive organization. Namely, consolidative activity would be characterized as taking both the hierarchic form and, viewed from a higher level of organization, the pars pro toto. As so characterized, these forms of constructive activity would indicate that the subject is structuring the object of knowledge both within, and simultaneously beyond, the explanatory limits of an already given knowing structure. (As I emphasized in Chapter 1, it is by virtue of characterizing cognitive activity in terms of its degree of hierarchization that we are able to say that these two forms of organization coexist in the subject's construction of the event. Thus we can say that the child's nonconserving response represents a solution to the conservation of quantity problem in terms of a perceptual mode of functioning that is a constituent of the older child's compensation rule, and, for that reason, can be designated as a pars pro toto. At the same time, this perceptual mode of functioning serves to integrate a variety of otherwise isolated particulars and, as such, can also be characterized as being hierarchic in nature, though at a different level of organization. That is, the sequential events "ball-into-sausage" are being integrated into "conserved" events by the non-conserver of quantity in accordance with Gestalt principles that govern perceptual functioning. From this viewpoint, the ball-deformed-into-sausage have been connected as continuous events in terms of spatial and temporal proximity, and in terms of similarity of color and texture.)[3] Thus, even while a given form of consolidative activity is serving to structure sequential events into a continuity-change relationship, this same activity is also serving to structure events as intrinsically connected forms of immutability and discontinuity. It is in this sense that such activity provides the basis for its own change. By virtue of the conflict that results from structuring sequential events as being discontinuous and simultaneously immutable, the pars pro toto form of consolidative activity serves as the essential condition for the second process that I am positing—a process similar to that suggested in White's view of imaginative synthesis—namely, developmental reorganization. I am suggesting that the conflict engendered by such contradictory forms of knowing constitutes the essential condition for a reorganization of the underlying cognitive structure—a reorganization which is manifested as a more hierarchically organized form of

[3] I am suggesting, then, that development, when understood as a trend of increasing hierarchization, implies the corollary of reorganization, namely, that prior activities become the constituents of a subsequent, more integrated form of functioning. It should also be noted that the processes being posited here apply only to behaviors that can be characterized as evidencing this developmental trend. This constraint is another indication that the orthogenetic principle has the status of a heuristic definition in my formulation. As Werner (1957) would express it, the principle itself is not subject to test but serves to define the formulation's range of applicability.

consolidative functioning and which thereby serves to reconcile the inconsistencies of the prior pars pro toto form of knowing activity.[4] Our constructionist presumption, moreover, imposes a fundamental constraint upon the way in which one can conceive of this process. For the event to be constructed in the more coherent form, it must, of course, be properly tuned to the new underlying structure. If, in constructing the event, the previous consolidative activity has served to change the event, the changed event must be so constituted that it can be constructed by the new structure that has resulted from this same prior activity of knowing. My solution would thus posit a particular, recursive relationship between the processes of consolidation and developmental reorganization: The activity of constructing the object of knowledge in terms of an already given structure can both change the object of knowledge and result in a developmental reorganization in the nature of the underlying structure. If the changed object of knowledge now represents a properly tuned reality, then it will be constructed in accordance with the newly formed structure and hence, in a more coherent, more hierarchically organized form. At the same time, however, this new form of consolidative activity, at another level of organization, will also take the form of a pars pro toto. That is to say, the subject will again be constructing the properly tuned event within, and simultaneously beyond, the explanatory limits of the newly formed structure; hence, contradictory ways of knowing will again be evidenced, etc.

In proposing this formulation as a solution to the constructionist dilemma, I am, by the same token, also maintaining that it represents a fundamental alternative to the Cartesian view of development and, in particular, to the

---

[4] The reader may well ask how the subject "recognizes" the conflict engendered by such contradictory forms of knowing. I will address this question at a somewhat later stage in my argument.

conceptions of classical and contemporary psychoanalytic theory. As a basis for further clarifying the nature of the proposed alternative, let us now compare the formulation first to the classical Freudian position and then to White's conflict-free version.[5] In Freud's theory, the immediate antecedent of development is a rise in instinctual tension that comes about as a result of primitive, inadequate functioning. The subject, governed by hydraulic id activity, is unable to anticipate the painful consequences—the rise in physiologic tension—of satisfying his instinctual needs in the direct, peremptory ways available to him. And development itself is understood as the behavioral acquisition of external, independently constituted properties that serve both to reduce such physiologic tension and to prevent this conflict from recurring. By virtue of mirroring the attributes of an external reality, an acquired ego activity serves to anticipate the consequences of such short-term satisfactions and thereby delays those id-governed behaviors that directly gratify instinctual needs. It may be seen, then, that the classical Freudian position posits a critical but derived relationship of antagonism between primitive and mature aspects of personality functioning. The antagonism between the hydraulic id and the purposive ego further reflects the more fundamental antagonism that Freudian theory presumes to exist between the primitive blind subject and an independently constituted punitive reality of mature interpersonal others. It is this antagonism between the subject and the external world which, in the final analysis, gives rise to conflict as the basic determinant of development.

[5] I should caution the reader at this point that the constructionist alternative I will so elaborate merely represents a set of possibilities. Thus, I will not attempt to identify the specific process by which the pars pro toto form of activity is reorganized into the hierarchic form of activity, nor will I attempt to apply my formulation to the dynamic interpersonal events with which Freudian theory has been so typically concerned. I leave those tasks for my planned further elaboration of the constructionist alternative.

As in the classical Freudian approach, so too in the constructionist alternative that I am proposing, conflict is the immediate antecedent of development. Moreover, my alternative similarly represents development as a succession of behavioral events in which a subsequent, more mature form of knowing serves to reduce the conflict generated by a prior, less mature form of activity. But I view such conflict as "cognitive" — as being generated by the activity of knowing the event in contradictory ways. That is to say, I derive such conflict not from the antagonism between an independently constituted reality and an "inadequate" subject who lacks the necessary qualities to know this reality. On the contrary, I am proposing that conflict stems from the *harmony* between a "competent" subject and a properly tuned event. The contradictory forms of knowing that constitute the basis for conflict can only occur when the subject constructs a reality that conforms to an underlying, already given cognitive structure. Thus, where Freudian theory posits an antagonism between primitive and mature aspects of personality, my conception assumes this antagonism to exist between activities at the same level of maturity. And where Freudian theory derives this antagonism from the relationship between the subject and the independently constituted object, my conception views this antagonism as intrinsic to mental activity itself — an activity that presumes a relationship of congruence between the subject and object. Finally, I am viewing development, not as an internal substitution for the mature external other, but as a reorganization of the pars pro toto form of activity such that this activity becomes a constituent of a hierarchically organized form of knowing. Thus, where Freudian theory views development as a behavioral acquisition from an external reality, my position views development as the behavioral expression of a new underlying structure — one that serves to resolve "cognitive conflict" by constructing the event in a reorganized, more coherent form.

I am suggesting, then, that my formulation differs fundamentally from that afforded by Freudian theory. At the same time, however, it should be noted that both formulations have an important feature in common—one that would seem to contradict my assertion regarding their essential difference. If Freudian theory encounters the immutability of giving the primitive subject those attributes that serve as a precondition for their own acquisition, so too does my alternative ascribe the same cognitive characteristics to all levels of maturity. Namely, I have asserted that at all levels of maturity constructive activity evidences hierarchic and pars pro toto forms of organization. And if Freudian theory encounters the discontinuity of ascribing polar contradictory characteristics to a given state, so too does my alternative ascribe such characteristics to cognitive functioning, only now explicitly rather than implicitly. Accordingly, it might be said that my formulation continues to encounter the very problems of immutability and discontinuity that I have posed for the Freudian position. Does this mean, then, that the respective formulations are, at root, the same? And that their differences are more apparent than real? I would suggest that this is not the case, but on the contrary, that these characteristics of the proposed alternative only serve to underscore the differences between our two positions. If my formulation does, indeed, encounter an immutability-discontinuity problem, it does so for good reason. Clearly, I cannot legislate that my conception be exempt from the rules to which I have held Freudian theory accountable. It follows from everything I have said that the constructionist alternative, as a form of refined cognition, can only serve to structure events within, and simultaneously beyond, its *own* explanatory limits. Accordingly, it would be cavalier, at the very least, were I to claim that my alternative can avoid the problems of immutability and discontinuity. I would suggest, however, that these problems represent something more than a superficial reworking of the preformism and logical contradiction that have been attributed to the Freudian position. For it also follows from my inquiry that if this alternative starts from an epistemology significantly different from that of Freudian theory, it must encounter the immutability-discontinuity problem in a significantly different form.

I can best distinguish between these forms of the immutability-discontinuity problem by considering them in relation to the child's developing conservation of quantity. As we have noted, the child is viewed as a conserver on Piaget's conservation task if he expresses the judgment that the amount of clay in the ball and deformed sausage is the same, and if he justifies this judgment in terms of the compensation rule. Now it has been observed that immediately prior to the attainment of conservation, there is a typical phase in the subject's behavior that is marked by a fluctuation among his various judgments.[6] The subject may say, for example, that the amount of clay in the sausage is successively "more," "less," and the "same," as compared to the amount of clay in the ball. This fluctuation, moreover, is accompanied by hesitation and conflict. The two different forms of the immutability-discontinuity problem can be exemplified by two different interpretations of this fluctuating, conflict-dominated phase. As might be expected, one interpretation is based on the alternative that I am proposing. The other, however, is not derived from the classical Freudian position as such. In order to highlight the essential differences between the two forms of the immutability-discontinuity problem, I will pose a hypothetical formulation instead — one that I am deliberately fashioning so that it encounters the immutability-discontinuity problem in precisely

---

[6] The reader may well ask how the child attains this phase of fluctuating judgments. In this regard, see my remarks at the end of this chapter.

the same form as that encountered by the Freudian position, even though it actually comes closer to my own position than it does to the Freudian view. This hypothetical formulation would share several important features with my alternative. It would posit, first of all, that the conflict of the subject serves as an antecedent condition for his subsequent conserving behavior. Moreover, it would derive this conflict from the contradiction between the child's different ways of knowing the event. That is, the formulation would maintain that the child is conflicted because he recognizes that he is being contradictory—that he is viewing the sausage at one time as having more clay than the ball, and at another time, as having less clay than the ball. In effect, the hypothetical formulation would suggest, as does my alternative, that the subject is asking himself: How can the *same* sausage have more *and* less clay than the ball? Where the two interpretations would differ is with respect to this question: How is the child able to recognize that a contradiction is, indeed, involved in his successive judgments? The hypothetical interpretation would suggest that the child recognizes the contradiction because he is able to conserve quantity in a form that he will later express in his overt behavior, but that at this earlier point, is expressed nascently or covertly. This view would have it that by virtue of implicitly coordinating the judgments "more" and "less" in terms of a nascent compensation rule, the subject can recognize that the sausage at time 1 and the sausage at time 2 are indeed the "same" and, therefore, that he is attributing opposite qualities to the same event.

Now I think it clear that this conception would encounter the immutability-discontinuity problem in very much the same form as it is encountered by Freudian theory. We have seen that Freudian theory posits a rise in instinctual tension as the fundamental determinant of development and derives this rise in tension, or conflict, from the inadequacy of an organism that is characterized as possessing certain attributes and as lacking their polar opposites. Yet in its conception of how these opposite qualities are acquired from the external world, Freudian theory is implicitly forced to give these characteristics in the same form to the organism prior to conflict and, indeed, from the very outset of functioning. (In Rapaport's terms, "The ego is both born out of the conflict, and party to the conflict" [1951a, p. 301].) Not only, then, does Freudian theory encounter the logical contradiction of ascribing opposite qualities to the same state, it also negates the very conflict that it has posited as necessary to development in the first place. By the same token, if the hypothetical formulation interprets the child's recognition of contradiction as being based on his ability to conserve quantity in terms of the compensation rule—however nascent this ability might be—it cannot at the same time posit that the recognition of contradiction and its accompanying conflict are the necessary conditions for this ability to come about. On the one hand, this conception would give to the organism the structurally more advanced form of cognition as a necessary condition for its own emergence and, in an infinite regress, would push that form of cognition back to the very onset of mental life. On the other hand, the conception would face the logical difficulty that the subject's conflict is based on the very structure that serves to resolve it. Conflict, as so conceived, would simultaneously negate itself.[7]

[7] Elkind (1968) is addressing himself to a similar problem when he notes that there is a seeming contradiction in Piaget and Inhelder's (1962) position that true conservation can only be assessed if one sets up the experimental conditions so as to elicit a "conflict" between the subject's immediate perceptual experience and his mental operations. He suggests that unless a distinction is made between a prior, more primitive form of conservation (in Piaget's sense, "the conservation of identity") and a more advanced form of conservation (the "operations"), then the "operations have to serve both as party to the conflict and the mediator of its resolution" (p. 468).

It should also be pointed out that there are a number of constructionist

Now let us interpret this phase in terms of the constructionist formulation that I am proposing as an alternative to the Freudian position. We have seen that my formulation also suggests that the child's recognition of contradiction requires that he conserve the sausage — judged at one time as having more clay than the ball and at another time as having

---

conceptions of development that, in my view, encounter the problem evidenced by our hypothetical formulation and, as such, realize the preformist potential of the constructionist root assumption. That is to say, they evidence a form of the immutability-discontinuity problem that, in the final analysis, cannot be distinguished from the Cartesian view represented by the Freudian position.. The significance of this issue for a constructionist alternative has been discussed elsewhere (Feffer, 1975). It is enough to indicate its importance here by noting its relevance to the very conception that has significantly influenced my own formulation — Piaget's view of the child's developing conservation of quantity. In characterizing the phase prior to the conservation response, Piaget (1957) states:

> With the third strategy, on the other hand, we meet with a *new* type of behavior wherein the subject hesitates among the responses "more," "less," or "equal" and which *thus* marks a beginning coordination between the two strategies ... or a beginning composition between the two opposed properties in the configuration [quoted by Flavell, 1963, p. 246; italics added].

As one may see, there is an implication here that Piaget is deriving conflict from the activity of a more advanced cognitive operation (the "beginning composition") that coordinates or otherwise integrates the antagonistic perceptual properties of the event. This implication is more clearly expressed in Flavell's (1963) rendition of Piaget's view. Flavell characterizes this same phase as

> The joint apprehension of both properties within a single cognitive act.... The typical *result* of this beginning *conceptual* coordination of length with width is a noticeable hesitation and conflict [p. 246; italics added].

Now, if Piaget were to posit that contradiction and conflict serve as the conditions for the conservation response (and I am not suggesting here that this is necessarily the case), then his formulation would face the same form of the problem as that encountered by our hypothetical conception.

less clay than the ball—as the same event over time. My alternative, however, would account for this "conservation," not in terms of a nascent compensation rule, but in terms of the less hierarchically organized level of functioning represented by *perceptual* activity. Indeed, my formulation suggests that the non-conserver of quantity is conserving the sausage as a stable event in terms of the same mode of activity that has led him to his different, distorting judgments of quantity in the first place. In this regard, I am interpreting the child's fluctuating contradictory judgments as solutions to an unsolvable problem—one that he is not yet able to solve in terms of the compensation rule but that he solves in terms of those constructive activities that *are* available to him. As so interpreted, the child's successive judgments of "more" and "less" are a function of perceptually focusing and refocusing on the isolated dimensions of length and circumference, all the while that this child, by virtue of his judgment that the sausage at time 1 and the sausage at time 2 are identical in terms of color and texture, is able to conserve the sausage as the "same" event over this same span of time.[8*]

    [8*] The reader is referred to Köhler's (1947) classic analysis of the perceptual constancies and, in particular, to his position that the Gestalt or "Ehrenfels" properties of perceptually organized units serve as the basis for such phenomenally experienced constancies as shape, size, and brightness. Note, moreover, that I have argued above (see pp. 262-263) that the sequential events "ball-into-sausage" are being integrated into conserved events by the non-conserver of quantity in accordance with Gestalt principles that govern perceptual functioning. That is to say, the non-conserver of quantity is still a conserver of what Piaget would term "identity." From this viewpoint, the ball-deformed-into-sausage have been connected as continuous events in terms of spatial and temporal proximity, and in terms of similarity of color and texture. Accordingly, when the subject states that there is the same amount of clay in the ball and sausage, I do not interpret this as necessarily indicative of his ability to conserve *quantity*. If this judgment occurs in the context of other contradictory judgments of "more" and "less," and if it is not accompanied by a justification in terms of the compensation rule (or any other indication of an "operational" reversibility [Piaget, 1950, p. 140]), I would interpret the statement as reflective of his ability to conserve the "sameness" of the events as perceptual entities.

My alternative, then, would suggest that the basis for the conflict lies in a contradictory relationship between already given constructive activities at the *same* level of organization—if you will, from a relationship of identity between the differentiating and connecting activity of the same perceptual mode of functioning. It would thus distinguish between the *generation* of conflict at one level of organization and the *resolution* of such conflict at a higher level of organization. Namely, it would distinguish between the generation of conflict that is based on a relatively primitive perceptual conservation and the resolution of such conflict by means of a more advanced form of conservation—one that serves to integrate the prior contradictory forms of perceptual activity in terms of the more hierarchically organized rule of compensation. By the same token, my view would suggest that in resolving the contradiction that has been encountered in the course of perceptually structuring the event, the rule of compensation will also serve to structure the event in contradictory ways; and this contradiction can be resolved, in turn, by means of a still more hierarchically organized rule or principle.[9] It may be seen, then, that whereas the hypothetical formulation assumes that individuals—regardless of their level of maturity—evidence exactly the same *form* of conserving activity, my alternative suggests that individuals evidence the same conserving *function* in *different* forms, and that this structural difference is precisely what defines their different levels of maturity. In

---

[9] As a case in point, I have noted that just as the subject is able to perceptually conserve the object through displacements in space but is not yet able to conserve quantity, so too is the conserver of quantity, at a certain point in his development, not yet able to conserve volume. Although he can apply the compensation rule in justifying his judgment that the ball-deformed-into-sausage has the same amount of clay, this subject will repeat his earlier form of contradictory behavior when confronted with the problem of comparing the respective amounts of water displaced by the ball and sausage.

other words, I have assumed that development takes the form of an increasing hierarchization of constructive activity, and that at all levels of organization such constructive activity serves to organize the world into stable units: That is to say, within the domain of his available constructs, the subject connects sequential particulars into a relationship of continuity and change. Moreover, I have assumed that in the course of so constructing this world, the subject encounters contradictory ways of knowing. And this, too, at all levels of organization. From this viewpoint, then, each conservation is built upon a prior, more primitive conserving activity and, as such, is evidenced in the form of increasingly hierarchized, progressively wider, and ever more stable constructions of reality. In short, where the immutability posited by the hypothetical formulation is one of *structural invariance* (and here it differs in no way from the Freudian conception), the immutability posited by my alternative is one of *functional invariance*. And where the hypothetical (and Freudian) conception encounters the discontinuity of unwittingly ascribing contradictory qualities to a given state, my alternative explicitly posits such polar contradictory qualities as an essential dynamic of development. And this precisely because it suggests that, as a functional invariant, contradictory ways of knowing are encountered at all levels of constructive activity.[10]

The implications of my formulation can be further clarified by now comparing it to the Cartesian view it most resembles, namely, White's dual concepts of competence-action and imaginative synthesis. In his view of competence-action, White suggests that developmental change comes about as a function of the subject's acting on a properly

[10] In this fundamental respect, my formulation derives directly from Piaget's (1952) view of intelligence and, in particular, his characterization of the functional invariants of intelligence—invariants that are expressed via a diversity of structures.

tuned world, thereby changing this responsive world and becoming "more like the adult" by virtue of acquiring, via feedback, the knowledge of the relationship of this changed world to his actions. His view of imaginative synthesis, on the other hand, suggests that the subject integrates less mature identifications into a more hierarchically organized structure—into "patterns as wholes." Notwithstanding the similarity between these concepts and my view of consolidative activity and developmental reorganization, there is a fundamental difference in our respective approaches to development. And this stems from the difference in our basic presumptions. In implicitly assuming that there is an independently constituted relationship between the subject's actions and the changes in reality produced by these actions, White isolates the subject's knowing activity from its consequences and, in the final analysis, produces a gap between subject and object that is identical to that in Freud's classical approach. As a result, White's view of development suffers a dual problem. His concept of competence-action not only encounters the Cartesian forms of immutability and discontinuity, but this conception, which derives developmental change from the independently constituted object, is isolated from his view of imaginative synthesis, which derives developmental change from the knowing activity of the subject.

My alternative similarly characterizes the subject of knowledge as one who can change a responsive reality by acting on it and who integrates less mature behaviors into more hierarchically organized units. In my view, however, the event, as so changed by the subject's knowing activity, is not independently constituted but is constructed by the subject; constructed, that is, precisely in terms of a new structure that has come into being by virtue of this same prior activity of knowing. The subject's structuring of an event in terms of a pars pro toto form of consolidative activity thus can not only change the event as a function of so constructing it, but, by virtue of the contradictory knowing activity it represents, can also provide the condition for the underlying structure to be reorganized into one by which the subject can construct the event in a more coherent way. But for this new structure to be evidenced as a more hierarchic form of consolidative activity, the event that has been so affected by the prior activity of knowing must now lend itself to being constructed in terms of the reorganized structure. If that is the case, then the event that has been changed by the prior form of consolidative activity can again be constructed by the subject, but now in terms of the new structure that has come into being by virtue of this same consolidative activity.[11] Thus, while White views the feedback from the changed event as the antecedent of development change, I view such feedback as being organized in terms of an already given structure. More precisely, while White views the change in the properly tuned event as a *determinant* of an acquired cognitive structure, I view the change in the properly tuned event as a *condition* for an already present, albeit newly formed, structure to manifest itself as a more integrated form of consolidative activity.[12]

[11] Note that I am not suggesting here that the activity of knowing must, of necessity, effect a change in the object. Rather, I am suggesting that if the activity of knowing *does* have such a consequence, then the change in the object can only be known in terms of an already given structure.

[12] It follows that if a prior form of consolidative activity leads both to a change in the object as well as to a newly formed underlying structure, and yet the changed object *cannot* be constructed in terms of the new structure, then the more hierarchically organized form of consolidative activity will not be manifested. The more advanced consolidative activity could be evidenced, however, under other circumstances — circumstances that I would interpret as representing a properly tuned reality for the newly emerged capacity to consolidate itself in actual performance, thereby providing the conditions for further change. In this respect, my view converges with Flavell and Wohlwill's (1969) distinction between "competence" and "performance." As a theoretical basis for this distinction, they have posited similar processes of consolidation and developmental reorganization.

In summary, my alternative restructures both poles of the subject-object relationship as it is defined by the Cartesian point of view. On the one hand, while rejecting the assumption that the object is independently constituted, it assumes, nevertheless, that the object is necessary to development. Thus, it suggests that consolidative activity, as the necessary basis for developmental reorganization, can occur only if there is an object that can be constructed by the subject in terms of this activity. The subject must have the "experience," as it were, of constructing a properly tuned world. Hence, while stressing the importance of an objective reality for development, the conception remains congruent with the Kantian assumption that objective reality must conform to the essential organization of mental activity in order to be known. On the other hand, in restructuring the Cartesian definition of the subject, my alternative posits a particular safeguard against the preformist tendency given in the constructionist assumption that we form our objects of knowledge. Rather than gratuitously attributing structures to the subject, my conception derives change from the organization of constructive activity itself, namely, from the conflict that is generated by the pars pro toto form of consolidation and from the reconciliation of this conflict at another level of organization, namely, in terms of a more hierarchically organized form of knowing. But this solution must adhere rigorously to the constructionist assumption if

---

That our distinction between consolidative activity and developmental reorganization is not new is further attested to by Nagel's (1957) characterization of development:

The connotation of *development* thus involves two essential components: the notion of a system possessing a definite structure and a definite set of pre-existing capacities; and the notion of a sequential set of changes in the system, yielding relatively permanent but novel increments, not only in the structure but in its mode of operation as well [p. 17].

we are to avoid any "backdoor" intrusion of the Cartesian epistemology. A prime case in point is White's view that development comes about via feedback from the changes produced by the subject's constructive activity. This view, I have argued, in implicitly assuming such changes to be independently constituted, formally isolates the subject from the product of his activity and, accordingly, the theoretical conceptions of competence and imaginative synthesis from each other. In contrast, my solution presumes that the changes produced by the subject's activity continue to be constructed by the subject if such changed events are properly tuned to an underlying structure. This reaffirmation of the constructionist assumption enables me to posit a particular relationship between the processes that have been isolated in White's view: Consolidation and developmental reorganization are the intrinsically connected processes of an interpenetrative dovetailing—or, as Piaget (1952) would express it, an "indissoluble relation"—between the subject and object. In the course of constructing the object, mental activity not only changes itself with respect to its underlying structure, but can also change the object in such a way that the object can be constructed anew; and this, precisely in terms of the new underlying structure.[13] Thus it may be seen

[13] Note the affinity that our conception has to the Marxist view of change. As with the proposed formulation, so too are the Marxist subject and object interpenetrative moments in individual development. Thus from Marx's early writings (as quoted by Fromm, 1961), we have the notion that "human sensibility and the human character of the senses . . . can only come into being through the existence of its object, through humanized nature" (p. 32) and, at another point, "the eye has become a human eye when its object has become a human social object, created by man and destined for him" (pp. 32–33). This relationship between subject and object has been dramatically expressed in the Marxist concept of socialist man—that man, in acting to change society, changes himself. The Marxist view of change, then, posits an intimate dovetailing between an external world that the individual creates, and the changes that occur in the individual as a function of so creating this world.

that, in so restructuring the relationship between the subject and object of knowledge, we have also redefined the classic and long-standing dichotomy between nature and nurture. We are viewing nurture, not as an independently constituted world that impresses itself in the form of mediating behavior on an inherently given human nature, but rather as the "experience" of actively constructing a properly tuned reality. Nurture, then, becomes synonymous with activity itself. And instead of viewing human nature as an immutable core of constitutional givens that exist prior to and beyond the reach of experience and, hence, beyond the reach of such

---

It may be seen, however, that this Marxist characterization of the subject-object relationship is open to the opposing interpretations that the object is a constructed one, and that it is independently constituted. On the one hand, there is the constructionist emphasis in Marx's view that the object is formed by man. Fromm (1961) has pointed out, for example, that Marx's conception of change can only be understood in terms of the notion that man, as an intrinsic aspect of creating his own history, creates his own objects. As Fromm expresses it, such objects in Marx's view serve to "confirm" man's faculties. On the other hand, there is also Marx's early view that man's senses "need to be formed by the objects outside of them" (p. 32). Accordingly, there is an implication similar to that in White's conception of development, namely, that the object, as changed by man, is an independently constituted event which, in turn, affects man by acting back on him via feedback. And, as Schaff (1970) has indicated, this implication has served as the basis for the crude or naïve materialism that has been set forth by some later Marxist theorists.

My formulation would attempt to reconcile these opposing interpretations by suggesting that while the object of knowledge is changed by man into something that is peculiarly attuned to him ("destined for him"), a new capacity comes into being ("the eye becomes a human eye") precisely by virtue of the conflict and resolution inherent in the activity of creating the object. And precisely because the object so created by man ("humanized nature") is peculiarly attuned to him, it can now serve to "confirm" this new capacity—the human eye can construct anew the human social object that man has created. It is in this sense that man's faculties need to be formed by the objects outside of them. Man's activity gives rise to an emergent or new capacity that requires a properly tuned reality to realize itself in actual performance—and this reality can only be one that has been created by man's own activity.

acquired "mediating behavior," nature in our view becomes this very same constructive activity, namely, the functional invariant of constructing and reconstructing a properly tuned world at all levels of organization.

Given these implications of the proposed alternative, we can now consider my contention that this formulation provides the basis for a conception of personality development that is more coherent than that afforded by the Freudian position. In this regard, I think it obvious that even if one were to grant that my formulation differs significantly from the Freudian position, this would merely constitute a necessary and not sufficient basis for saying that my alternative is the more coherent of the two. What, then, are the grounds for my assertion? Essentially, my contention rests on the persuasiveness of my critique of the Freudian position. I do not mean by this that I draw support from the mere fact that I am able to point to problems of immutability and discontinuity in Freudian theory. For it follows from my own conception that one can recognize a contradiction in terms of the same type of functioning that has led to the contradiction in the first place. Indeed, it is on this basis that I have suggested that Allport and Bertocci were able to recognize the immutability-discontinuity problem in each other's theory even though each was doing so from the vantage point of the same epistemology; and that Hartmann was able to recognize the discontinuity in classical Freudian theory even while accepting Freud's metapsychological assumptions. Clearly, then, the fact that I am able to recognize the preformism and logical contradiction in Freudian theory does not necessarily imply that I am doing so from the vantage point of a more coherent perspective. Rather, I draw support for my contention from the fact that my formulation serves to connect these problems of immutability and discontinuity in the Freudian position in a particular way. And, in my view, being able to so connect these otherwise isolated problems requires a more integrated vantage point than the perspective that has produced them in the first place.[14]

In effect, then, I am basing my assertion on a particular relationship that obtains between the Freudian conception and my alternative. We have seen that Freudian theory is forced to ascribe contradictory polar qualities to the same event, thereby negating the very condition of conflict that it posits as being necessary to development in the first place. The preformism and logical contradiction that are so encountered by Freudian theory have a particular status in my formulation. Rather than representing a set of implicit and unanticipated difficulties as they do in the Freudian conception, these problems serve, in my alternative, to particularize a general principle — namely, that mental activity at any level of organization will structure events beyond its explanatory limits as a pars pro toto and, accordingly, into a form of the immutability-discontinuity problem. In this sense, the Freudian problems of preformism and logical contradiction are functionally equivalent to, and structurally different from, the forms of immutability and discontinuity that are evidenced in the non-conserver's construction of quantity. They represent a particular form of an invariant function that my position ascribes to cognitive activity in general. Indeed, therein lies a significant implication of my critique of "Freudian thought." Seen in this light, the Freudian problems of preformism and logical contradiction have

---

[14] Thus, in terms of my formulation, the child — while still a non-conserver — will be able, at some point, to see the contradiction in his own performance, but will not be able to resolve the conflict engendered by this recognition. And this, by virtue of having "conserved" the sausage as an "immutable" event in terms of the same mode of activity that has led him to his different distorting judgments of quantity in the first place. Only a conserver — by virtue of connecting these polar dimensions in a particular way — is able to resolve this conflict, namely, in terms of a construct more inclusive than that afforded by the non-conserver's perceptual activity.

a positive implication. As antagonistic, contradictory ways of knowing beyond the explanatory limits of the theory, these problems can be seen as constituting the necessary basis for a theoretical reorganization that can serve to structure the problem of development in a more coherent way.[15] In thus being an explicit instance of what, in my formulation, is a general principle of development, the contradiction encountered by Freudian theory can be said to serve as a constituent of my alternative. To the extent, then, that my formulation is persuasive — to the extent that it serves to clarify the basis of the immutability-discontinuity problem evidenced by Freudian theory — to that extent I can say that, as compared to the Freudian conception of development, the constructionist alternative is the more coherent or more hierarchically organized.

THE TASK FOR THE FUTURE

It need hardly be emphasized that the constructionist alternative that has been outlined here merely represents a set of possibilities. For these to be realized as a conception of personality development, the formulation must at the very least be elaborated in two interdependent ways. First, the relationship between the concepts of functional invariance and structural diversity must be clarified. It is not enough to say that, as functional invariants, conserving ac-

[15] This evaluation of Freudian theory departs sharply from the position of those critics who, given the fundamental nature of the problems encountered by the Freudian position, simply reject the whole enterprise (Stannard [1980] is the most recent example of this genre). Indeed, as some would have it, the mistakes and excesses of the Freudian position reflect the local aberrance of an arrogant genius and, consequently, are disarticulated from the mainstream of the history of ideas. In opposition to this view, my thesis would suggest that the weakness of the Freudian position is, in a significant sense, a measure of its strength: that Freud was stretching the Cartesian view to its limits — and beyond — thereby encountering the problems of immutability and discontinuity in a particularly sharp form.

tivity and contradictory ways of knowing provide the basis for a reorganization into structurally diverse and increasingly hierarchic forms of constructive behavior. The processes involved have to be explicated both theoretically and empirically — while adhering to the basic view that development derives from the organization of constructive activity itself. As I see it, such clarification is particularly required in the following problem areas: With respect to consolidative activity, there is the question as to how the act of constructing the event, as such, serves as the essential condition for the fluctuating polar ways of knowing that I have posited are evidenced at every level of cognitive organization. To use the child's developing conservation of quantity as an example: How does the very activity of perceptually constructing the deformed sausage in terms of its increased length prepare or "prime" the child to shift to the opposite dimension in constructing the event in terms of its decreased width? Another issue in regard to consolidative activity is the question of how these initially isolated polar forms of constructive activity become connected to one another such that the subject becomes conflicted with respect to his contradictory ways of knowing. Again using the child's developing conservation of quantity: How do the temporally isolated and mutually antagonistic perceptual constructions of the deformed sausage become connected with the perceptual conservation of the same event such that the child faces the contradiction that the same sausage has more and less clay than the ball? And not the least of the problems the formulation faces has to do with the process of developmental reorganization itself, namely, the problem of clarifying the nature of the relationship between the subject's recognition of his contradictory ways of knowing and the subsequent reorganization whereby he conserves the event on a more inclusive, hierarchically organized level.[16]

---

[16] Because it requires a substantially different background from that provided by my critique of the Freudian position, I am deferring any discussion of the relationship between the discontinuity problem and the concept

Second, I have assumed, as the basis for the projected alternative, that my formulation applies to the dynamic interpersonal events with which Freudian theory has been so typically concerned. Thus, I have assumed that my assertions apply to constructive activity in general, including the affectively loaded activity of constructing the attributes of an interpersonal other. From this point of view, it is possible to suggest that the subject knows the interpersonal other insofar as this other can be organized in accordance with patterns of activity that are available to the subject, and to characterize such subject-other (interpersonal) relationships in the same way that I have characterized subject-object (impersonal) relationships, namely, as evidencing the two forms of organization that are open to cognitive activity in structuring a sequence of events. As so understood, a given interpersonal relationship can evidence a fluctuating pars pro toto form of organization that gives rise to contradiction and conflict, an organization that thus constitutes the essential condition for its own development into a more hierarchically organized form of conserving interpersonal behavior.[17] Yet in advancing the present formulation, I have confined myself to such impersonal events as the child's developing notion of quantity and refined Freudian thought. If, then, there is a crucial problem of clarifying the relationship between the functional invariance and the structural diversity of constructive activity, our second task is no less critical. And that is to understand, and to demonstrate empirically, how these processes are involved in the development of interpersonal functioning, or what is the same thing, personality development.

---

of developmental reorganization until my intended elaboration of the constructionist alternative.

[17] For a preliminary extension of the constructionist alternative to interpersonal development and psychopathology, see Feffer (1967, 1970).

It should be noted, moreover, that even if one were to grant the validity of my formulation with respect to the domain of neutral impersonal events, one clearly could still question my assumption that this formulation can be applied to the affective dynamics of interpersonal relationships. Indeed, some psychoanalytic theorists, such as Wolff (1960), have made a strong argument against the appropriateness of such an extension. There is no question, therefore, but that any elaboration of the present formulation into a theory of personality development will have to come to grips with this issue. And this will have to be done precisely in the context of refining this formulation and extending its implications to the particulars of interpersonal life.

REFERENCES

Alexander, F. (1932), *The Medical Value of Psychoanalysis.* New York: Norton.

Allport, G. W. (1937), The functional autonomy of motives. *Amer. J. Psychol.,* 50:141–156.

Arieti, S. (1959), Schizophrenia: The manifest symptomatology, the psychodynamic and formal mechanisms. In: *American Handbook of Psychiatry,* Vol. 1, ed. S. Arieti. New York: Basic Books, pp. 455–485.

Asch, S. (1952), *Social Psychology.* Englewood Cliffs, N. J.: Prentice-Hall.

Bartlett, F. C. (1932), *Remembering.* Cambridge, Eng.: Cambridge University Press.

Bertocci, P. A. (1940), A critique of Gordon W. Allport's theory of motivation. *Psychol. Rev.,* 47:501–532.

Breuer, J., & Freud, S. (1893–1895), *Studies on Hysteria. Standard Edition,* 2. London: Hogarth Press, 1955.

Burtt, E. A. (1924), *The Metaphysical Foundations of Modern Science.* Garden City, N.Y.: Doubleday, 1954.

Cassirer, E. (1923), *The Philosophy of Symbolic Forms,* Vol. 1. New Haven: Yale University Press, 1953.

Dixon, N. (1971), *Subliminal Perception: The Nature of a Controversy.* London: McGraw-Hill.

Dollard, J., & Miller, N. (1950), *Personality and Psychotherapy.* New York: McGraw-Hill.

287

Elkind, D. (1968), Piaget's conservation problems. In: *Logical Thinking in Children,* ed. I. S. Sigel & F. H. Hooper. New York: Holt, Rinehart and Winston, pp. 460–472.

Erikson, E. H. (1959), *Identity and the Life Cycle.* [*Psychological Issues,* Monogr. 1.] New York: International Universities Press.

Feffer, M. (1967), Symptom expression as a form of primitive decentering. *Psychol. Rev.,* 74:16–38.

—— (1970), A developmental analysis of interpersonal behavior. *Psychol. Rev.,* 77:197–215.

—— (1975), Comments on role-taking and moral development. Paper presented at Eastern Psychological Association, New York.

—— & Gourevitch, V. (1960), Cognitive aspects of role-taking in children. *J. Personal.,* 28:383–396.

Fenichel, O. (1945), *The Psychoanalytic Theory of Neurosis.* New York: Norton.

Flavell, J. (1963), *The Developmental Psychology of Jean Piaget.* Princeton: Van Nostrand.

—— & Wohlwill, J. (1969), Formal and functional aspects of cognitive development. In: *Studies in Cognitive Development,* ed. D. Elkind & J. Flavell. New York: Oxford University Press, pp. 67–121.

Freud, S. (1895), Project for a scientific psychology. In: *The Origins of Psycho-Analysis: Letters to Wilhelm Fliess, Drafts and Notes, 1887–1902.* New York: Basic Books, 1954, pp. 355–445.

—— (1900), *The Interpretation of Dreams. Standard Edition,* 4 & 5. London: Hogarth Press, 1953.

—— (1905), Three essays on the theory of sexuality. *Standard Edition,* 7:135–243. London: Hogarth Press, 1953.

—— (1909), Analysis of a phobia in a five-year-old boy. *Standard Edition,* 10:5–149. London: Hogarth Press, 1955.

—— (1911a), Psycho-analytic notes on an autobiographical account of a case of paranoia (dementia paranoides). *Standard Edition,* 12:9–82. London: Hogarth Press, 1958.

—— (1911b), Formulations on the two principles of mental functioning. *Standard Edition,* 12:218–226. London: Hogarth Press, 1958.

_____ (1913), *Totem and Taboo. Standard Edition,* 13:1-161. London: Hogarth Press, 1953.

_____ (1914a), On the history of the psycho-analytic movement. *Standard Edition,* 14:7-66. London: Hogarth Press, 1957.

_____ (1914b), On narcissism: An introduction. *Standard Edition,* 14:73-102. London: Hogarth Press, 1957.

_____ (1915a), Repression. *Standard Edition,* 14:146-158. London: Hogarth Press, 1957.

_____ (1915b), The unconscious. *Standard Edition,* 14:166-215. London: Hogarth Press, 1957.

_____ (1917a), Mourning and melancholia. *Standard Edition,* 14:243-258. London: Hogarth Press, 1957.

_____ (1917b), Introductory lectures on psycho-analysis.*Part III. Standard Edition,* 16:243-496. London: Hogarth Press, 1963.

_____ (1921), Group psychology and the analysis of the ego. *Standard Edition,* 18:69-143. London: Hogarth Press, 1955.

_____ (1923), The ego and the id. *Standard Edition,* 19:12-59. London: Hogarth Press, 1961.

_____ (1925), A note upon the 'mystic writing-pad.' *Standard Edition,* 19:227-232. London: Hogarth Press, 1959.

_____ (1926), Inhibitions, symptoms and anxiety. *Standard Edition,* 20:87-172. London: Hogarth Press, 1959.

_____ (1933), *New Introductory Lectures on Psycho-Analysis. Standard Edition,* 22:5-182. London: Hogarth Press, 1964.

_____ (1940), An outline of psycho-analysis. *Standard Edition,* 23:144-207. London: Hogarth Press, 1964.

Fromm, E. (1961), *Marx's Concept of Man.* New York: Frederick Ungar.

Gibson, J. J. (1968), *The Senses Considered as Perceptual Systems.* London: Allen and Unwin.

Goldstein, K. (1939), *The Organism.* Boston: Beacon Press, 1963.

_____ (1940), *Human Nature in the Light of Psychopathology.* New York: Schocken Books, 1963.

Hanfmann, E. (1939), Analysis of the thinking disorder in a case of schizophrenia. In: *Contemporary Psychopathology,* ed. S.

Tomkins. Cambridge, Mass.: Harvard University Press, pp. 319-331, 1947.

Hartmann, H. (1939), Ego psychology and the problem of adaptation. In: *Organization and Pathology of Thought,* ed. D. Rapaport. New York: Columbia University Press, 1951, pp. 362-396.

_____ (1952), The mutual influences in the development of the ego and id. *The Psychoanalytic Study of the Child,* 7:9-30. New York: International Universities Press.

_____ (1955), Notes on the theory of sublimation. *The Psychoanalytic Study of the Child,* 10:9-29. New York: International Universities Press.

_____ (1956), Notes on the reality principle. *The Psychoanalytic Study of the Child,* 11:31-53. New York: International Universities Press.

_____ Kris, E., & Loewenstein, R. M. (1946), Comments on the formation of psychic structure. *The Psychoanalytic Study of the Child,* 2:11-38. New York: International Universities Press.

Holt, R. (1967), The development of the primary process: A structural view. In: *Motives and Thought: Psychoanalytic Essays in Honor of David Rapaport,* ed. R. Holt. [*Psychological Issues,* Monogr. 18/19.] New York: International Universities Press, pp. 345-383.

Howie, D. (1952), Perceptual defense. *Psychol. Rev.,* 59:308-315.

Kaplan, B. (1960), Lectures on developmental psychology. Unpublished manuscript, Worcester State Hospital, Worcester, Mass.

Kasanin, J. (1944), *Language and Thought in Schizophrenia.* New York: Norton.

Kelly, G. A. (1955), *The Psychology of Personal Constructs,* Vol. 1. New York: Norton.

Köhler, W. (1947), *Gestalt Psychology.* New York: Liveright.

Langer, J. (1969), *Theories of Development.* New York: Holt, Rinehart and Winston.

Lehrman, D. (1970), Semantic and conceptual issues in the nature-nurture problem. In: *Development and Evolution of Behavior,* ed. L. Aronson, E. Tobach, D. Lehrman, & J. Rosenblatt. San Francisco: W. H. Freeman, pp. 17-52.

MacIntyre, A. (1970), *Herbert Marcuse: An Exposition and a Polemic.* New York: Viking.

McGinnies, E. (1949), Emotionality and perceptual defense. *Psychol. Rev.,* 56:244-251.

Nagel, E. (1957), Determinism and development. In: *The Concept of Development,* ed. D. B. Harris. Minneapolis: University of Minnesota Press, pp. 15-25.

Paul, I. H. (1967), The concept of schema in memory theory. In: *Motives and Thought: Psychoanalytic Essays in Honor of David Rapaport,* ed. R. Holt. [*Psychological Issues,* Monogr. 18/19.] New York: International Universities Press, pp. 219-258.

Pepper, S. (1942), *World Hypotheses.* Berkeley: University of California Press, 1961.

Peters, R. S. (1958), *The Concept of Motivation.* London: Routledge and Kegan Paul.

Piaget, J. (1950), *The Psychology of Intelligence.* New York: Harcourt Brace.

———— (1952), *The Origins of Intelligence in Children.* New York: International Universities Press.

———— (1957), Logique et équilibre dans les comportements du sujet. In: *Logique et équilibre,* ed. L. Apostel, B. Mandelbrot, & J. Piaget. [*Etudes d'épistémologie génétique,* Vol. 2.] Paris: Presses Universitaires, pp. 27-211.

———— & Inhelder, B. (1962), *Le développment des quantités physiques chez l'enfant.* Paris: Delachaux et Niestlé.

Rank, B., & Macnaughton, D. (1950), A clinical contribution to early ego development. *The Psychoanalytic Study of the Child,* 5:53-56. New York: International Universities Press.

Rapaport, D. (1951a), The autonomy of the ego. In: *The Collected Papers of David Rapaport,* ed. M. M. Gill. New York: Basic Books, 1967.

———— , Ed. (1951b), *Organization and Pathology of Thought.* New York: Columbia University Press.

———— (1958), The theory of ego autonomy: A generalization. *Bull. Menn. Clin.,* 22:13-35.

———— (1959), The structure of psychoanalytic theory. In: *Psychology: A Study of a Science.,* ed. S. Koch. New York: McGraw-Hill, pp. 55-183.

Sanford, N. (1955), The dynamics of identification. *Psychol. Rev.*, 62:106–118.

Schaff, A. (1970), *Marxism and the Human Individual*. New York: McGraw-Hill.

Schilder, P. (1920), On the development of thoughts. In: *Organization and Pathology of Thought*, ed. D. Rapaport. New York: Columbia University Press, pp. 497–518, 1951.

Stannard, D. (1980), *Shrinking History: On Freud and the Failure of Psychohistory.* New York: Oxford University Press.

Von Domarus, E. (1944), The specific laws of logic in schizophrenia. In: *Language and Thought in Schizophrenia,* ed. J. S. Kasanin. New York: Norton, pp. 104–114, 1964.

Werner, H. (1957), The concept of development from a comparative and organismic point of view. In: *The Concept of Development,* ed. D. B. Harris. Minneapolis: University of Minnesota Press, pp. 125–148.

White, R. W. (1959), Motivation reconsidered. *Psychol. Rev.,* 66: 297–333.

–––––– (1963), *Ego and Reality in Psychoanalytic Theory.* [*Psychological Issues,* Monogr. 11.] New York: International Universities Press.

–––––– (1972), *The Abnormal Personality.* New York: Ronald Press.

Windelband, W. (1901), *A History of Philosophy,* Vol. 2. New York: Harper, 1958.

Wolff, P. (1960), *The Developmental Psychologies of Piaget and Psychoanalysis.* [*Psychological Issues,* Monogr. 5.] New York: International Universities Press.

–––––– (1967), Cognitive considerations for a psychoanalytic theory of language acquisition. In: *Motives and Thought: Psychoanalytic Essays in Honor of David Rapaport,* ed. R. Holt. [*Psychological Issues,* Monogr. 18/19.] New York: International Universities Press, pp. 300–343.

INDEX

Energy
libidinal, 88–89, 101–104,
115–117, 168–172, 176–
177, 184–186, 214, 225–
234
neutral, 234–236, 240, 247
neutralization of, 162–163,
171–172, 175, 214, 220–
221, 225–234
Energy-structure dichotomy, 6,
80, 205, 213–214, 222–234,
251; see also Metapsychology of Freudian theory
Erikson, E. H., 246–247, 288

Feffer, M., 13, 33, 271, 284, 288
Fenichel, O., 96, 130, 163, 288
Fixation, 95–97, 100, 107, 118
Flavell, J., 271, 276, 288
Freud, S., passim
Fromm, E., 278-279, 289
Functional autonomy of mo-
tives, see Allport-Bertocci
controversy
Functional equivalence, 15, 17–
19, 28-29, 281; see also
Functional invariance
Functional invariance, 18, 274,
281

Galileo, 56–59
Gibson, J. J., 165, 289
Goldstein, K., 33, 63, 289
Gourevitch, V., 13, 288

Habit, 52, 55–56, 67, 159, 161
Hanfmann, E., 33, 289

Hartmann, H., 6, 107, 131–
134, 152, 205–210, 212–
215, 219–220, 225, 235–
236, 280, 290
Hierarchic form of organization, 12–14, 22–27, 30, 39–
40, 262-264, 266, 273–277
Hobbes, T., 139
Holt, R., 80, 114, 225, 229–
230, 232, 290
Howie, D., 166, 290
Hypnoid state, 84–85

Id, 82, 112–119, 126, 209, 211
in anxiety-defense paradigm,
163–165, 168, 171–174,
178, 180–182, 185–186,
190–203
as reflection of Cartesian
world view, 141–145
summary of status in conflict
development, 158–161
see also Sexual-ego instinct
polarity; Sexual instincts
Immutability-discontinuity
problem, 2–6, 13, 22, 31–
34, 39, 140–141
in behaviorist theory, 67–78,
158–162, 201–202
in the constructionist alternative, 267–274
in ego psychology, 205, 215–
221
in Freud's anxiety-defense
paradigm, 162–167, 185–
203, 253–257
in Freud's view of development, 119, 131–139,
150–162, 253–257